"Charles Spurgeon is well knwell known for his passion a1is wonderfully resolved in thi̟ing. Well researched. A model for the twenty-first- century evangelical church. I cannot commend a book more highly than this one."
—Daniel L. Akin, president of Southeastern Baptist Theological Seminary

"What's the relationship between gospel ministry and mercy ministry? With the rise of social gospel movements in the twentieth century, evangelicals have held firmly to the former while tending to be nervous about the latter. But here is where church history can provide a helpful corrective. Alex DiPrima presents the forgotten example of Charles Haddon Spurgeon, the preeminent preacher and philanthropist of his day. Amid all the social ills of nineteenth-century London, Spurgeon models how to uphold the primacy of gospel preaching while pursuing social activism as the necessary fruit of the gospel. As Christians and church leaders navigate the challenges of our day, this book provides us with a mentor who will help us both guard the gospel and live out its implications."
—Geoff Chang, associate professor of historical theology and curator of the Spurgeon Library, Midwestern Baptist Theological Seminary

"For years I have known that Charles Spurgeon was one of the greatest preachers of all time. But I did not realize until now how energetic, diverse, and relentless was his life of benevolent ministry to the needy. Alex DiPrima's excellent work on Spurgeon reveals him as not only 'a greater and grander man' but also a role model for a beautiful harmony between proclaiming the true gospel in words and living out a Christlike compassion for the suffering. The river of Spurgeon quotes enables the great man Spurgeon to speak for himself, and the result was electric in my soul. I was cut to the heart and often needed to repent. I heartily commend this book and pray that it will result in a harvest of good works leading to a harvest of souls for Christ."
—Andrew M. Davis, senior pastor of First Baptist Church in Durham, North Carolina

"There remains a large storehouse of untold treasures of wisdom from the life of C. H. Spurgeon for believers in the twenty-first century, and Alex DiPrima's book gives readers wheelbarrows full of those treasures. DiPrima is convinced that Spurgeon can help us wed faithful gospel preaching and social concern. I agree and commend this book as a wonderful tool to help retrieve from Spurgeon wisdom for contemporary spiritual renewal."
—Jason G. Duesing, provost and professor of historical theology, Midwestern Baptist Theological Seminary

"Words and actions. Creeds and deeds. So often, believers are tempted to tear asunder what the Lord brings together. Charles Spurgeon shows us a better

way with his commitments to sound doctrine, evangelistic urgency, and good works. In this helpful book, Alex DiPrima demonstrates that gospel proclamation and gospel-driven social ministry were both essential to Spurgeon's view of the Christian life and his vision for faithful ministry. I trust this book will be of enormous benefit to both students of the Prince of Preachers and, more importantly, to contemporary pastors who desire to preach the gospel and 'to do good' that is animated by that gospel. Highly recommended."
—Nathan A. Finn, provost and dean of the university faculty,
North Greenville University

"C. H. Spurgeon was perhaps the greatest Protestant preacher since the Reformation. But he also had an all-round ministry of compassion and mercy that touched throngs of the poor and disadvantaged in Victorian England. This well-researched book brings to light an oft-neglected aspect of his life and work. A welcome addition to Spurgeon studies."
—Timothy George, distinguished professor at Beeson Divinity
School of Samford University and the general editor of the
twenty-nine-volume Reformation Commentary on Scripture

"When Christians think about Charles Spurgeon, they naturally recall his stirring sermons and energetic evangelism. Spurgeon is not often remembered as an advocate for ministry to the poor and suffering, but as Alex DiPrima's book convincingly shows, he should be. To Spurgeon, caring for the 'least of these' was the inevitable fruit of God's regenerating work in the hearts of the saints. DiPrima's work is a timely reminder that for the church, there should be no artificial separation between the proclamation of the gospel and Christlike works of mercy."
—Thomas Kidd, research professor of church history,
Midwestern Baptist Theological Seminary

"The best way to address the fear we have about the true gospel being morphed into a social gospel is by seeing how men like C. H. Spurgeon, who were true to the gospel, did mercy ministries. Alex DiPrima gives us a glimpse of this in his well-researched book. Spurgeon remained a true gospel preacher to his dying day. Read this book and see how the gospel he preached fired his heart with loving zeal for the poor and needy in his own day."
—Conrad Mbewe, pastor of Kabwata Baptist Church and founding
chancellor of the African Christian University in Lusaka, Zambia

"This is quite simply an outstanding book. Many Christians are familiar with Charles Spurgeon and his extensive preaching ministry, but few (including myself) are aware of the depth of his love and compassion for the poorest members of society. This book contains twelve immensely instructive and easily readable chapters and packs a powerful punch. How I wish I'd had this book in my hands twenty years ago as I embarked on pastoral ministry. I honestly don't have enough superlatives to adequately express how good this book is. In an age of fierce and ongoing debate in Christian circles about the relationship between the gospel and mercy ministry, this book helps us to see how Spurgeon cut across the divide and lived a life fully devoted to the gospel of Christ, with a heart fully devoted to relieving the suffering of, quite literally, thousands of lost and needy souls.

"If you have a love for the Lord, read this book. If you have a love for the lost, read this book. If you have a love for the neediest and most deprived members of society, read this book. Come and sit at the feet of a man who did more for the cause of the gospel among the poor and working class in his own lifetime than has been done by practically every pastor who has lived from the moment of his death until the present day.

"Truly inspirational. It moved me and renewed my own faith in terms of continuing to fight for the least, the last, and the lost in the UK and further afield."

—Mez McConnell, founder and director of 20schemes

"Christians who have always admired C. H. Spurgeon as the Prince of Preachers may be surprised to discover his benevolent interests ran deep. In *Spurgeon and the Poor*, Alex DiPrima proves that the nineteenth century's most famous pastor led his congregation to serve the poor, widows, orphans, and pastors-in-training. Spurgeon did more than raise money; he equipped the members of a growing, thriving congregation to roll up the sleeves of their heart and love their neighbors in tangible ways. Gospel proclamation is preeminent—Spurgeon made that clear. But if you want to see how faithful gospel preaching can produce active social concern, you will be greatly helped by DiPrima's excellent research and pastoral reflections."

—Aaron Menikoff, senior pastor, Mount Vernon Baptist Church

"My enthusiasm for this book is high and genuine. Mr. DiPrima has done excellent work in revealing Spurgeon's benevolent ministries in their biblical and gospel foundations, their variety, their relation to the fundamental calling of evangelism, and how they should flow naturally from the Christian heart as an expression of mercy. His thorough engagement with the primary source drives his thesis, while his knowledge of secondary sources—an impressively wide variety of them—sustains his thesis, puts it in context of other scholarship, and shows how needed his work is. His attention to practical implications for today that flow from precise descriptions of Spurgeon's theology and practice are really workable. They can aid, therefore, in helping Christian churches today bear a more biblically full ministry in the places God has planted them."

—Tom J. Nettles, senior professor of historical theology,
The Southern Baptist Theological Seminary

"Alex DiPrima serves the church well in *Spurgeon and the Poor*. Spurgeon is primarily remembered as the Prince of Preachers, and for good reason. His preaching stands front and center in his overall ministry. But it must not be imagined that Spurgeon was only a preacher; he was also the primary overseer and facilitator of some sixty-six benevolent social ministries at his church. How did such a program of social concern work itself out in Spurgeon's church? DiPrima argues that all of Spurgeon's church-focused ministries were 'downstream' from his gospel preaching. Spurgeon and the Poor is timely, gospel-centered, well written, balanced, and a welcomed addition to the Spurgeon canon. I heartily commend DiPrima's excellent book for your consideration."
—Ray Rhodes Jr., author of *Yours, till Heaven: The Untold Love Story of Charles and Susie Spurgeon* and *Susie: The Life and Legacy of Susannah Spurgeon*

"Christians have disagreed over how to address social concern and cultural and political engagement for centuries. Today is no different. That's why I'm excited to recommend Alex DiPrima's *Spurgeon and the Poor*. In this book, DiPrima offers lessons from the life and ministry of Charles Spurgeon that provide a way to maintain the priority of gospel proclamation while also recognizing that Christian social concern and cultural and political engagement flow naturally from the new birth, follow the example of Jesus's ministry and teaching, and strengthen the church's witness for the good of the gospel and the glory of God."
—Juan R. Sanchez, senior pastor, High Pointe Baptist Church, Austin, Texas

"Charles Spurgeon was accused of many things in his day; some would probably dismiss him as a social justice warrior in ours. (Spoiler alert: he was not.) But he did insist that social concern—even social activism—is not optional. Nor is it simply preferable. It is essential—necessary evidence that we ourselves have internalized gospel grace. In this fascinating book, Alex DiPrima sheds light on Spurgeon's bigheartedness toward the poor and marginalized. The Savior of sinners was mighty in both 'deed and word' (Luke 24:19). So was the Prince of Preachers. So must we be."
—Matt Smethurst, pastor, River City Baptist Church, Richmond, Virginia; managing editor, The Gospel Coalition; author, *Before You Share Your Faith*, *Before You Open Your Bible*, and *Deacons*

"There is rampant confusion in evangelicalism on the relationship between the gospel and social activism. If we're not careful, the latter risks consuming the former, which is why examples are needed to show their proper relationship and their proper ordering. Alex DiPrima's work on Charles Spurgeon as a faithful exemplar of gospel-focused social action is a welcome resource in a sea of confusion. As DiPrima demonstrates in the life of Spurgeon, Christians are called to the social sphere of mercy ministry and cultural engagement but chastened by the supremacy of the gospel as the catalyst."
—Andrew T. Walker, associate professor of Christian ethics, The Southern Baptist Theological Seminary

SPURGEON
AND THE POOR

SPURGEON
AND THE POOR
How the Gospel Compels Christian Social Concern

Alex DiPrima

Foreword by Jonathan Leeman

Reformation Heritage Books
Grand Rapids, Michigan

Spurgeon and the Poor
© 2023 by Alex DiPrima

All rights reserved. No part of this book may be used or reproduced in any manner whatsoever without written permission except in the case of brief quotations embodied in critical articles and reviews. Direct your requests to the publisher at the following addresses:

Reformation Heritage Books
3070 29th St. SE
Grand Rapids, MI 49512
616-977-0889
orders@heritagebooks.org
www.heritagebooks.org

Printed in the United States of America
23 24 25 26 27 28/10 9 8 7 6 5 4 3 2 1

Library of Congress Cataloging-in-Publication Data

Names: DiPrima, Alex, author. | Leeman, Jonathan, other.
Title: Spurgeon and the poor : how the gospel compels Christian social concern / Alex DiPrima ; foreword by Jonathan Leeman.
Description: Grand Rapids, Michigan : Reformation Heritage Books, [2023] | Includes bibliographical references.
Identifiers: LCCN 2022042101 (print) | LCCN 2022042102 (ebook) | ISBN 9781601789457 (paperback) | ISBN 9781601789464 (epub)
Subjects: LCSH: Spurgeon, C. H. (Charles Haddon), 1834-1892. | Evangelicalism. | Poor--Biblical teaching. | Suffering--Religious aspects--Christianity. | Church and social problems. | Church and the world.
Classification: LCC BX6495.S7 D57 2023 (print) | LCC BX6495.S7 (ebook) | DDC 270.8/2--dc23/eng/20221014
LC record available at https://lccn.loc.gov/2022042101
LC ebook record available at https://lccn.loc.gov/2022042102

For additional Reformed literature, request a free book list from Reformation Heritage Books at the above regular or email address.

To Jenna,

I have led her home,
My love, my only friend.
There is none like her,
None.
—Alfred Lord Tennyson

Table of Contents

Timeline... ix
Foreword.. xi
Preface.. xvii
Acknowledgments.. xxv

Part 1: Spurgeon's Teaching

Chapter 1: The Prince of Preachers 3
Chapter 2: The Grace Effect 19
Chapter 3: Followers of Christ, Lovers of Men............ 31
Chapter 4: Gospel Proclamation and Social Ministry....... 45
Chapter 5: The Church: A City on a Hill.................. 61
Chapter 6: Political Preaching?.......................... 75

Part 2: Spurgeon's Practice

Chapter 7: The Priority of Soul Winning 93
Chapter 8: The Pastors' College 111
Chapter 9: A Benevolent Ministry....................... 129
Chapter 10: The Metropolitan Tabernacle 147
Chapter 11: The Good Samaritan in London.............. 163
Chapter 12: Social and Political Activism............... 177

Conclusion 195
Appendix: Spurgeon and Social Ministry in
    Historical Perspective 205

Timeline

June 19, 1834—Charles Spurgeon is born in Kelvedon, Essex, to John and Eliza Spurgeon.

January 1836—Moves in with his grandparents in Stambourne, where he lives between the ages of one and six years old. Is first introduced to the Puritans in his grandfather's study.

1840—Returns to his parents' home in Colchester.

January 6/13, 1850—Converted at the age of fifteen in a Primitive Methodist chapel through a sermon preached on Isaiah 45:22.

May 3, 1850—Baptized at Isleham Ferry, a few miles outside of Cambridge, by the Reverend W. H. Cantlow.

June 17, 1850—Moves to Cambridge.

August 1850—Begins preaching in a local Cambridge lay preacher's association; preaches his first sermon in Teversham Cottage.

October 1851—Accepts a call to pastor Waterbeach Chapel outside of Cambridge at the age of seventeen.

April 19, 1854—Accepts a call to pastor New Park Street Chapel in London at the age of nineteen.

January 1855—Begins publishing his weekly sermons.

July 1855—Begins to mentor T. W. Medhurst, who will eventually be the first student in the Pastors' College.

TIMELINE

January 8, 1856—Marries Susannah Thompson.

September 20, 1856—Susannah gives birth to twin boys, Charles and Thomas.

October 19, 1856—Disaster takes place at the Surrey Gardens Music Hall, killing seven people and injuring twenty-eight more.

1857—The Pastors' College is founded.

March 18, 1861—The Metropolitan Tabernacle opens for services.

June 5, 1864—Preaches his controversial sermon on baptismal regeneration.

January 1, 1865—Begins publishing his monthly magazine, the *Sword and the Trowel*.

August 1866—Meets Anne Hillyard; plans for the Stockwell Orphanage are put in place.

November 1, 1866—The Colportage Association is founded for the widespread distribution of affordable Christian literature.

September 9, 1869—The Stockwell Orphanage opens.

September 1875—Mrs. Spurgeon's Book Fund is established.

1879—The Girls' Orphanage is established.

March 1887—The Downgrade Controversy commences with two articles published in the *Sword and the Trowel*.

January 18, 1888—Officially resigns from the Baptist Union and is subsequently censured.

June 7, 1891—Preaches his last sermon at the Metropolitan Tabernacle.

January 31, 1892—Dies peacefully in Mentone, France, surrounded by his wife and several of his closest friends and associates.

Foreword

If you're a genuinely converted pastor or a church member, I trust you want to be faithful to God's call on your life. You want your faith to be characterized by deeds. You want to be zealous for good works. You want your love of God to express itself in love of neighbor, especially among those belonging to the household of God. You want to be obedient. The Holy Spirit of God has wonderfully planted these new desires in your heart.

Yet sometimes you wonder, how much time and money do you need to give up? And are you giving enough?

You recognize that Jesus calls you to give up everything and follow Him. You mean to do so. But let's get practical. Now you're looking at your family budget spreadsheet, and you're wondering, Is now the time to buy a new car? If so, would it be better to get the older car so that you're paying less monthly and can give away more, or the newer car that will last longer but has a higher monthly payment, leaving less to give away?

If you're a pastor, maybe you're wondering how to spend your week. Do you spend twenty hours preparing Sunday's sermon, or just ten so you can use those ten saved hours helping your church serve in more hands-on ways?

With everyday questions like these, what exactly does faithfulness to Jesus and His Word require?

To help answer such questions, you might turn to the literature that's been written on topics like *mission of the church* or *how*

Christians should engage politically or *what justice requires*. I've contributed at length to those very conversations and think they're worthwhile.

Yet, together with this kind of topical study, you should also walk up to older saints or pastors and ask what they've done. What can you learn from their example? With other members of your church, take Paul's advice: "Imitate me, just as I also imitate Christ" (1 Cor. 11:1 NKJV; also, 4:16–17; Heb. 6:12; 13:7).

Then again, every once in a while, God blesses history with a truly astounding example of faithfulness, someone *greater and grander*, as John B. Gough puts it. We may never be these greater men or women, but we can all learn from them. They set a pattern we can follow. Alex DiPrima's presentation of Charles Spurgeon, the nineteenth-century pastor of London's Metropolitan Tabernacle, shows that Spurgeon's example of caring for the poor and needy and engaging the social issues of the day is worthy of emulation, as is the example of his church.

Friends, Spurgeon is that older saint and pastor whose hand is worth taking and can lead us.

You will sell yourself short by treating this book merely as a piece of history. Rather, engage with it personally and ecclesiastically. That's the author's goal. What can *you* learn? How can *your church* follow?

DiPrima reasonably conjectures in the appendix that twentieth- and twenty-first-century conservative evangelicals sometimes avoid conversations about mercy ministry and preaching politics because that territory has been occupied by theological liberals for over a century. Liberals sold their birthright for a mess of pottage by prioritizing an earthly handout over an eternal inheritance. The trouble, DiPrima continues, is that conservatives can react against these gospel-compromising errors by eschewing talk of caring for the poor or social engagement altogether. We can be like someone reacting against the ditch of legalism by crossing the road and falling into the ditch of antinomianism.

Some evangelicals try to make up for this latter error by pulling their car back onto the center of the road. To switch metaphors, they preach a gospel of both/and. As in, we need both faith and deeds—or, churches must both preach and seek justice. John Stott famously articulated this instinct with his illustration of the "two wings of a bird." The church's mission requires both wings: gospel words and good deeds. And like a bird's wings, he says, these things are symmetrical and equally important. Each exists for its own sake, he says.[1]

Yet slightly more careful contributors to these conversations realize that faith and deeds, preaching and good works, don't play the same role. They aren't equal. Rather, the first must be our priority because the first creates the second, while the second proves and illustrates the first. Everything needs to be set in its proper place.

This is the picture DiPrima offers us of Spurgeon. For a book dedicated to Spurgeon's personal and church-conducted philanthropy, you might be surprised by how much space DiPrima devotes to Spurgeon's preaching and the priority Spurgeon gave to making disciples. Yet that's because DiPrima, like Spurgeon before him, recognizes that churches won't get their social ministries and political engagement right without properly setting these activities inside the larger gospel and disciple-making context. You make good the enemy of great when you don't explain the good in the context of the great.

Among other things, this means we must eschew all talk of "transforming the city" or "renewing the culture," as has been popular in some evangelical circles over the last couple of decades. Sure, Christians can make an "impact." We can make a "difference." We can leave our corner of the garden better than how we found it. Yet "transformation" talk, at least in the Bible, is Holy Spirit talk. He's the one who regenerates, and He's the one who will remove the curse. In the meantime, we cannot transform anything. We can only point to

---

1. John Stott and Christopher J. H. Wright, *Christian Mission in the Modern World*, updated and expanded (Downers Grove, Ill.: InterVarsity, 2015), 44.

the one who does. DiPrima's Spurgeon doesn't entertain such eschatologically over-realized ambitions.

Rather, our benevolence ministries, first and foremost, are evidence of the gospel and the Spirit's work in us. Second, they are part of what makes the converted life and the church attractive in their witness. DiPrima writes, "Perhaps more would be won to the faith if Christians showed forth a commitment to compassionate concern for the poor and the afflicted, not necessarily as a means of transforming the culture or eradicating poverty from the world, but simply as a way of living out the new nature in Christ." Later, he writes, "Spurgeon believed that works of charity adorn and beautify the testimony of Christ in the world." His use of the verb "adorn" reminds me of Paul and Peter's instructions for how godly wives will "adorn" themselves with good deeds and not just fine jewelry (1 Tim. 2:9–10; 1 Peter 3:3–5). The lesson applies to churches generally: if your church possesses real faith, it will be adorned by caring for the vulnerable among us.

In short, there is a both/and when it comes to faith and deeds. The two are inseparable. Yet there's also an asymmetry between them since faith is prior and foundational. Faith creates deeds, while deeds prove and adorn faith. Can you see the flowchart?

Particularly challenging in this book is how much Spurgeon wove his emphases on benevolence and mercy ministry, as well as his very occasional forays into preaching politics, into the life of the Metropolitan Tabernacle. In one or two places, DiPrima's Spurgeon sets more weight onto the shoulders of the entire church for doing mercy ministry than I have been willing to recommend in my own theological writing on the mission of the church. Individual church members? Of course. But the whole church together? That's a tougher question. When does social ministry or political engagement threaten to overtake a congregation's primary call to leverage their collective resources for disciple-making?

Yet, once again, I'm happy to let this greater saint from a previous century, whose battles weren't my own but who lived in a city where poverty and the ravages and exploitations of early industrialization were palpable on every street corner, lead and challenge me. I hope you will as well.

I haven't said it plainly yet, so let me say it: this is a wonderful, worthy, and soul-edifying book. DiPrima has done a remarkable job of collecting a ton of historical material on Spurgeon's life and ministry. Yet he also presents all his data with pastoral mindfulness. You might not agree with every line Spurgeon drew or failed to draw, but I'm confident you'll be convicted and challenged by his example. As we think about the mission of the church and what faithfulness should look like in our own lives, Spurgeon can help us overcome our own theological parochialism. God has things to teach us from saints in different times because the blinders of our own times sometimes keep us from seeing what should be obvious.

So read this book. Then go back to your budget spreadsheet or your weekly calendar, pray, and ask yourself, should anything change?

—Jonathan Leeman
Elder at Cheverly Baptist Church
and editorial director at 9Marks

Preface

The American temperance activist John B. Gough stepped off the train in London. He had come to visit England's greatest preacher, Charles Haddon Spurgeon. The year was 1879, and the preacher was at the height of his powers. Gough himself had described Spurgeon's ministry as "a career thus far unparalleled in the history of ministers."[1] Indeed, there had never been a preacher like him. In his teenage years, he gained a reputation as the famous "boy preacher of the Fens."[2] He arrived in London at the age of nineteen to command the pulpit of the city's most historic Baptist church in the heart of the metropolis, just south of the Thames. He preached for nearly forty years from that pulpit to thousands upon thousands, winning souls, planting churches, and ministering to the poor.

During Gough's visit, Spurgeon provided him with a tour of the Stockwell Orphanage. Ten years prior, Spurgeon began this ministry to orphaned boys with the help of an elderly widow who will appear later in these pages. While the two men were visiting the orphanage, Spurgeon received a call to the bedside of a boy who was terminally ill. As he sat with the dying boy, Spurgeon placed the child's hand in

---

1. John B. Gough, *Sunlight and Shadow; or, Gleanings from My Life Work* (Hartford, Conn.: A. D. Worthington, 1881), 407.
2. *C. H. Spurgeon's Autobiography, Compiled from His Diary, Letters, and Records by His Wife and His Private Secretary* (London: Passmore and Alabaster, 1897), 1:199–212. The Fens (or the Fenlands) is a relatively flat and marshy region of East Anglia comprising parts of the counties of Cambridgeshire, Norfolk, and Lincolnshire. It is the region where Spurgeon did most of his early preaching and is just north of where Spurgeon grew up.

his and told him, "Jesus loves you. He bought you with His precious blood, and He knows what is best for you. It seems hard for you to lie here and listen to the shouts of the healthy boys outside at play. But soon Jesus will take you home, and then He will tell you the reason, and you will be so glad."[3] Spurgeon then inched forward in his chair, laid his hand on the boy's head, and quietly prayed aloud, "O Jesus, Master, this dear child is reaching out his thin hand to find thine. Touch him, dear Saviour, with thy loving, warm clasp. Lift him as he passes the cold river, that his feet be not chilled by the water of death; take him home in thine own good time. Comfort and cherish him till that good time comes. Show him thyself as he lies here, and let him see thee and know thee more and more as his loving Saviour."[4] After a moment's pause, he said with a warm smile, "Now, dear, is there anything you would like? Would you like a little canary in a cage to hear him sing in the morning? Nurse, see that he has a canary tomorrow morning. Goodbye, my dear; you will see the Saviour perhaps before I shall."[5] Gough, who had quietly witnessed the scene, recorded his recollections in his autobiography, writing, "I had seen Mr. Spurgeon holding by his power sixty-five hundred persons in a breathless interest; I knew him as a great man universally esteemed and beloved; but as he sat by the bedside of a dying pauper child, whom his beneficence had rescued, he was to me a greater and grander man than when swaying the mighty multitude at his will."[6]

The book in your hands is about this *greater and grander man*—a man who, in a sense, history has obscured amid the widely chronicled sensation his preaching genius created. Ask many evangelicals today about Spurgeon, and they can likely tell you something about

---

3. Gough, *Sunlight and Shadow*, 407–8.
4. Gough, *Sunlight and Shadow*, 408.
5. Gough, *Sunlight and Shadow*, 408. This was not an unusual occurrence. Arnold Dallimore notes that Spurgeon "made it a particular point to call on any children who might be in the infirmary, to pray for them and show whatever special kindness he could." Arnold Dallimore, *Spurgeon: A New Biography* (Edinburgh: Banner of Truth, 1985), 129.
6. Gough, *Sunlight and Shadow*, 408.

his storied preaching. However, how many have heard of Spurgeon's activities as a philanthropist, activist, or friend of poor orphans and needy widows? How many would imagine that Spurgeon, the famous Prince of Preachers, whose preaching commanded the rapt attention of tens of thousands, took appointments to pray hand in hand with sick children? Yet this is the Spurgeon who was and who must again be reintroduced to the church today.

From the very beginning of his Christian experience, Spurgeon zealously devoted himself to good works. Within days of his conversion at the age of fifteen, Spurgeon began giving his time to ministry among the needy of his community in Cambridgeshire. He filled his days distributing tracts, ministering to the poor, and teaching Bible classes to young children. Spurgeon said of this period in his life, "I could scarcely content myself even for five minutes without trying to do something for Christ."[7]

The same was true when he arrived in London in 1854 at the age of nineteen. The sprawling metropolis was, to Spurgeon, one towering monument to human need. Almost immediately, Spurgeon established himself as a friend to London's indigent. Just a few months into his new pastorate at New Park Street Chapel (later to change its name to the Metropolitan Tabernacle), Spurgeon found London in the midst of a deadly cholera epidemic, which would claim the lives of over ten thousand of its citizens. Without hesitation, Spurgeon threw himself into the fray, traveling from house to house to visit the sick and dying. He did this for weeks on end, all the while expecting that he would die from the disease himself, as many in those days believed cholera to be contagious. This concern was insignificant to him in the face of the tremendous need all around him.

As Spurgeon gained more exposure to the acute and diverse exigencies facing London, he aggressively launched dozens of ministries and organizations to combat suffering and poverty in the city. By 1884, these benevolent ministries numbered sixty-six in total and included an orphanage, a ministerial college, subsidized housing

---

7. *C. H. Spurgeon's Autobiography*, 1:181.

for poor widows, a clothing bank, a ministry to prostitutes, several street missions, and a host of children's ministries.[8] Whether it was London's widows and orphans, the poor of her many crowded slums and back alleys, or the city's forgotten blind, Spurgeon opened his arms wide to the needy and the afflicted. In addition, his private philanthropy was prodigious, from supporting needy saints out of his own pocket to providing the means for new churches to be planted. Throughout his life, money flowed freely through his hands into the many benevolent institutions he himself founded.

Still more remarkable is that Spurgeon was not content to advocate only for the afflicted and the oppressed of his homeland. On the eve of the American Civil War, Spurgeon spoke out courageously against the evils of slavery, leading to significant personal criticism, financial loss, and even occasional death threats. Spurgeon's godly stand against the wicked institution of slavery (which will be considered in greater depth in chapter 11) provides a striking example of what it looks like to fight injustice from biblical convictions and principles.

Even from his deathbed in Mentone, France, when most men would be attending to the details of their estate, Spurgeon steadfastly gave to the church and the poor. His last conscious act was to give one hundred pounds to the Metropolitan Tabernacle thank offering for the support of the church and its various ministries. His final telegram before he died read, "Self and wife, £100, hearty thank-offering towards Tabernacle General Expenses. Love to all Friends." Spurgeon's secretary, Joseph Harrald, recorded, "That was his last generous act, and his last message."[9]

Spurgeon lived a life filled to the brim with good works of benevolence and charity. However, too few today are familiar with this vital aspect of his life and ministry nor the theological convictions

---

8. *Memorial Volume, Mr. Spurgeon's Jubilee: Report of the Proceedings at the Metropolitan Tabernacle on Wednesday and Thursday Evenings, June 18th and 19th, 1884* (London: Passmore and Alabaster, 1884), 7–8; C. H. Spurgeon, "Mr. Spurgeon's Jubilee Meetings," *Sword and the Trowel*, July 1884, 373.

9. *C. H. Spurgeon's Autobiography*, 4:371.

that undergirded it. I have written this book because I find in Spurgeon a most compelling example of the proper wedding of faithful gospel preaching with earnest social concern. Evangelicals have frequently failed to correctly understand the relationship between these two biblical burdens. I am convinced that Spurgeon can help us. He eagerly invites pastors and churches to devote themselves to the fervent preaching of evangelical truth while showing us how that truth moves Christians toward practical concern for the needy. As the subtitle of this book suggests, the gospel compels Christian social concern (Titus 2:11–14).

Part 1 of this book explains how Spurgeon grounded evangelical mercy ministry in the teaching of the Bible. Spurgeon's philanthropy, benevolence, and concern for the poor were prominent features of his ministry, but they did not represent its central locus. At the heart of Spurgeon's ministry was the earnest preaching of the gospel unto the winning of souls. He understood this to be the primary call of the preacher and the principal mission of the church, from which all other aspects of ministry flow.

Spurgeon's commitment to gospel preaching gave social ministry its proper place. He believed that care for the poor and the oppressed grows naturally out of the preaching of the gospel. Social concern was not an optional add-on for Spurgeon. Instead, it is the fruit of a life transformed by the grace of God through the new birth. Churches are not faithful if they do not manifest the power of the gospel through heartfelt compassion for the needy and benevolent care for the poor. Though such good works do not embody the church's central mission, they nonetheless are essential to the church's ministry as the necessary fruit and vindication of the power of the gospel. As Spurgeon once put it, "Works of charity must keep pace with the preaching of faith or the church will not be perfect in its development."[10]

In part 2 of this book, I will tell the story of the "Forgotten Spurgeon." Iain Murray famously used this name as the title of his

---

10. Spurgeon, "Notes," *Sword and the Trowel*, November 1879, 544.

excellent book on Spurgeon the controversialist. I am borrowing it to refer to Spurgeon the philanthropist, the activist, and the friend of the poor. This is the Spurgeon who John B. Gough referred to as the "greater and grander man." We should seek to know this man better, as he can provide something of a model to evangelicals who wish to be faithful to Christ and His Word.

Therefore, part 1 is more theoretical, focusing on Spurgeon's teaching regarding benevolence and mercy ministry. Part 2 is more practical, focusing on how Spurgeon applied his convictions in these vital areas. Part 1 is word; part 2 is deed.

For those who wish to read a biography of Spurgeon alongside this book, I recommend Arnold Dallimore's *Spurgeon: A New Biography*[11] and an older but no less accessible work by W. Y. Fullerton titled *C. H. Spurgeon: A Biography*.[12] I have consulted both in the research and writing of this book, along with all the major biographies of Spurgeon written since his death. I have also drawn heavily from Spurgeon's four-part autobiography, which is an invaluable source for students of Spurgeon. Additionally, I have spent hours in *The New Park Street Pulpit* and *The Metropolitan Tabernacle Pulpit*, both collections of Spurgeon's sermons.[13] These indispensable volumes have largely determined the course of this book's argument, especially in part 1.

One of the unique features of this book is that I make liberal use of Spurgeon's monthly magazine, the *Sword and the Trowel*, which has historically been underutilized in books about Spurgeon. Spurgeon referred to the *Sword and the Trowel* as "in some sense our

---

11. Arnold Dallimore, *Spurgeon: A New Biography* (Edinburgh: Banner of Truth, 1985).

12. W. Y. Fullerton, *C. H. Spurgeon: A Biography* (London: William and Norgate, 1920).

13. *The New Park Street Pulpit: Containing Sermons Preached and Revised by the Rev. C. H. Spurgeon, Minister of the Chapel*, 6 vols. (Grand Rapids: Baker Book House, 2007); *The Metropolitan Tabernacle Pulpit: Sermons Preached and Revised by C. H. Spurgeon*, Vols. 7–62 (Pasadena, Tex.: Pilgrim Publications, 1969–90).

autobiography."[14] Finally, I have accessed scores of articles, dissertations, and chapters on Spurgeon found in larger works, along with other secondary sources related to Spurgeon and the Victorian era.

Though I wrote my doctoral thesis on matters related to Spurgeon's social ministries, the book in hand is not primarily a work of scholarship. I have provided footnotes mainly for students, historians, and theologians who would like to retrace the footprints of my research and wish to build upon what I have written here. Nonetheless, this book is primarily for pastors and church members who desire to think more carefully about the role of benevolence and social ministry in the life of the individual Christian and the mission and ministry of the local church. I hope I have succeeded in producing a book that is both careful in historical research and accessible and edifying to the average Christian.

On Sunday morning, November 9, 1862, Spurgeon preached on Job's words in Job 30:25, "Did I not weep for him that was in trouble? Was not my soul grieved for the poor?"[15] Spurgeon proclaimed to the assembled congregation, "If there were nowhere else a heart that had sympathy for the needy there should be one found in every Christian breast.... To me a follower of Jesus means a friend of man. A Christian is a philanthropist by profession, and generous by force of grace; wide as the reign of sorrow is the stretch of his love, and where he cannot help he pities still."[16] Spurgeon believed these words should describe every true Christian. He perhaps embodied them better than anyone else. Spurgeon's love embraced the suffering and the needy of almost every sort and variety. He was a man zealous for good works. Moved by the love of Christ and the grace of God, Spurgeon devoted himself eagerly to helping the poor, the needy, and the oppressed. We turn now to tell his story.

---

14. Spurgeon, "Notice of Books," *Sword and the Trowel*, January 1885, 35.

15. Unless otherwise noted, all Scripture quotations will be from the King James Version.

16. C. H. Spurgeon, "Christian Sympathy," in *The Metropolitan Tabernacle Pulpit: Sermons Preached and Revised by C. H. Spurgeon* (Pasadena, Tex.: Pilgrim Publications, 1969), 8:628.

Acknowledgments

This book does not come into existence without the contribution of many helpers along the way. I'd like to thank Nathan Finn, my dear friend and once doctoral supervisor, who first awakened my interest in church history and later supervised my research into Spurgeon's life and ministry while I was his PhD student. I also wish to thank the community of Spurgeon scholars who encouraged my research, including Christian George, Geoff Chang, Ray Rhodes, and Tom Nettles. I owe an immeasurable debt to Iain Murray, first, for the many books he's written that have informed, edified, and inspired me, and second, for his warm support for and endorsement of this project when it was still only a book proposal. I'm thankful as well to those who assisted me throughout my research for this book, including Philip Ort from the Spurgeon Center in Kansas City, who coordinated my visits to the Spurgeon Library; Helen Compston from the Metropolitan Tabernacle in London, who arranged for me to have access to the Tabernacle archives; and Annabel Haycraft from Spurgeon's College in London, who pulled a number of rare resources for me. Special thanks also belong to Jeremy Walker, a Spurgeon expert in his own right, who hosted my wife and me on our visits to England during the research and writing of this book. I also owe thanks to David Woollin, Jay Collier, Ethan Fuller, and the whole team at Reformation Heritage. It has been nothing but a joy to work with them. I also want to thank Emma Collins for her beautiful artwork that dons the cover of this book, which is based on a monument that used to stand outside Spurgeon's orphanage.

I want to thank a number of faithful friends who provided me with careful and thoughtful input along the way as well. I am deeply grateful to Robert Fisher—a pastor, a mentor, and one of my dearest friends. His input and guidance contributed greatly to the direction of this project. I also owe a tremendous debt to Lydia Schaible for her careful editing and thoughtful feedback on early drafts of the manuscript. Thanks belong to Zack DiPrima, Debbie Clark, and Jason Finley, who provided excellent input as well. I also wish to express my gratitude to the officers and members of Emmanuel Church, who have made me the happiest of pastors and have blessed me greatly through their prayers and encouragements to write.

Most of all, I wish to thank my wife, Jenna. No man has ever had a more supportive life companion. Thank you for your love and devotion to our children and me. If this book bears any fruit, it is fruit I share with you.

PART 1

Spurgeon's Teaching

The Prince of Preachers

John B. Gough described Spurgeon's ministry as "a career thus far unparalleled in the history of ministers."[1] This achievement is evident nearly a century and a half after his death, but it appears that even those who observed Spurgeon's life as it unfolded were well aware they were witnessing something singular in Christian history. The first biography of Spurgeon appeared in print in 1856 when he was only twenty-one years old.[2] After Spurgeon died in 1892, a new biography of him surfaced every month for the next two years.[3] The tale of his storied ministry has instructed and inspired millions around the world and continues to attract both popular and scholarly attention today.[4]

In order to properly appreciate Spurgeon's views on Christian social concern, we first have to understand something of his basic story. This chapter provides a brief survey of Spurgeon's life, highlighting some of the major events and aspects of his ministry. This

---

1. John B. Gough, *Sunlight and Shadow; or, Gleanings from My Life Work* (Hartford, Conn.: A. D. Worthington, 1881), 407.

2. E. L. Magoon, *"The Modern Whitfield": Sermons of the Rev. C. H. Spurgeon, of London; With an Introduction and Sketch of His Life* (New York: Sheldon, Blakeman, 1856).

3. Christian T. George, "Jesus Christ, the 'Prince of Pilgrims': A Critical Analysis of the Ontological, Functional, and Exegetical Christologies in the Sermons, Writings, and Lectures of Charles Haddon Spurgeon (1834–1892)" (PhD diss., University of St. Andrews, 2011), 18.

4. As this book was being written, there were more doctoral students studying Spurgeon's life, ministry, and theology than at any time since his death in 1892.

short account of Spurgeon's biography will supply us with context so that we can better understand the role that good works and mercy ministry played in Spurgeon's overall view of the Christian life and the ministry of the church.

Childhood and Conversion (1834–1850)

Charles Haddon Spurgeon was born on June 19, 1834, in Kelvedon, Essex, about fifty miles east of London. He was the oldest of seventeen children, only eight of whom survived infancy. Spurgeon's family was, for generations, part of England's rural working class. Spurgeon's father, John, earned a living as a clerk in a coal merchant's office and also served churches as a Congregationalist lay minister. His mother, Eliza, devoted herself to the spiritual nurture of her children and had a remarkable impact on Spurgeon's spiritual life as a child. Spurgeon once wrote of her, "I cannot tell how much I owe to the solemn words of my good mother.... I am sure that, in my early youth, no teaching ever made such an impression on my mind as the instruction of my mother."[5]

From the time he was eighteen months old until he was age six, Spurgeon lived with his grandparents in the village of Stambourne. The precise reason for the change of house is not known, but it likely had to do with his parents' slender means and growing family. Whatever the reason, it is not hard to trace God's hand of providence in these events. The years spent in his grandparents' home proved to be tremendously formative in shaping Spurgeon's earliest spiritual impressions.

His grandfather, James Spurgeon, who served as a Nonconformist minister for more than a half century, profoundly influenced the precocious young Charles. It was in his grandfather's study that Spurgeon first discovered Puritan classics, such as Bunyan's *Pilgrim's*

---

5. C. H. *Spurgeon's Autobiography, Compiled from His Diary, Letters, and Records by His Wife and His Private Secretary* (London: Passmore and Alabaster, 1897), 1:67–69.

Progress, Foxe's *Book of Martyrs*, and Baxter's *Call to the Unconverted*. Like his grandfather, Spurgeon would remain a lifelong admirer of the Puritans. In light of how early Spurgeon began to encounter such works, it would only be a slight exaggeration to say that Spurgeon took in the theology of the Puritans with his mother's milk. Even the region of East Anglia where Spurgeon grew up was known as a true Puritan stronghold, populated as it was with old churches associated with well-known Puritans, such as John Rogers, John Owen, and William Gurnall.

By the time Spurgeon entered his teenage years, he had begun to wrestle intensely with what he described as "a deep and bitter sense of sin."[6] In his autobiography, compiled and published posthumously, Spurgeon chronicled a protracted internal struggle with doubt and fear over the state of his soul.[7] This internal wrestling persisted until January 1850, when the fifteen-year-old Spurgeon experienced the new birth. Historians dispute the exact date of this event. Spurgeon himself dated his conversion to January 6, 1850, but some scholars contend that he was mistaken about the date and was actually converted a week later, on January 13, 1850.[8]

The morning of his conversion, Spurgeon walked out of his parents' home (then in Colchester) to attend a nearby church, possibly to hear his father preach. He set out that morning in the midst of a terrible blizzard. He started to hike up the long hill lane leading to the church where he intended to worship that day. However, as conditions began to worsen, Spurgeon realized he needed to move

---

6. *C. H. Spurgeon's Autobiography*, 1:76.

7. *C. H. Spurgeon's Autobiography*, 1:75–96.

8. As Peter Morden notes, the reason some dispute Spurgeon's reckoning of the date of his conversion is that there is no record of a snowstorm in Colchester on January 6, 1850. However, there is a record of a snowstorm the following Sunday, January 13. Also, Robert Eaglen, the man who was widely believed to have preached the Isaiah 45:22 sermon that Sunday, was scheduled to preach on January 13 according to the Primitive Methodist circuit schedule. See Peter J. Morden, *Communion with Christ and His People: The Spirituality of C. H. Spurgeon* (Eugene, Ore.: Pickwick Publications, 2013), 50–51.

quickly indoors. He decided to enter the local Primitive Methodist chapel on Artillery Street.

As Spurgeon recounted, the minister who was to preach that day was unable to make it due to the storm, so a poor man of little learning stepped up into the pulpit and began to preach in a lowly style with a humble country accent. His text was Isaiah 45:22, "Look unto me, and be ye saved, all the ends of the earth: for I am God, and there is none else." Spurgeon described the man's sermon, saying,

> Just fixing his eyes on me, as if he knew all my heart, he said, "Young man, you look very miserable.... And you will always be miserable—miserable in life and miserable in death—if you don't obey my text; but if you obey now, this moment, you will be saved." Then lifting up his hands, he shouted, as only a Primitive Methodist could do, "Young man, look to Jesus Christ. Look! Look! Look! You have nothing to do but look and live."... I saw at once the way of salvation.... There and then the cloud was gone, the darkness had rolled away, and that moment I saw the sun; and I could have risen that instant, and sung with the most enthusiastic of them of the precious blood of Christ, and the simple faith which looks alone to Him.[9]

And so it was, with a look to the Savior, that Spurgeon found new life in Christ. The verse from Isaiah 45:22 was one that Spurgeon returned to repeatedly throughout his ministry. He would go on to tell his conversion story countless times and often utilized it as the basis for his own evangelistic appeals to sinners.[10] The call of the Primitive Methodist preacher on that winter morning to "look to Jesus Christ" would one day become the central theme of Spurgeon's own ministry.

---

9. C. H. Spurgeon's *Autobiography*, 1:106.

10. Eric Hayden has observed that Spurgeon gave an account of his conversion in every one of the fifty-six volumes of *The Metropolitan Tabernacle Pulpit* and did so an average of five times per volume. Cited in Geoff Thomas, "The Conversion of Charles Haddon Spurgeon: January 6 1850," *Banner of Truth*, January 1, 2000, https://banneroftruth.org/us/resources/articles/2000/the-conversion-of-charles-haddon-spurgeon-january-6-1850/.

Early Ministry in Cambridgeshire and Call to London (1850–1854)

Almost immediately after his conversion, Spurgeon began to evidence intense spiritual vitality. Many of his extant letters and diary entries from 1850 document his early spiritual formation and his fervent commitment to Christian work during this period. In a letter to his mother dated February 19, 1850, he wrote, "Oh, how I wish that I could do something for Christ!"[11] Mark Hopkins notes how quickly Spurgeon began to devote himself to various forms of Christian activity in the days following his conversion:

> Spurgeon lost no time in channelling this rush of spiritual life into practical Christian commitment and work. By February 1850 he was distributing tracts, in April he was admitted to church membership, in May he was baptized by immersion (in accordance with convictions arrived at before his conversion) and began teaching a Sunday school class, and by June he was visiting seventy people regularly on Saturdays to converse on spiritual things. He started lay preaching soon after moving to Cambridge…and began his first ministry a year later in the nearby village of Waterbeach when only seventeen.[12]

Spurgeon's zeal as a new believer erupted and overflowed into numerous avenues of ministry. Of this early phase of his Christian experience, George Needham wrote, "Having thus publicly devoted himself to the service of God, he was more earnest than ever.… He was instant in season, and indeed, seldom out of season, in his efforts to do good."[13]

---

11. C. H. Spurgeon's Autobiography, 1:118.
12. Mark Hopkins, *Nonconformity's Romantic Generation: Evangelical and Liberal Theologies in Victorian England* (Eugene, Ore.: Wipf and Stock, 2006), 127.
13. George Needham, *The Life and Labors of Charles H. Spurgeon: The Faithful Preacher, the Devoted Pastor, the Noble Philanthropist, the Beloved College President, and the Voluminous Writer, Author, Etc., Etc.* (Boston, Mass.: D. L. Guernsey, 1887), 41.

Spurgeon began to preach at the age of sixteen for the local Cambridge lay preachers' association. He preached his first sermons in cottages, in barns, and in the open air. By the time the small congregation in the rural village of Waterbeach called Spurgeon to be their pastor in the autumn of 1851, he had already developed a reputation in the surrounding region as a dynamic preacher. Upon taking up his first ministerial charge at the age of seventeen, Spurgeon immediately adopted a busy pastoral schedule, preaching frequently and carrying on a regular regiment of pastoral visitation from house to house. Hopkins writes, "His success was immediate and immense."[14] The village warmly received the ministry of their young pastor, and he became something of a local legend as the church speedily grew from forty to over four hundred members.[15] Before long, fabled accounts of the teenage preacher began to spread far and wide.

Spurgeon's pastorate at Waterbeach would be brief and ultimately preparatory for a larger sphere of ministry that the "boy preacher of the Fens" could not possibly have anticipated. After only eighteen months at Waterbeach, in January 1854, Spurgeon received a call to pastor one of London's most eminent Baptist congregations in New Park Street, Southwark. Three venerable Baptist theologians—Benjamin Keach, John Gill, and John Rippon—had previously pastored the church for one and a half centuries. Yet the church's greatest days lay ahead as Spurgeon would go on over the next four decades to draw larger crowds than not only his predecessors but any other preacher in the Christian world of his day.[16]

---

14. Hopkins, *Nonconformity's Romantic Generation*, 127.
15. H. L. Wayland, *Charles H. Spurgeon: His Faith and Works* (Philadelphia: American Baptist Publication Society, 1892), 26; Peter J. Morden, *C. H. Spurgeon: The People's Preacher* (Farnham, U.K.: CWR, 2009), 44; Eric W. Hayden, *Highlights in the Life of C. H. Spurgeon* (Pasadena, Tex.: Pilgrim Publications, 1990), 2.
16. Hayden, *Highlights*, 17.

New Park Street Chapel: Early Success, Criticism, and Adversity (1854–1860)

Immediately after Spurgeon embarked upon his new pastorate at New Park Street, the church started to grow by the hundreds. It was not long before they began to explore options for how to accommodate better the large crowds that came to hear Spurgeon preach. This effort led the church to rent larger venues, including Exeter Hall and later the newly erected Surrey Gardens Music Hall, while they worked to build a more permanent location in South London.

As Spurgeon's profile grew, so did criticism of him in the popular religious press of the day. Many of his critics seemed to view his ministry as sensational at best and superficial at worst.[17] Biographer Peter Morden writes, "Spurgeon, [the newspapers] said, was like a comet which blazed across the sky—he would burn brightly for a while but would disappear just as quickly as he had appeared."[18] Certainly, Spurgeon's youth, his unconventional preaching style, and his willingness to use secular venues for his services contributed to the press's portrayal of him as a sort of nine days' wonder. Steady criticism persisted through the mid-1850s but tended to die down as it became increasingly evident that Spurgeon's ministry had staying power.

It was during these years that Spurgeon met, courted, and married Susannah Thompson.[19] Within the first year of their marriage, Susannah gave birth to twin boys, Thomas and Charles, who would both go on to be ministers themselves.[20] By all accounts, the Spurgeons enjoyed a wonderful and happy marriage, though one marked

---

17. For examples and excerpts of criticism of Spurgeon by the religious press of his day, see *C. H. Spurgeon's Autobiography*, 2:33–61. However, not all coverage of Spurgeon was negative; see *C. H. Spurgeon's Autobiography*, 2:63–80.

18. Morden, *C. H. Spurgeon*, 55.

19. For more on the Spurgeons' marriage, see Ray Rhodes Jr., *Yours, till Heaven: The Untold Love Story of Charles and Susie Spurgeon* (Chicago: Moody, 2021).

20. Charles Jr. pastored South Street Baptist Church in Greenwich, London, while Thomas pastored first in Auckland, New Zealand, before succeeding his father at the Metropolitan Tabernacle from 1894 to 1908.

by considerable trials of poor health. Susannah, for her part, was essentially an invalid who spent most of their married life at home.[21] As for Spurgeon himself, he suffered greatly for much of his adult life from rheumatic gout and chronic kidney problems (later diagnosed as Bright's disease). By the time he reached his forties, Spurgeon had begun regularly to experience protracted seasons of ill health that often required him to be out of the pulpit for months at a time.[22]

Poor health was not the only trial that the Spurgeons endured together. Not even a year after they married, Spurgeon experienced one of the greatest tragedies of his life. On October 19, 1856, Spurgeon preached his first service at the newly rented Surrey Gardens Music Hall. Many criticized the decision to rent the hall, including some of the members of the New Park Street Chapel.[23] Some viewed it as extravagant to rent such a large venue, and others saw it as sacrilegious to make use of a space that hosted secular concerts and events during the week. Undaunted by his critics, Spurgeon went forward with securing the venue, believing it to provide a significant opportunity to proclaim the gospel to a wider audience. As Spurgeon was preaching on the night of the first service, someone in the crowd raised a false alarm by shouting, "Fire!" Mass confusion ensued. As many tried to flee the venue, a stairwell collapsed, and seven people were trampled to death, with many more injured. The tragedy left an indelible mark on Spurgeon's psyche, and he later referred to the experience as "a night which time will never erase from my memory."[24]

The episode at the Surrey Gardens Music Hall notwithstanding, Spurgeon experienced extraordinary fruitfulness in his ministry during the late 1850s. His church grew by hundreds of new mem-

---

21. The details of her condition are largely unknown, except that she underwent a fairly serious operation by one of England's leading obstetricians in 1868; see Ray Rhodes Jr., *Susie: The Life and Legacy of Susannah Spurgeon, Wife of Charles H. Spurgeon* (Chicago: Moody, 2018), 125–30.

22. Morden, *Communion with Christ*, 259.

23. Morden, *C. H. Spurgeon*, 67–68.

24. *C. H. Spurgeon's Autobiography*, 2:195.

bers each year, and he eventually began raising funds to erect a new building that could accommodate his burgeoning congregation. Spurgeon also founded the Pastors' College during these years. This training center for ministers would end up being one of his foremost institutions, and he served as its president and one of the lecturers. Kenneth Brown estimated that by Spurgeon's death in 1892, over 20 percent of all the Baptist ministers in England and Wales had trained at the Pastors' College.[25] Through this considerable alumni base and an annual conference the college held, Spurgeon developed a close-knit network of like-minded pastors all over England.

It is hard to overstate just how significant the Pastors' College was to Spurgeon's life and ministry. One of his biographers quotes him as saying of the college, "This is my life's work, to which I believe God has called me."[26] David Gracey, principal of the college from 1881 to 1893, said that "the Pastors' College was the first of [Spurgeon's] philanthropic institutions" and the one that was "dearest to his heart."[27] During Spurgeon's lifetime, the Pastors' College trained nearly nine hundred men, and its graduates planted nearly two hundred new churches in Britain alone.[28] We will consider the Pastors' College in greater depth in chapter 8.

The Metropolitan Tabernacle: Sustained Success, Expansion, and Writing (1861–1887)

On March 25, 1861, Spurgeon preached his first sermon in the newly erected Metropolitan Tabernacle near the Elephant and Castle station in South London. He began his sermon with these words,

---

25. Kenneth D. Brown, *A Social History of the Nonconformist Ministry in England and Wales 1800–1930* (Oxford: Clarendon, 1988), 33, 98.

26. W. Y. Fullerton, *C. H. Spurgeon: A Biography* (London: William and Norgate, 1920), 227.

27. David Gracey, "Mr. Spurgeon's First Institution," *Sword and the Trowel*, June 1892, 277.

28. Eric W. Hayden, *A History of Spurgeon's Tabernacle* (Pasadena, Tex.: Pilgrim Publications, 1971), 18; Morden, *C. H. Spurgeon*, 151; Mike Nicholls, *C. H. Spurgeon: The Pastor Evangelist* (Didcot, U.K.: Baptist Historical Society, 1992), 175–77.

> I would propose that the subject of the ministry of this house, as long as this platform shall stand, and as long as this house shall be frequented by worshippers, shall be the person of Jesus Christ. I am never ashamed to avow myself a Calvinist.... I do not hesitate to take the name of Baptist.... But if I am asked to say what is my creed, I think I must reply—"It is Jesus Christ."[29]

Spurgeon would preach Christ from this pulpit weekly to crowds of over six thousand on Sundays in both the morning and the evening for the next thirty years. The Metropolitan Tabernacle also became the center for many of Spurgeon's benevolent ministries. As has already been noted, by 1884, the list of active ministries operating out of the Tabernacle numbered sixty-six. These ministries engaged a vast array of material, social, and economic needs.[30] Spurgeon himself either founded, chaired, or financially supported many of these institutions. One of the foremost of these benevolent ministries was the Stockwell Orphanage, founded in 1867. The orphanage housed roughly five hundred orphans at any given time and provided care of the highest quality. Spurgeon frequently visited the orphanage and would often spend his Christmas mornings with the children who, as he said, "compassed me about like bees."[31] We will learn more about the Stockwell Orphanage as well in chapter 9.

The Tabernacle membership grew in almost every year of Spurgeon's tenure as pastor. Over his thirty-eight years in London, Spurgeon saw the church grow from 232 members when he first arrived in 1854 to 5,311 in 1892.[32] Altogether, 14,461 people became members during his ministry, an average of more than 1 person

---

29. C. H. Spurgeon, "The First Sermon in the Tabernacle," in *The Metropolitan Tabernacle Pulpit: Sermons Preached and Revised by C. H. Spurgeon* (Pasadena, Tex.: Pilgrim Publications, 1969), 7:169.

30. Spurgeon, "Mr. Spurgeon's Jubilee Meetings," *Sword and the Trowel*, July 1884, 373.

31. *C. H. Spurgeon's Autobiography*, 3:179.

32. Figures recorded in the annual membership roles in the archives of Metropolitan Tabernacle in London.

per day.[33] This sort of sustained growth was without precedent in Spurgeon's era. His power to draw large crowds was only exceeded by his ability to keep them, and he did so for nearly four decades.

Spurgeon's publishing career became more prolific during this period as well. One facet of this was the weekly publication of his sermons, a routine he began while at New Park Street.[34] These sermons achieved a consistent weekly readership of twenty-five thousand in Spurgeon's day.[35] In 1865, Spurgeon also began publishing a monthly magazine, the *Sword and the Trowel*, which, by 1871, reached a regular circulation of fifteen thousand.[36] And it was in these years that Spurgeon published some of his most famous books, including *John Ploughman's Talk*, *Morning by Morning*, *Evening by Evening*, and his magnum opus, *The Treasury of David*, which was a popular commentary on the Psalms.[37]

The Downgrade Controversy and Final Days (1887–1892)

In his final years, Spurgeon found himself embroiled in the most intense controversy of his life. What has come to be known as the Downgrade Controversy began in 1887 with a series of articles published in the *Sword and the Trowel*. Spurgeon detected what he

---

33. Hopkins, *Nonconformity's Romantic Generation*, 155.

34. These sermons are now contained in sixty-three volumes as *The New Park Street Pulpit: Containing Sermons Preached and Revised by the Rev. C. H. Spurgeon, Minister of the Chapel*, 6 vols. (Grand Rapids: Baker Book House, 2007) and *The Metropolitan Tabernacle Pulpit: Sermons Preached and Revised by C. H. Spurgeon*, Vols. 7–62 (Pasadena, Tex.: Pilgrim Publications, 1969–90).

35. Hopkins, *Nonconformity's Romantic Generation*, 154; Spurgeon, "To You," *Sword and the Trowel*, January 1871, 1–3.

36. Spurgeon, "To You," 3.

37. C. H. Spurgeon, *John Ploughman's Talk or Plain Talk for Plain People* (London: Passmore and Alabaster, n.d.); Spurgeon, *Morning by Morning: Or, Daily Readings for the Family or the Closet* (London: Passmore and Alabaster, 1865); Spurgeon, *Evening by Evening: Or, Readings at Eventide for the Family or the Closet* (London: Passmore and Alabaster, 1868); Spurgeon, *The Treasury of David: Containing an Original Exposition of the Book of Psalms; A Collection of Illustrative Extracts from the Whole Range of Literature; A Series of Homiletical Hints upon Almost Every Verse; And List of Writers upon Each Psalm*, 7 vols. (London: Passmore and Alabaster, 1869–85).

considered to be a disturbing downgrade in the theological convictions among Baptists on crucial doctrines such as the inspiration and infallibility of Scripture, the necessity and substitutionary nature of the atonement, and the existence and eternity of hell.[38] The controversy pitted Spurgeon against Baptist Union leadership who believed that Spurgeon's claims were largely unfounded. As Spurgeon gradually realized that his concerns were not widely shared among his opponents and that the prospects for reform were grim, he chose to resign from the Baptist Union. After receiving his resignation in early 1888, the Baptist Union responded by censuring Spurgeon for what they regarded as divisive behavior. This was a tough blow for Spurgeon, made all the more bitter by his failure to receive broad support from many of his friends and former students.

Spurgeon believed to his death that he was warranted in his stand against what he perceived as doctrinal decline among the Baptists of his day. Reflecting on the conflict, he said, "I am quite willing to be eaten of dogs for the next fifty years, but the more distant future shall vindicate me."[39] With the benefit of hindsight, it is evident that Spurgeon's assessment has proved true. Though he felt assured that his stand was right, he nonetheless suffered deep discouragement over the controversy. Susannah described the affair as the "deepest grief of his noble life," and she suggested that the Downgrade Controversy contributed to his premature death at the age of fifty-seven.[40]

Spurgeon spent his last days in relative peace in Mentone, France, which was a regular retreat site for him and his associates. He died there at the Hotel Beau Rivage on January 31, 1892, of kidney complications. A week later, the Metropolitan Tabernacle held a series of

---

38. Hopkins, *Nonconformity's Romantic Generation*, 234. See also Spurgeon, "Our Reply to Sundry Critics and Enquirers," *Sword and the Trowel*, September 1887, 465, where Spurgeon writes, "We cannot hold the inspiration of the Word, and yet reject it; we cannot believe in the atonement and deny it;... we cannot recognize the punishment of the impenitent and yet indulge the 'larger hope.'"

39. Spurgeon, "The Preacher's Power, and the Conditions of Obtaining It," *Sword and the Trowel*, August 1889, 420.

40. C. H. *Spurgeon's Autobiography*, 4:255.

memorial services, and on February 11, 1892, Spurgeon was finally laid to rest in West Norwood Cemetery, London. Observers estimated that more than one hundred thousand people attended these services.[41] Today, hundreds still visit his grave each year. At the foot of the grave is a sculpture of a Bible opened to 2 Timothy 4:7–8, which reads, "I have fought a good fight, I have finished my course, I have kept the faith: Henceforth there is laid up for me a crown of righteousness, which the Lord, the righteous judge, shall give me at that day: and not to me only, but unto all them also that love his appearing."

Legacy

Spurgeon's career was remarkable by any measure. In his many endeavors, such as preaching, pastoral training, church planting, publishing, and mercy ministry, he experienced ministerial fruitfulness to an unprecedented degree. Though it has been well over a century since his death, Spurgeon's sermons and other writings are still tremendously popular in the twenty-first century among evangelicals of all stripes. Christians across the globe still admire and appreciate Spurgeon's legacy. Three particular aspects of this legacy stand out for further comment.

Without question, Spurgeon's legacy shines most brightly today *in his printed sermons*. There are nearly four thousand of his sermons currently in print, and they are still tremendously popular among Christians all over the world. They have been published in a host of different collections and editions, and most of them are available free online. Their popular appeal is due, in part, to Spurgeon's singular command of the English language. President John F. Kennedy famously said of Winston Churchill, "He mobilized the English language and sent it into battle." It might be said of Spurgeon that he mobilized the English language and sent it to church. Spurgeon admired many of England's greatest poets, playwrights, and authors.

---

41. J. C. Carlile, *C. H. Spurgeon: An Interpretive Biography* (London: Kingsgate, 1933), 11.

He owned a complete set of Dickens's works, enjoyed the poetry of Wordsworth and Tennyson, and could recite long portions of Shakespeare from memory.[42] His mind was well stocked with muscular vocabulary and poignant metaphors, which he skillfully marshaled to capture the doctrines of the Bible, the beauty of the gospel, and the breadth of Christian experience.

The warmth, depth, and richness of even his earliest sermons give testimony to a preaching brilliance that is hard to account for by any natural explanations. God's anointing was plainly upon the minister and the message. Though he lacked a college degree and any formal training whatsoever, Spurgeon was nonetheless able to draw five-figure crowds in his early twenties. Yet he was no flash in the pan. His preaching had staying power and carried whole generations of his hearers for decades. Today, volumes of his sermons line the bookshelves not only of ministers but of ordinary Christians across the globe. Spurgeon's sermons are read by more people today than at any time during his life, and it is these sermons more than anything else that have kept his legacy alive well into the twenty-first century.

I have enjoyed the opportunity of talking to countless Christians who are familiar with the sermons of Charles Spurgeon. I often ask them to identify the quality or characteristic of these sermons that they find most personally and spiritually helpful. Answers vary, but they almost always will cite something related to Spurgeon's preeminent focus on the person and work of Christ. In his preaching, Spurgeon exuded something of the posture and disposition of the Lord Jesus toward sinners, and he did this in a way that brought the reality of the grace and mercy of God to his audience with profound existential power. Simply put, Spurgeon's sermons brought Christ to the hearer. One of the reasons his sermons remain so popular today

---

42. Readers interested in seeing Spurgeon's personal collection of Dickens along with several other classic works can find them on display at the Spurgeon Library on the campus of Midwestern Baptist Theological Seminary in Kansas City, Missouri.

is because they have so much of Jesus in them, emanating His love for needy sinners.

Spurgeon's legacy also continues today *through his published books*. Spurgeon wrote nearly 150 books, most of them directed to a popular Christian readership. Though some of his books have faded with time, many are still widely read by Christians today. Among the most popular of Spurgeon's books are his devotional classics such as *Morning and Evening*, his commentaries such as *The Treasury of David*, and his books on the Christian life such as *All of Grace*. Many students of preaching and pastoral theology still make use of Spurgeon's *Lectures to My Students*, as well as his pastors' conference addresses recorded in *An All-Round Ministry*. Many of these books are more popular than ever and are enjoying a far wider and more diverse readership than at any other time in history.

A third prominent aspect of Spurgeon's legacy is simply *his faithful example as a preacher, pastor, and church leader*. Spurgeon's story continues to instruct and edify pastors and other Christians in a myriad of ways. Many preachers have appreciated and imitated the profound christocentrism of Spurgeon's preaching, with its focus on the person and work of Christ and an emphasis on the universal call of the gospel. Many Christians have found much to applaud in Spurgeon's catholicity, both in his private friendships and in the fellowship he shared among other churches. Others still have derived help and comfort from Spurgeon's perseverance through suffering of various kinds, whether it be his internal struggles with depression, his trials of ill health, or his experiences of unjust criticism. Spurgeon's steadfast endurance through the hardships of life and ministry has inspired many Christians to persevere through their own trials.

Spurgeon's legacy has blessed and instructed millions over the years and speaks more loudly than ever to Christians today. However, though Spurgeon is so well known and so widely beloved, his work in benevolence and social activism is lesser known and, thus, underappreciated. Yet these burdens occupied much of his attention and played a substantial part in his overall ministry. My hope is that through the chapters that follow, Christians will come to appreciate, and even better still, imitate Spurgeon's example in his eager care and concern for the poor and the needy. We begin with a consideration of his teaching on this vital subject.

The Grace Effect

Charles Spurgeon was an eager student of church history. He read deeply in the Reformers, especially Luther and Calvin, and greatly admired the Puritans, who occupied a special place in both his heart and library. His appreciation for the Puritans began in his grandfather's study, where he first pored over the massive, age-worn folio volumes of the works of Puritan giants such as Owen, Bunyan, and Baxter. Eventually, Spurgeon came to possess his own copies of such volumes, and by the end of his life, he boasted one of the largest Puritan libraries in the world. He took great pride in the Reformed and "puritanic" theology taught in his Pastors' College.[1] The great prime minister, and Spurgeon's personal friend, William Gladstone famously referred to Spurgeon as the "last of the Puritans."[2] As a Baptist, Spurgeon saw himself squarely in the Particular Baptist tradition, even republishing the Second London Baptist Confession of Faith with his own preface in 1855 shortly after arriving at New Park Street.[3] From the outset of his career in London, he made it clear

---

1. See *C. H. Spurgeon's Autobiography, Compiled from His Diary, Letters, and Records by His Wife and His Private Secretary* (London: Passmore and Alabaster, 1898), 2:149; Spurgeon, "College and Orphanage," *Sword and the Trowel*, March 1881, 133; and W. Y. Fullerton, *C. H. Spurgeon: A Biography* (London: Williams and Norgate, 1920), 235.

2. Christian T. George, "A Man behind His Time," in *The Lost Sermons of C. H. Spurgeon: His Earliest Outlines and Sermons Between 1851 and 1854*, ed. Christian T. George (Nashville: B&H Academic, 2016), 1:18.

3. *Thirty-Two Articles of Christian Faith and Practice; or, Baptist Confession of Faith, with Scripture Proofs, Adopted by the Ministers and Messengers of the General*

that his ministry would be distinctly Reformed, trumpeting the doctrines of grace and the great *solas* of the Reformation.

However, though Spurgeon embraced Reformed and Baptist distinctives, he loved most of all to preach basic evangelical doctrines such as the necessity of the atonement, the authority of the Bible, and the priority of the new birth. This latter doctrine was a favorite subject of George Whitefield, the foremost preacher of the evangelical movement. Whitefield preached on the new birth hundreds of times and famously said, "It is the very hinge on which the salvation of each of us turns, and a point too in which all sincere Christians, of whatever denomination, agree."[4] For Spurgeon's part, he referred to Whitefield as his chief model and said that he endeavored to "follow his glorious track."[5] Throughout his lifetime, Spurgeon was often compared to Whitefield.[6] This comparison emerged almost immediately after Spurgeon entered the public view, as the first biography of Spurgeon, published when he was just twenty-one years old, was titled *"The Modern Whitfield": Sermons of the Rev. C. H. Spurgeon*.[7]

Just as the theme of the new birth was prominent in Whitefield's preaching and that of other early evangelical preachers, so it was in Spurgeon's ministry as well. And just as the early evangelical movement's preaching of the new birth led to an explosion of benevolent and charitable activity in Britain, so it did in Spurgeon's ministry. Indeed, Spurgeon believed that one of the effects of the new birth was that it transforms the individual sinner into a purveyor of mercy. Those who experience the grace and compassion of Christ through

---

Assembly, Which Met in London in 1689, with a Preface by the Rev. C. H. Spurgeon (London: Passmore & Alabaster, 1855).

4. George Whitefield, *The Nature and Necessity of Our New Birth in Christ Jesus, in Order of Salvation: A Sermon Preached in the Church of St. Mary Radcliffe in Bristol* (London, 1738), 1.

5. *C. H. Spurgeon's Autobiography*, 2:66.

6. *C. H. Spurgeon's Autobiography*, 2:47, 66, 104–5.

7. E. L. Magoon, *"The Modern Whitfield": Sermons of the Rev. C. H. Spurgeon, of London; with an Introduction and Sketch of His Life* (New York: Sheldon, Blakeman, 1856).

regeneration will themselves become gracious and compassionate toward others.

The New Birth and Concern for the Poor

The new birth factored prominently in Spurgeon's preaching on the priority of good works of benevolence and mercy. He strongly believed that the experience of divine grace in the heart should lead to the expression of Christian grace toward others, especially those in need. Thus, Spurgeon maintained that genuine compassion and sympathy for the poor are marks of true conversion. He believed that all Christians should exhibit practical expressions of benevolence and charity toward others that prove their authenticity as true believers. Spurgeon exhorted his congregation, saying, "Called with a nobler calling, let us exhibit as the result of our regenerate nature a loftier compassion for the suffering sons of men."[8]

Spurgeon was not surprised if a stranger to God's saving grace disregarded the poor. He thought it would be consistent with a sinful nature for people to think primarily of themselves and be generally indifferent to the needs of others. However, he believed the new birth brings about genuine heart transformation that produces a host of new attitudes and dispositions, including a heightened concern for the poor. He viewed a Christian without compassion for the needy as a walking contradiction. Spurgeon argued, "Sympathy is especially a Christian duty. Consider what the Christian is, and you will say that if every other man were selfish he should be disinterested; if there were nowhere else a heart that had sympathy for the needy there should be one found in every Christian breast."[9]

It is important to understand that Spurgeon did not view Christian charity as the province of a special subset of Christians. Rather, he believed that every Christian, by virtue of his regenerate nature,

---

8. C. H. Spurgeon, "Christian Sympathy," in *The Metropolitan Tabernacle Pulpit: Sermons Preached and Revised by C. H. Spurgeon* (Pasadena, Tex.: Pilgrim Publications, 1969), 8:627.

9. Spurgeon, "Christian Sympathy," 8:627.

should love his fellow men and labor for their welfare. "Love," Spurgeon said, "should shine throughout the Christian character."[10] Love is the sine qua non of true Christian piety. Moreover, Spurgeon believed love for the needy, in particular, is a distinctive mark of a renewed nature. In a sermon preached in 1873 from Jesus's words in Matthew 5:7, "Blessed are the merciful, for they shall obtain mercy," Spurgeon said, "No merciful man could forget the poor. He who passed by their ills without sympathy and saw their suffering without relieving them, might prate as he would about inward Grace, but Divine Grace in his heart there could not be! The Lord does not acknowledge as of His family one who can see his brother has needs and shuts up 'his heart of compassion from him.' The apostle John rightly asks, 'How dwells the love of God in him?' No, the truly merciful are considerate of those who are poor."[11] In the above quotation, Spurgeon strongly stated his belief in a correlation between the experience of divine grace in the heart and the commensurate character of life that shows itself in mercy and compassion toward the poor. In other words, Spurgeon believed true conversion inevitably leads to the exercise of Christian charity. Thus, he understood sympathy for the poor as a litmus test for true saving faith.

Spurgeon frequently stressed that one of the results of regeneration is authentic love for one's neighbor, including love for the poor and needy. In 1876, he said, "If Christ has saved you, he will save you from being selfish. You will love your fellow men; you will desire to do them good. You will endeavor to help the poor; you will try to instruct the ignorant. He who truly becomes a Christian becomes in that very same day a practical philanthropist. No man is a true Christian who is un-Christlike.... The true Christian lives for others: in a word, he lives for Christ."[12] The new birth brings about a fundamentally new nature, with love toward others as one of its principal

---

10. Spurgeon, "The Good Samaritan," in *Metropolitan Tabernacle Pulpit*, 23:350.
11. Spurgeon, "The Fifth Beatitude," in *Metropolitan Tabernacle Pulpit*, 55:400.
12. Spurgeon, "Aeneas," in *Metropolitan Tabernacle Pulpit*, 22:539.

qualities. Spurgeon thus believed that one of the surest signs of the new birth is genuine love for one's fellow men.

A Warning to the Cold-Hearted

Spurgeon reserved the sternest words for professing Christians who show little regard for the needs of the poor. He viewed indifference toward the needy as sub-Christian, something utterly alien to an authentic profession of faith. Spurgeon feared that some in his large congregation in London possessed this type of indifference.[13] He often sought to bring such people to conviction through severe warnings. The following admonition from an 1866 sermon is emblematic of the sort of rebuke Spurgeon would issue to such people:

> You may talk about your religion till you have worn your tongue out, and you may get others to believe you; and you may remain in the Church twenty years, and nobody ever detect you in anything like an inconsistency; but, if it be in your power, and you do nothing to relieve the necessities of the poor members of Christ's body, you will be damned as surely as if you were drunkards or whoremongers. If you have no care for God's Church this text applies to you, and will as surely sink you to the lowest hell as if you had been common blasphemers.[14]

Spurgeon did not mince words. He believed a person truly acquainted with the saving grace of God could never close his heart to the needy.

---

13. Spurgeon's congregation drew heavily from the working class of London and was thus predominately lower-middle class in social distribution, though he did attract some among the poor of London. See Joseph S. Meisel, *Public Speech and the Culture of Public Life in the Age of Gladstone* (New York: Columbia University Press, 2001), 130–31; Patricia Stallings Kruppa, *Charles Haddon Spurgeon: A Preacher's Progress* (New York: Garland, 1982), 134–38, 496–97. Generally speaking, the social location of the Tabernacle membership was in keeping with trends among Victorian Baptists. See Hugh McLeod, *Class and Religion in the Late Victorian City* (London: Croom Helm, 1974), 69–70; and J. H. Y. Briggs, *The English Baptists of the Nineteenth Century* (Didcot, U.K.: Baptist Historical Society, 1994), 3:268–78.

14. Spurgeon, "The Reward of the Righteous," in *Metropolitan Tabernacle Pulpit*, 12:46.

In this particular sermon, Spurgeon sought to convince professing Christians not to neglect the needs of others within the body of Christ. Christians should have a special regard for their brothers and sisters in the family of God. Spurgeon embraced the words of the apostle Paul from Galatians 6:10: "As we have therefore opportunity, let us do good unto all men, especially unto them who are of the household of faith." However, Spurgeon did not believe Christians should limit their charity to those within the church alone. He argued, "The Christian's sympathy should ever be of the widest character."[15] Spurgeon described Christian sympathy as a "precious stone of love" cast into the "crystal pool of a renewed heart." This stone of love should generate "ever-widening circles of sympathy." The first ring is the Christian's household. The second is the household of faith, namely the church. Spurgeon then said, "Look once more, for the ever-widening ring has reached the very limit of the lake, and included all men in its area."[16] Indeed, in Spurgeon's mind, there ought to be no limit to the sphere of Christian love. Surely members of the Lord's family have special priority for the believer, but Christian love must nonetheless extend beyond the church to include all members of the human family.

Spurgeon believed that benevolence and good works are essential to the Christian life by virtue of the new birth. Just as a good tree bears good fruit, so too Christian faith ought to result in love for the poor and regard for the needy. In one of his most concise and lucid statements on this subject, cited earlier in this book, Spurgeon said, "To me, a follower of Jesus means a friend of man. A Christian is a philanthropist by profession, and generous by force of grace; wide as the reign of sorrow is the stretch of his love, and where he cannot help he pities still."[17] He went on to say, "Time was when, wherever a man met a Christian he met a helper. 'I shall starve!' said he, until

---

15. Spurgeon, "Christian Sympathy," 8:628.
16. Spurgeon, "Christian Sympathy," 8:628.
17. Spurgeon, "Christian Sympathy," 8:628.

he saw a Christian's face, and then he said, 'Now shall I be aided.'"[18] Spurgeon believed that every Christian is, in some sense, a philanthropist. This did not mean, as in the modern sense of the word, that every Christian gives large sums of money to aid the poor (though some are certainly called to this). However, it did mean that every Christian should naturally be disposed to show compassion toward the poor and should seek, as opportunity affords, practical steps to relieve human oppression, suffering, and need. Spurgeon understood this to be the product of the new birth. "Where God has given a man a new heart and a right spirit," he said, "there is great tenderness to all the poor."[19]

A Call to All Christians

We must appreciate just how universal Spurgeon understood this call to Christian compassion for the poor and needy to be. He did not see this as optional or preferable but as essential and fundamental to regenerate humanity. He believed that the call to Christian social concern is not limited to the privileged few or to a small number of individuals who felt uniquely called. Rather, the call to Christian concern for the needy is part of the call to basic discipleship. Every Christian, Spurgeon believed, should have a heart of compassion and love for the poor and the destitute. Love for needy neighbors is part of the very fabric of the Christian life.

Of course, Spurgeon believed compassion and concern for the needy ought to produce action on their behalf. He once said, "I would rather create an ounce of help than a ton of theory."[20] He urged Christians to devote themselves to practical service as they have opportunity. This was clearly the expectation he had for his congregants, as he said, "Every member who joins my church

---

18. Spurgeon, "Christian Sympathy," 8:634.
19. Spurgeon, "Fifth Beatitude," 55:400.
20. Spurgeon, "The Blind Man's Eyes Opened; or, Practical Christianity," in *Metropolitan Tabernacle Pulpit*, 29:677.

is expected to do something for his fellow creatures."[21] Writing in 1933, one of Spurgeon's biographers and former students, J. C. Carlile, summarized, "What is now familiarly known as Social Service, from Spurgeon's point of view, was the ordinary expression of Christian character."[22] This is not to say that Spurgeon was an advocate of large-scale government-sponsored social welfare. However, it is to say that Spurgeon believed there is a special burden on Christians to care for the poor by nature of their new birth. Practical care and concern for the needy, the afflicted, and the oppressed ought to be natural to the Christian by virtue of regeneration.

Spurgeon enjoined every true Christian to practical ministry among the poor and afflicted with the utmost urgency, saying, "Now learn this lesson, all ye followers of Christ. Whenever you see suffering, I hope you will each one feel 'I must work, I must help.' Whenever you witness poverty, whenever you behold vice, say to yourself, 'I must work, I must work.' If you are worthy of the Christ whom you call leader, let all the necessities of men impel you, compel you, constrain you to be blessing them."[23] The widespread suffering of men and women ought to drive Christians to labor on their behalf. Spurgeon would not allow his hearers to satisfy themselves with rote adherence to religious forms. It is not enough to participate in church services and apprehend sound preaching. Nor is it sufficient to develop mere sympathies and burdens for those in need. Compassion has to melt into action. Spurgeon went on to say, "Oh that I could lay my hand—or, better far, that my Master would lay his pierced hand on every true Christian here and press it upon him until he cried out, 'I cannot sit here. I must be at work as soon as this

---

21. Eric W. Hayden, *A Centennial History of Spurgeon's Tabernacle* (London: Clifford Frost, 1962), 80.

22. J. C. Carlile, *C. H. Spurgeon: An Interpretive Biography* (London: Kingsgate, 1933), 228.

23. Spurgeon, "Blind Man's Eyes Opened," 29:682.

service is done. I must not only hear, and give, and pray, but I must also work.'"[24]

Spurgeon often referred to the Metropolitan Tabernacle as a "working church."[25] The members of the congregation embraced this identity. It would be difficult, perhaps impossible, to calculate with precision the number of volunteers required to sustain the many ministries, missions, classes, societies, and institutions that operated out of the Tabernacle. William Olney, one of Spurgeon's deacons, speculated that the number of members who were out conducting meetings of various kinds among the poor of London on Sunday evenings was at least one thousand.[26] The wide-ranging and multifaceted work of the church could not have succeeded as it did without a high degree of volunteer recruitment and coordination. Spurgeon expected all the church's members to engage in this kind of Christian work. Spurgeon's contemporary Charles Booth, in his famous sociological study of the London poor, commented, "Such was the power [Spurgeon] exercised that, as one admirer phrases it, 'you could not hear him without saying, What can I do for Jesus?'"[27]

A Needed Word for the Church

Christians today have tended to neglect Spurgeon's teaching on the relationship between the new birth and how Christians relate to the needy, with detrimental consequences for the church. Failure to understand how the new birth affects our view of the afflicted and the disenfranchised will not only stymie otherwise healthy efforts to

---

24. Spurgeon, "Blind Man's Eyes Opened," 29:682.
25. For examples, see Spurgeon, "The Arrows of the Lord's Deliverance," in *Metropolitan Tabernacle Pulpit*, 10:276; Spurgeon, "A Bright Light in Deep Shades," in *Metropolitan Tabernacle Pulpit*, 18:274; Spurgeon, "A Plea for the Pastors' College," *Sword and the Trowel*, June 1875, 253; Spurgeon, *Annual Report of the Stockwell Orphanage for Fatherless Boys* (London: Passmore & Alabaster, 1879), 16.
26. Arnold Dallimore, *Spurgeon: A New Biography* (Edinburgh: Banner of Truth, 1985), 159.
27. Charles Booth, *Life and Labour of the People in London*, 3rd ser., vol. 4, *Religious Influences, Inner South London* (London: Macmillan, 1902), 74.

promote benevolence and mercy ministry but will also cripple the church's witness. Spurgeon preached a new birth that produces compelling mercy and love toward those in need, spilling over into works of charity and benevolence. These works not only provided aid and relief to thousands but also set forth a striking witness to the power of the gospel to change people and make them truly new.

Spurgeon's teaching on this subject presents us with several valuable lessons. Foremost among them is the idea that Christians should not view care for the needy as merely optional or preferable for the believer but as basic and essential to the new nature produced by regeneration. This is a manifestly biblical idea (e.g., Titus 2:14; 3:3–8, 14; James 1:27; 1 John 3:16–18). Experiencing God's kindness, compassion, and mercy ought to transform people. The new birth causes selfish and self-absorbed sinners to become loving toward their neighbors, tender toward the poor, and compassionate toward the needy. True Christians are generous, warmhearted, and beneficent toward others. They delight in mercy, treasure kindness, and are eager to do good to needy people. They are not stingy, parsimonious, or miserly. When they encounter people who are afflicted and in genuine need, their regenerate instinct is to provide aid and relief (see Luke 10:25–37). The virtues of mercy, kindness, and love should radiate from the Christian's life and character. All of this is the product of the new birth.

The second important lesson Christians can glean from Spurgeon is that such transformation is a vital part of the Christian witness in the world. The experience of supernatural regeneration made manifest in one's merciful and compassionate disposition toward others is one of the most compelling demonstrations of the power of the gospel to change men and women. The new birth transmutes people from being entirely consumed with the love of self to being consumed with the needs of others. Spurgeon reminds us that regeneration should produce something universally attractive and compelling to a world full of sorrows and misery. What a credit it would be to the gospel's appeal if the world saw in the people of God a universal predisposition of compassion in the face of deprivation and want. How the testimony of the church would be improved if it were true that "wherever a man met a Christian he met a helper." Perhaps more would be won to the faith if Christians showed a commitment to compassionate concern for the poor and the afflicted, not necessarily as a means of transforming the culture or eradicating poverty from the world, but simply as a way of living out their new nature in Christ.

Few things poison the Christian witness as much as cruelty and hard-heartedness toward the poor and the oppressed. A lack of compassion among Christians for needy people paralyzes the church's testimony in the world and bears false witness about the power of the new birth and the sweetness of the grace of God. Because of the gospel, Christians should be the most gracious people in the world. Such is the inevitable effect of experiencing God's love in regeneration.

3

Followers of Christ, Lovers of Men

Charles Spurgeon did not rely on one silver bullet text to encourage social concern among his congregation. Instead, he promoted benevolence and care for the needy by bringing a variety of scriptural burdens to bear upon his hearers. As we saw in the last chapter, Spurgeon believed Christian compassion and charity, particularly for the poor, are inevitable consequences of the new birth. However, regeneration represents only the beginning. The new birth transforms the individual from a rebellious sinner into a loving follower of the Lord Jesus Christ. Once converted, the work of discipleship commences. As part of this work, the believer embarks on a lifetime of following the teachings and example of Jesus. In so doing, Spurgeon maintained, faithful Christians will demonstrate practical concern and care for the poor and the needy according to the model that Jesus set for His followers.

Preaching Jesus as a Model for Believers to Follow

Most students of Spurgeon agree that the most prominent feature of his preaching was his emphasis on the person and work of Christ. Lewis Drummond comments, "He always lifted up who Jesus Christ was and what He did so that people might be attracted to Him as Lord and Savior."[1] Christian George notes, "From the beginning of his ministry to its conclusion, Spurgeon preached Christ frequently

---

1. Lewis A. Drummond, *Spurgeon: Prince of Preachers*, 3rd ed. (Grand Rapids: Kregel Publications, 1992), 291.

and thoroughly."[2] Few preachers in church history—let alone the nineteenth century—were more thoroughly Christ-centered in their preaching than he was. While Spurgeon consistently promoted Christ as a savior to whom sinners must come by faith for the forgiveness of their sins, he also repeatedly commended Christ as a model for Christians to follow. Spurgeon argued that Christians should be imitators of Christ and always seek to follow His example.

However, some view with suspicion the practice of preaching Jesus as a model for Christians to follow. They argue that we should consider the person of Christ and His effect on our lives only through the lens of His substitutionary death on our behalf. After all, this is what secures our redemption. Christ's example is only relevant insofar as He lived the perfect life we could never live so that we could receive the record of His righteous life imputed to us as a gift by faith. Preaching Jesus as a model for believers to follow in their daily lives has no place and inevitably engenders a kind of dead moralism that will leave Christians discouraged and deflated as they fail to live up to His example.

This shallow (and unbiblical) way of thinking fails to take into account the fact that Jesus frequently set patterns for His disciples to follow and even expressly commanded them to imitate His example at a number of points. After washing the disciples' feet in the upper room, Jesus said in John 13:15, "For I have given you an example, that ye should do as I have done to you." Jesus's call to His disciples

---

2. Christian T. George, "Jesus Christ, the 'Prince of Pilgrims': A Critical Analysis of the Ontological, Functional, and Exegetical Christologies in the Sermons, Writings, and Lectures of Charles Haddon Spurgeon (1834–1892)" (PhD diss., University of St. Andrews, 2011), 46. Many others have identified the christocentric theme in Spurgeon's preaching as well. See Mark Hopkins, *Nonconformity's Romantic Generation: Evangelical and Liberal Theologies in Victorian England* (Eugene, Ore.: Wipf and Stock, 2006), 153–54; Peter J. Morden, *Communion with Christ and His People: The Spirituality of C. H. Spurgeon* (Eugene, Ore.: Pickwick Publications), 14; Nathan A. Finn and Aaron Lumpkin, eds., *The Sum and Substance of the Gospel: The Christ-Centered Piety of Charles Haddon Spurgeon* (Grand Rapids: Reformation Heritage Books, 2020), 27–28.

to take up their cross and follow Him is, in part, a call for believers to imitate Him in His suffering and self-denial (see Matt. 16:24; Mark 8:34; Luke 9:23). Furthermore, the apostles often directed believers to follow the example of Christ. The apostle Paul exhorted the Christians in Corinth, "Be ye followers of me, even as I also am of Christ" (1 Cor. 11:1). The apostle Peter, writing of Christ's example in suffering, said, "For even hereunto were ye called: because Christ also suffered for us, leaving us an example, that ye should follow his steps" (1 Peter 2:21). The apostle John could write confidently, "He that saith he abideth in him ought himself also so to walk, even as he walked" (1 John 2:6).

The Bible plainly teaches that a large part of Jesus's ministry while He was on earth was to set a model for His followers to imitate. This is precisely why His followers are referred to as "disciples" and why the primary directive He gives them is the simple command "Follow me." Disciples follow the model set by their teacher. Servants follow the example of their master. Christians follow the pattern laid out for them by Christ Himself.

The Example of Christ in Caring for the Needy

It is no surprise, therefore, that one of the themes that recurred most often in Spurgeon's preaching on the subject of Christian benevolence and social concern was the need for Christians to imitate the example of Christ. Jesus set the ultimate pattern for His disciples to imitate. Spurgeon said in an 1883 sermon, "[Jesus] is the Worker, the Chief Worker and the Example to all workers."[3] For Spurgeon, engaging in active Christian work on behalf of the needy was part of being faithful to the example set by the Lord Himself. Spurgeon once summarized Jesus's work in this way,

---

3. C. H. Spurgeon, "The Blind Man's Eyes Opened; or, Practical Christianity," in *The Metropolitan Tabernacle Pulpit: Sermons Preached and Revised by C. H. Spurgeon* (Pasadena, Tex.: Pilgrim Publications, 1973), 29:675.

He went about, not discoursing upon benevolence, but "doing good;" he itinerated not to stir up a missionary spirit, but "to preach glad tidings to the poor." Where others theorized he wrought, where they planned he achieved, where they despaired he triumphed! Compared with him, our existence is a mere windbag; his life was solid essential action, and ours a hazy dream, an unsubstantial would-be which yet is not. Most blessed Son of the Highest, thou who workest evermore, teach us also how to begin to live, ere we have stumbled into our graves while prating about purposes and resolves![4]

Spurgeon often referred to Jesus as the "great Philanthropist."[5] For example, in a message on the shortest verse in the Bible—"Jesus wept" (John 11:35)—he said, "Jesus was far more tender towards humanity than any other man has ever been. He was the great Philanthropist!"[6] In another sermon, he said, "Every real philanthropist is a copy of the Lord Jesus; for though it is too low a term to apply to his infinite excellence, yet truly the Son of God is the grandest of all philanthropists."[7] Spurgeon held Jesus forth as the ultimate friend of man and the model for all those who are called by Him to love their neighbors.

Spurgeon preached that Christ perfectly exemplified mercy, compassion, service, and love and thus provided a model for Christians to follow. In a sermon preached in 1873, Spurgeon said, "[A Christian] understands that as his Lord and Master sought after that which was

---

4. C. H. Spurgeon, "Acta Non Verba," *Sword and the Trowel*, January 1873, 2.

5. For examples, see Spurgeon, "For Whom Did Christ Die?" in *Metropolitan Tabernacle Pulpit*, 20:498; Spurgeon, "Our Hiding Place," in *Metropolitan Tabernacle Pulpit*, 49:537; Spurgeon, "Mourning at the Cross," in *Metropolitan Tabernacle Pulpit*, 50:451. In the Victorian era, the word *philanthropist* had a broader meaning than simply an affluent individual giving money to charity. Philanthropy was understood more generally as helping the needy. Such help could come in a variety of forms and was not limited to financial aid. This broader usage of the term represents the way in which Spurgeon used the word.

6. Spurgeon, "Jesus Wept," in *Metropolitan Tabernacle Pulpit*, 35:338.

7. Spurgeon, "By All Means Save Some," in *Metropolitan Tabernacle Pulpit*, 20:243.

wounded, bound up that which was broken, healed that which was sick and brought again that which was driven away, even so ought all His servants to imitate their Master by looking with the greatest interest after those who are in the saddest plight. O children of God, if ever you are hardhearted towards any sorrowful person, you are not what you ought to be! You are not like your Master!"[8] Spurgeon believed Christians ought to observe the manner in which Jesus ministered to the needy and follow His example by ministering to others. As Christ looked with interest upon the poor and the downtrodden, so also Christians are to have sympathy for those in distress.

Spurgeon did not hesitate to appeal to the emotions of his audience in this regard. He would often paint scenes of the most devastating and abject need before his listeners in order to impel them to Christian charity. By eliciting compassion for human need, Spurgeon believed himself to be attuned to the humanity of Christ. He argued that as a man, Christ was never cold or indifferent to human suffering. He said, "It is not so with Jesus. He has a quick eye to see the blind beggar if he sees nothing else.... He is all eye, all ear, all heart, all hand, where misery is present. My Master is made of tenderness: he melts with love. O true souls who love him, copy him in this, and ever let your hearts be touched with a fellow feeling for the suffering and the sinning."[9]

Spurgeon held that Jesus's experience of humanity through His incarnation conditioned Him to be sensitive to the needs of the poor and the afflicted. Jesus took on frail human flesh and, in so doing, became sympathetic to human weakness. Spurgeon set forth the significance of this aspect of Jesus's ministry when he said, "If he cannot go with us through all the rough places of our pilgrim-way, how can he be our guide? If he has never traveled in the night himself, how can he whisper consolation to us in our darkest hours? We have a fully qualified High Priest in our Lord Jesus Christ: he is perfect

---

8. Spurgeon, "The Fifth Beatitude," in *Metropolitan Tabernacle Pulpit*, 55:402.
9. Spurgeon, "Blind Man's Eyes Opened," 29:675.

in that capacity."[10] Jesus was thus able to be a faithful high priest, in part, because He had developed sympathy with mankind in His incarnation. Furthermore, the incarnation enabled Jesus to provide a model for Christians to follow. Because He experienced humanity Himself, He was able to provide an example for Christians of how they ought to live.

In an 1862 sermon on the subject of Christian sympathy, Spurgeon said, "Beloved, will you remember the blessed example of our Lord and Saviour Jesus Christ?... His heart is made of tenderness, his bowels melt with love. In all our afflictions he is afflicted. Since the day when he became flesh of our flesh, he hath never hidden himself from our sufferings."[11] Spurgeon also argued that Jesus, though risen and ascended, was still conditioned by the incarnation and thus continues to have ongoing sympathy for those in need. His argument was that just as Christ is perpetually sympathetic to human frailty, so Christians ought always to be compassionate toward human weakness and distress.

Spurgeon believed that part of the reason why so few follow the example of Jesus in this regard is because they are willfully ignorant of the needs around them. Spurgeon described his own community in the sprawling metropolis of London as a "wicked, wretched city," full of scenes of "abject misery." He said, "There are sights in this metropolis that might melt a heart of steel, and make a Nabal generous."[12] Spurgeon believed that in the face of these sorts of scenes, believers ought to imitate Christ by showing Christian compassion. He said to his congregation, "If but for one night you could see the harlotry and infamy, if you could but once see the rascality of London gathered into one mass, your hearts would melt with woe and bitterness."[13] On another occasion, he said to his church, "I want

---

10. Spurgeon, "Our Sympathizing High Priest," in *Metropolitan Tabernacle Pulpit*, 32:590.
11. Spurgeon, "Christian Sympathy," in *Metropolitan Tabernacle Pulpit*, 8:628.
12. Spurgeon, "Blind Man's Eyes Opened," 29:675.
13. Spurgeon, "Christian Sympathy," 8:632. Many Victorians wrote about the

you to help the heathen world, but I want you to begin with caring for this great heathen world of London."[14]

Spurgeon maintained that the abiding example of Jesus toward the poor is one of the greatest motivations for Christian activism. In the sermon on Christian sympathy mentioned above, Spurgeon went on to say, "But if ye profess to be followers of the Man of Nazareth, be ye full of compassion; he feeds the hungry lest they faint by the way; he bindeth up the broken in heart and healeth all their wounds; he heareth the cry of the needy and precious shall their blood be in his sight; therefore be ye also tenderhearted also very affectionate the one toward the other."[15] Clearly Spurgeon felt that Christ's example of compassion and benevolence ought to loom large in the minds and hearts of His disciples. Jesus called believers to imitate His "splendid life of disinterested philanthropy."[16] Thus, Spurgeon sought to compel his hearers to Christian activism through the model set by Jesus. If Christians are called to follow Jesus, they are then called to Christ-like compassion and activism on behalf of the needy.

---

plight of the poor of London in the nineteenth century. In 1851, the journalist Henry Mayhew published the first installment of an immense project of social research on the plight of London's poor. See Henry Mayhew, *London Labour and the London Poor: A Cyclopedia of the Condition and Earnings of Those That Will Work, Those That Cannot Work, and Those That Will Not Work*, 3 vols. (London: George Woodfall and Son, 1851–61). The Congregational Union, in an effort to inspire work among the poor, published Andrew Hearns, *The Bitter Cry of Outcast London: An Inquiry into the Condition of the Abject Poor* (London: James Clarke, 1883). In 1890, William Booth, founder of the Salvation Army, documented the impoverished state of many, as well as his proposal for addressing mass poverty in England. See William Booth, *In Darkest England and the Way Out* (London: Funk and Wagnalls, 1890). One of Spurgeon's brightest students, closest friends, and his eventual successor, Archibald G. Brown, a powerful preacher in his own right, pastored in London's East End at the East London Tabernacle. He experienced firsthand much of the poverty and degradation of East End life and wrote a great deal about it. See Iain Murray, *Archibald G. Brown: Spurgeon's Successor* (Edinburgh: Banner of Truth, 2011), 50–53, 103–21.

14. Spurgeon, "A Desperate Case—How to Meet It," in *Metropolitan Tabernacle Pulpit*, 10:24.

15. Spurgeon, "Christian Sympathy," 8:628–29.

16. Spurgeon, "Seeing Is Not Believing, but Believing Is Seeing," in *Metropolitan Tabernacle Pulpit*, 12:364.

The Good Samaritan

On Sunday morning, June 17, 1877, Spurgeon preached to the Metropolitan Tabernacle from Luke 10:25–37. This particular sermon is noteworthy for a number of reasons. In the first place, it was rare that Spurgeon preached a single sermon on more than a verse or two, as he himself acknowledged in the opening of the sermon.[17] It is also noteworthy because of the dedication inserted just below the title of the message that reads, "On behalf of the Hospitals of London."[18] This sermon's significance for the theme of this book is enhanced by the fact that it was preached in 1877 in the latter half of Spurgeon's ministry in London when he was well into his forties. Also, many of Spurgeon's most prominent benevolent ministries were not only fully operational but were flourishing by this time. Accordingly, this sermon makes an excellent case study for Spurgeon's understanding of the place of benevolence and mercy ministry in the Christian life.

In the message, Spurgeon commended the Good Samaritan as an example for all believers to follow. He argued that the Good Samaritan represents how Christians ought to fulfill the second great commandment, to love one's neighbor. Thus, the Good Samaritan provides believers with a practical example of how one might engage in Christian benevolence and charity toward those in need.

Spurgeon observed in the narrative of Luke 10:25–37 that the man who fell among thieves was a victim of the sins of others. At this point in the sermon, Spurgeon drew a parallel with some in London society in his own day who would have also been properly considered victims:

---

17. Spurgeon, "The Good Samaritan," in *Metropolitan Tabernacle Pulpit*, 23:349.

18. In the same month as the preaching of this sermon on behalf of London's hospitals, Spurgeon announced in the *Sword and the Trowel* that a group of young women from the Tabernacle established the Flower Mission, which was founded to deliver flowers to hospitals with texts of Scripture appended to them; see Spurgeon, "Notes," *Sword and the Trowel*, June 1877, 286. Spurgeon himself donated flowers to the Tabernacle Flower Mission from his own gardens at Westwood; see Ray Rhodes Jr., *Susie: The Life and Legacy of Susannah Spurgeon, Wife of Charles H. Spurgeon* (Chicago: Moody, 2018), 163.

> When we see innocent persons suffering as the result of the sin of others our pity should be excited. How many there are of little children starving, and pining into chronic disease through a father's drunkenness, which keeps the table bare! Wives too, who work hard themselves are brought down to pining sickness and painful disease by the laziness and cruelty of those who should have cherished them. Work-people, too, are often sorely oppressed in their wages and have to work themselves to death's door to earn a pittance. Those are the people who ought to have our sympathy when accident or disease bring them to the hospital gates, "wounded and half dead."[19]

Spurgeon's benevolent ministries addressed a wide array of needy individuals and groups, but Spurgeon seemed to be particularly eager to help those who were in some way neglected or oppressed. His compassion extended especially to those who found themselves in need as the result of the sins of others.

During the message, Spurgeon cited Jerome, who claimed that the path between Jerusalem and Jericho where the poor man fell among thieves had been known in that day as the "path of blood."[20] Here, Spurgeon drew another parallel to nineteenth-century London:

> Long hours in ill-ventilated work-rooms are accountable for thousands of lives, and so are stinted wages, which prevent a sufficiency of food from being procured. Many a needle-woman's way of life is truly a path of blood. When I think of the multitudes of our work people in this city who have to live in close, unhealthy rooms, crowded together in lanes and courts where the air is stagnant, I do not hesitate to say that much of the road which has to be trodden by the poor of London is as much deserving of the name of the way of blood as the road from Jerusalem to Jericho. If they do not lose their money it is because they never have it: if they do not fall among thieves, they fall among diseases which practically wound them, and leave them half dead.... Do you not agree with me

---

19. Spurgeon, "Good Samaritan," 23:351.
20. Spurgeon, "Good Samaritan," 23:352.

that such persons ought to be among the first to receive of our Christian kindness?[21]

Spurgeon called upon the men and women of the Metropolitan Tabernacle to reach out in compassion to the poor, the oppressed, and the disenfranchised in London society. He believed it would not be difficult to find such needy people in the city.

Spurgeon spent a large portion of the message analyzing the priest and the Levite who passed by the poor man who fell among thieves. He sharply condemned these men and those like them who disregard the needs of the poor, saying, "So you do know that there is poverty and sickness around you, and if you pass by on the other side you will have looked at it, you will have known about it, and on your heads will be the criminality of having left the wounded man unhelped."[22] Spurgeon addressed many of his points of application to the rich among his listeners. Similar to Paul in 1 Timothy 6:17–19, Spurgeon argued that one of the main reasons God makes a man rich is so that he can use his affluence to bless the poor. He said, "Now, you that are wealthy are sent into our city on purpose that you may have compassion upon the sick, the wounded, the poor, and the needy. God's intent in endowing any person with more substance than he needs is that he may have the pleasurable office, or rather let me say, the delightful privilege, of relieving want and woe."[23]

Additionally, observing that the Good Samaritan was helping a man who presumably was a Jew, Spurgeon noted, "We are to relieve real distress irrespective of creed, as the Samaritan did."[24] Spurgeon practiced what he preached. His benevolence efforts extended to needy men and women regardless of denominational and, in some cases, religious background.

---

21. Spurgeon, "Good Samaritan," 23:352.
22. Spurgeon, "Good Samaritan," 23:354.
23. Spurgeon, "Good Samaritan," 23:353.
24. Spurgeon, "Good Samaritan," 23:356.

In Spurgeon's view, the Good Samaritan was a striking example of the sort of Christian charity for which followers of Christ ought to be known. Spurgeon concluded his exposition of the text by commending the Good Samaritan as a model of Christian benevolence:

> The Samaritan was personally benevolent, and therein he is a mirror and model to us all.... Brethren, let what we do for others always be done in the noblest style. Let us not treat the poor like dogs to whom we fling a bone, nor visit the sick like superior beings who feel that they are stooping down to inferiors when they enter their rooms; but in the sweet tenderness of real love, learned at Jesu's feet, let us imitate this good Samaritan.[25]

In Luke 10:25–37, Spurgeon found a compelling example of Christian philanthropy and kindness. For him, the text was a paradigm of how Christians should love their neighbors and serve the needy.

Following Jesus

Spurgeon's focus on the example and teaching of the Lord Jesus with respect to benevolence, love of neighbor, and concern for the poor highlights some important lessons for Christians today. First, *Spurgeon recognized that care and concern for the needy and the afflicted is a matter of faithfully following in the footsteps of Jesus. It is thus a matter of basic Christian discipleship.* Just as the Lord Himself compassionately attended to the needs of those around Him, so His servants ought to imitate His example. It was customary for Jesus to meet the pressing physical demands of the poor as He went about teaching from town to town. He fed the hungry, healed the sick, and helped those in distress, thereby setting an example for His disciples to follow. Though no follower of Christ can ever meet the needs of others in precisely the same way that Jesus did, all Christ-followers can imitate His basic compassion for the needy around them and pursue practical ways of meeting real needs.

---

25. Spurgeon, "Good Samaritan," 23:357–58.

As Christians follow Jesus's example, they represent Him to the world. Thus, Christians, by their conduct, inevitably say something to others about who they understand Christ to be. Therefore, if Christians are insensitive, hard-hearted, and ruthless in their dealings with their neighbors, many will conclude that they have learned this from the one whom they profess to follow. By the same token, if Christians show compassion for the needy and concern for the oppressed and the afflicted, some will conclude that this is what Christ must be like.

Christians must remember that Jesus called men and women not only to repentance and faith but to a life of discipleship. The gospel call includes a call to follow Jesus, and part of following Jesus in basic discipleship is imitating His example. Part of the pattern He left behind for His disciples is that He was sensitive to the felt needs and burdens of those whom He served. He had a heart of compassion for the suffering and the afflicted. All those who profess to follow Christ must follow Him in this.

A second lesson Spurgeon teaches us is that *Jesus reveals Himself to humanity as one who is sympathetic and compassionate toward human suffering and need.* Of course, Jesus's primary work was revealing who He was as the Son of God and the long-expected Messiah. Moreover, Jesus repeatedly emphasized that He was the God-appointed Savior to whom sinners must look in repentance and faith, trusting in His blood alone to secure their redemption. We should emphasize these aspects of Jesus's person and ministry above all else. The focus of the gospel message is on the incarnation, death, and resurrection of the Son of God by which He has made a way of salvation for sinners. Christians should never suggest that Jesus's primary concern during his earthly ministry was to engage in social work or alleviate poverty. This is not ultimately why He came. Simply put, He came to reveal Himself as the Christ, to die and to rise, and to call men and women into a saving relationship with Himself.

Nonetheless, as Jesus revealed Himself to the world, one of the things He disclosed about Himself was that He is compassionate in His disposition toward human suffering. It is a matter of significance that Jesus performed most of His miracles to meet the pressing physical and material burdens of the people around Him. He usually performed His miracles on behalf of people who were severely afflicted. He healed the sick, raised the dead, and fed the hungry.

Though there are significant theological reasons why Jesus performed these miracles that we must appreciate, we mustn't miss something very basic going on in these episodes: Jesus loved people, cared about their suffering, and purposed to intervene. He genuinely wanted to help people and provide for their relief. Of course, He ultimately wanted to bring about their spiritual salvation whereby they could be spared everlasting suffering in hell. Yet, he also expressed concern for people experiencing present suffering in this life. In some instances, it was precisely His concern for their present suffering that manifested His concern for their eternal suffering as well (see John 6). The material point is that as Jesus came to reveal who He is, one of the things He revealed about Himself was that He cares about the suffering and sorrow of needy men and women.

This leads to a third lesson Spurgeon teaches us: *practical care and concern for the poor and the needy is part of living out a distinctly Christian ethic.* Caring for our neighbors and those in need is simply what Christians do. It is what they do because it is what Christ did and what He commanded His disciples to do. After giving the parable of the good Samaritan, Jesus concluded by telling the man, "Go, and do thou likewise" (Luke 10:37). In other words, Jesus essentially said that this is what His followers will do. This is how they will treat others. They will care for the needs of their neighbors and will seek to provide aid and relief for the destitute and the afflicted.

Through the parable of the good Samaritan, Jesus taught something about the ethics of the kingdom of heaven. Jesus taught that members of His kingdom will live lives of sacrificial love that issue forth in practical concern for the needs of others. Just like their master, the Lord's people will work to undo suffering and relieve sorrow. This is part of what Jesus revealed through His miracles. The miracles of Christ were nothing short of the spontaneous inbreaking of the kingdom of heaven into the present age. What we learn through the Lord's miracles is that He came to reverse the effects of sin and the curse. His miracles often undid some form of human suffering and sorrow, and as such, they anticipated the power of His coming kingdom.

One of the implications of this reality for the present is that we who are the Lord's people should hate sin and all its effects, including all forms of human suffering. Christians, in the deepest way and for the deepest reasons, should hate human suffering and misery because it is not how this world was meant to be. All human suffering and misery are the product of the fall. The new heavens and new earth will see the ending of all such suffering and misery. This means that when Christians, following Christ's example, seek to alleviate sorrow in the present, they are pointing not only to the example of Christ but to something that is distinct about His kingdom. In His kingdom, suffering and sorrow will have no place. This is one of the most significant reasons why Christians help the poor, love their needy neighbors, and provide relief for those in distress. In doing so, they are living out a distinctly Christian ethic.

Christ was always to be found at the center of Spurgeon's preaching. Spurgeon, without fail, gave pride of place in his sermons to the primary events of the gospel—namely, the incarnation, death, and resurrection of Jesus. Yet, Spurgeon also faithfully presented Christ's teaching and His example for disciples to follow. He believed faithful Christian discipleship required believers to give attention to the pattern of life and godliness set by the master. Part of that pattern was a life that was ever marked by tender compassion and concern for the poor and the needy. "O true souls who love him," Spurgeon would say, "copy him in this."[26]

---

26. Spurgeon, "Blind Man's Eyes Opened," 29:675.

4

Gospel Proclamation and Social Ministry

Understanding the proper relationship between gospel proclamation and social ministry is a matter that has been notoriously fraught for many Christians throughout church history. This is especially the case among evangelicals in the past one hundred years or so. From its beginnings in the early eighteenth century, the evangelical movement has had a strong activist impulse and a high regard for social ministry.[1] The movement in its early days erupted with a profusion of benevolent societies, associations, and organizations designed to address all kinds of social needs, such as education, poverty alleviation, and caring for society's most vulnerable groups. This impulse among evangelicals carried into the twentieth and twenty-first centuries, manifesting in diverse approaches to social ministry. However, evangelicals have not always agreed on how good works and social concern fit within the mission and ministry of the local church. It is an issue frequently debated and has been understood in a myriad of ways in various contexts among evangelicals.

This chapter will more narrowly analyze Spurgeon's understanding of the relationship between gospel proclamation and social ministry. On this complex issue, Spurgeon provides pastors and churches with a faithful model to follow. One biographer writes, "Almost unparalleled in church history, the ministry of Charles

---

1. David W. Bebbington, *Evangelicalism in Modern Britain: A History from the 1730s to the 1980s* (New York: Routledge, 1989), 10–12, 105–50; David W. Bebbington, *The Dominance of Evangelicalism: The Age of Spurgeon and Moody* (Downers Grove, Ill.: InterVarsity, 2005), 36–40.

Haddon Spurgeon epitomized the perfect blending of evangelistic fervency and deep social concern."[2] Spurgeon believed that the mission of the church is primarily bound up in evangelism and disciple-making. He was suspicious of missional drift and did not believe the church should ever become primarily consumed with social activism. However, Spurgeon did believe social concern occupies an important place in the ministry of the church, but it is always subordinate to and, indeed, flows out of gospel proclamation and the ministry of the Word. In this way, Spurgeon promoted social ministry as a necessary fruit of true gospel ministry. Care for the poor and needy is not an optional add-on but an indispensable part of the individual Christian's witness and of the church's ministry.

The Mission of the Local Church

The local church was paramount in Spurgeon's thinking about ministry and mission (as the next chapter will argue). Of all his agencies and institutions, it was his own local church that was the central locus for all of his other activities. As such, Spurgeon gave considerable attention to studying and articulating the mission and purpose of the local church. For him, the Bible clearly laid out the basic platform for the church's mission. Understanding Spurgeon on this crucial subject is vital to appreciating his understanding of the relationship between gospel proclamation and social ministry.

The essence of Spurgeon's view of the mission of the church is helpfully summarized by Spurgeon scholar Geoff Chang, who writes, "The church's mission was to bear witness to Christ and to advance the truth of the gospel for the salvation of the world."[3] Chang is undoubtedly correct that Spurgeon held gospel proclamation to be at the heart of the church's mission. However, this conviction did not lead Spurgeon to conclude that benevolence and social concern

---

2. Lewis A. Drummond, *Spurgeon: Prince of Preachers*, 3rd ed. (Grand Rapids: Kregel Publications, 1992), 398.

3. Geoffrey Chang, "The Militant Ecclesiology and Church Polity of Charles Haddon Spurgeon" (PhD diss., Midwestern Baptist Theological Seminary, 2020), 230.

have no part in the mission of the church. As Spurgeon believed the church is called to bear witness to the gospel, he believed one of the most vital ways the church does this beyond the preaching of the Word is through its care and regard for the poor and the needy. Spurgeon never understood social ministry to be superior to, or even on par with, gospel proclamation. However, social ministry serves the preaching of the gospel by validating the message and providing a tangible expression of Christ's love toward those in need. Thus, social ministry supports gospel proclamation, and thereby, the two are inextricably linked together. Let us consider both in turn.

Gospel Proclamation

In Spurgeon's view, the proclamation of the gospel through the ministry of the Word is at the very center of the mission of the church. He said, "As long as there is a church in the world the obligation to preach the gospel will remain, and if that church should ever come to consist of but one or two, it must still, with all its might, go on promulgating the gospel of Jesus Christ. Preaching is to be for all time; and until Jesus Christ himself shall come, and the dispensation shall close, the mission of the church is to go into all the world—all of you—and tell out the gospel to every creature."[4] In another sermon, he stated, "[Christ's] church, when she understands her work, will perceive that she is not here to gather to herself wealth or honor, or to seek any temporal aggrandisement and position; she is here unselfishly to live, and if need be, unselfishly to die for the deliverance of the lost sheep, the salvation of lost men.... To rescue souls from hell and lead to God, to hope, to heaven, this is her heavenly occupation."[5] Simply put, the mission of the church is bound up in the preaching of the gospel unto the salvation of souls.

---

4. C. H. Spurgeon, "Preach, Preach, Preach Everywhere," in *The Metropolitan Tabernacle Pulpit: Sermons Preached and Revised by C. H. Spurgeon* (Pasadena, Tex.: Pilgrim Publications, 1970), 15:629.

5. Spurgeon, "The First Cry from the Cross," in *Metropolitan Tabernacle Pulpit*, 15:596–97.

Spurgeon endeavored to proclaim the gospel in every sermon he preached. In fact, if one were to pull almost any sermon at random from one of the many volumes of *The Metropolitan Tabernacle Pulpit*, one would invariably find the sermon would not only include a simple and direct presentation of the gospel somewhere in the message but would also include an impassioned evangelistic appeal at the conclusion of the sermon. Spurgeon's sermons always featured clear and simple summaries of the gospel. But how did Spurgeon define the gospel? He summarized the good news in this way,

> When we preach the gospel, then, we must declare to the sons of men that they are fallen, they are sinful, they are lost, but Christ has come to seek and to save that which was lost; that there is in Christ Jesus, who is now in heaven, grace all sufficient to meet each sinner's need, that whosoever believeth in him shall be forgiven all his sins, and shall receive the Holy Ghost, by which he shall be helped to lead a new life, shall be preserved in holiness, and shall be brought safely to heaven. To preach the gospel is to preach up Christ.... The first message we have to preach to every creature is that there is a Savior: "Life; for a look at the Crucified One, life at this moment," for all who look to him. This is the gospel which we have to preach.[6]

Spurgeon's vision for gospel proclamation was very much a corporate one. The mission to preach the gospel is for the whole church body, not merely for those who stand to preach in the gathered assembly week by week.[7] Spurgeon's expectation was that all of the church's members would be engaged on some level in sharing the gospel. He believed that every Christian has an individual mandate to evangelize and, moreover, was required to participate in the church's corporate mission of proclaiming the gospel to the world.

---

6. Spurgeon, "Preach, Preach, Preach Everywhere," 15:627.

7. Even in the context of the regular gathering of the church as the congregation assembled to hear Spurgeon preach, Spurgeon trained his congregation to always be "watching for souls" and to be ready to commend the gospel themselves as they interacted with unbelievers in their midst. See C. H. Spurgeon, "Opening the Campaign," *Sword and the Trowel*, October 1872, 441.

Spurgeon deprecated the notion of a sharp distinction in this respect between an ordained preacher and a lay person. He did not believe that proclaiming the gospel should be understood as being limited to a clerical activity only. He could never tolerate such a professionalization of gospel proclamation. All were called in some sense to tell of the good news. He said, "We are not all called to preach in these boxes called pulpits, but we may preach more conveniently and much more powerfully behind the counter or in the drawing-room, or in the parlor, or in the field, or wherever providence may have placed us. Let us endeavor to make men mark what kind of gospel we believe."[8] In another message, Spurgeon declared, "Every Christian here is either a missionary or an impostor. Recollect that you are either trying to spread abroad the kingdom of Christ, or else you do not love him at all. It cannot be that there is a high appreciation of Jesus, and a totally silent tongue about him.... You are either doing good, or you are not yourself good. If thou knowest Christ, thou art as one who has found honey, and thou wilt call others to taste of it."[9]

Spurgeon's congregation eagerly responded to such exhortations as these. Whether it was through Sunday schools, evangelists' associations, or the church's many street missions, the Tabernacle presented its members with a host of outlets for the ministry of evangelism and gospel proclamation. Hundreds of volunteers from among the Tabernacle membership rushed to staff these ministries. They did so because they believed, along with their pastor, that their "great Commander's marching orders to his troops are—'Go ye into all the world, and preach the gospel to every creature.'"[10]

---

8. Spurgeon, "The Glorious Gospel of the Blessed God," in *Metropolitan Tabernacle Pulpit*, 13:371.

9. Spurgeon, "A Sermon and a Reminiscence," in *Metropolitan Tabernacle Pulpit*, 54:476.

10. Spurgeon, "Preach, Preach, Preach Everywhere," 15:629.

Social Ministry

As prominent as gospel proclamation and Word ministry were in Spurgeon's understanding of the church's mission, he did not believe the church is only to be concerned with the spiritual needs of the world. He believed the church ought to address temporal suffering and material needs as well and plainly understood ministry to the poor and needy to form a vital part of the church's work. However, it must be emphasized that he did not believe the church was called to embrace what the next generation would commonly refer to as the *social gospel*.[11]

The social gospel is often associated with the teaching of Walter Rauschenbusch, an American Baptist who ministered in the early 1900s in the Hell's Kitchen neighborhood of Manhattan.[12] However, the phrase *social gospel*, along with its concomitant ideas, began to appear near the end of Spurgeon's life, reaching its full bloom in the generation following his death. Though the social gospel did not truly come of age until the early 1900s, some Baptists in Britain, such as John Clifford, "had this worldview before it became articulate."[13] Clifford was Spurgeon's primary sparring partner in the Downgrade Controversy. In 1888, after the Baptist Union censured Spurgeon in

---

11. Patricia Stallings Kruppa, *Charles Haddon Spurgeon: A Preacher's Progress* (New York: Garland, 1982), 360–61.

12. See Walter Rauschenbusch, *A Theology for the Social Gospel* (New York; Macmillan, 1917); and Christopher H. Evans, *The Social Gospel in American Religion: A History* (New York: New York University Press, 2017).

13. Mark Hopkins, *Nonconformity's Romantic Generation: Evangelical and Liberal Theologies in Victorian England* (Eugene, Ore.: Wipf and Stock, 2006), 184; see also 179–85, 191. For a contextual study of Clifford's thought, particularly as it relates to socialism and the social gospel, see Matthew Erwin Brandt, "Baptist Social Christianity in Victorian England: The Individual and Society in the Theology of Dr. John Clifford" (PhD diss., Marquette University, 1999); and D. M. Thompson, "John Clifford's Social Gospel," *Baptist Quarterly*, 31 (1986): 199–217. For more on the history of the emergence of the social gospel in Britain among Nonconformists, see David W. Bebbington, "The City, the Countryside and the Social Gospel in Late Victorian Nonconformity," in *The Church in Town and Countryside*, ed. Derek Baker (Oxford: Blackwell, 1979), 415–26.

the midst of the controversy, Clifford gave the presidential address at the Union's annual assembly and titled his message "The New City of God; Or the Primitive Christian Faith as a Social Gospel."[14] Clifford's views on the social implications of the gospel were not especially original. By the mid- to late 1880s, contemporary thinkers like the Anglican B. F. Westcott, the Methodist Hugh Price Hughes, and the Congregationalist R. W. Dale had also begun to articulate similar perspectives on what they understood to be the gospel's social implications.[15]

The phrase *social gospel* is hard to define. At its heart, however, it is usually an understanding of the gospel that views social reform as central to the church's work. Thus, the goal of the church's ministry is social activism leading to widespread social renewal. The church's primary aim is to improve society as a whole, especially the material conditions of the poor, rather than saving souls.

Though there is little evidence Spurgeon ever encountered the full-blown social gospel, there is no doubt he would have rejected it. Had he become familiar with the concept in his day, he almost certainly would have agreed with the sentiments expressed by his student, protégé, and intimate friend, Archibald G. Brown, who said not long after Spurgeon's death, "Among the working classes what is known as the Social Gospel has done as much harm as anything. I hate the expression Social Gospel. Sometimes I think it must have been invented by the devil."[16]

Spurgeon never preached anything approximating a social gospel. Social renewal and economic betterment were not at the heart of the gospel for Spurgeon. Rather, the gospel Spurgeon preached

---

14. John Clifford, *The New City of God: Or the Primitive Christian Faith as a Social Gospel* (London: Alexander & Shepheard, 1888).

15. B. F. Westcott, *Social Aspects of Christianity* (London: Macmillan, 1887); W. M. King, "Hugh Price Hughes and the British 'Social Gospel,'" *Journal of Religious History* 13, no. 1 (June 1984): 66–82; R. W. Dale, "Political and Municipal Duty," in *Laws of Christ for Common Life* (London: Hodder and Stoughton, 1884), 187–204.

16. Iain Murray, *Archibald G. Brown: Spurgeon's Successor* (Edinburgh: Banner of Truth, 2011), 120.

was one of personal salvation and spiritual renewal, leading to a transformed life that expresses itself in good works of benevolence. Christian social concern comes into play as a demonstration of the Christian's renewed nature, a manifestation of the character and love of Christ, and a vindication of the gospel message. Spurgeon believed ministry to the poor, though not the gospel itself, nonetheless enhances the witness of the gospel. In this sense, social concern serves gospel ministry.[17] For those who embrace the social gospel, social ministry is at the heart of the gospel. For Spurgeon, social ministry flows out of the gospel.

As noted at the start of the chapter, it has frequently been a matter of debate as to how the burden to preach the gospel and the burden to help the poor ought to interact with one another in the ministry of the church. How to balance and integrate these priorities in his own ministry was a subject of great importance to Spurgeon. He viewed both gospel proclamation and social ministry as urgent biblical concerns. Ultimately, Spurgeon's brand of evangelical Christianity had room for a well-developed social conscience. This social conscience did not lead Spurgeon to embrace the social gospel, but it did move him to embark upon a program of Christian benevolence that issued aid to a broad array of needy Londoners.

Spurgeon was undoubtedly a powerful preacher, renowned for his proclamation of the gospel, but he was also an outstanding philanthropist whose charitable organizations and ministries provided aid and relief to thousands of people. For Spurgeon, gospel preaching and mercy ministry had to go together. In one of his most penetrating statements on the subject, Spurgeon commented in an 1879 issue of the *Sword and the Trowel* that "works of charity must keep pace with the preaching of faith or the church will not be perfect in its development."[18] This sentiment lay behind the explosion of

---

17. See David Nelson Duke, "Charles Haddon Spurgeon: Social Concern Exceeding an Individualistic, Self-Help Ideology," *Baptist History and Heritage* 22, no. 4 (October 1987).

18. Spurgeon, "Notes," *Sword and the Trowel*, November 1879, 544.

benevolent activity that poured forth from the Tabernacle throughout Spurgeon's ministry. Spurgeon believed there was something deficient in any preaching that failed to produce work for Christ on behalf of the poor and the needy. Regular efforts in benevolence and mercy ministry should proceed from the sustained, faithful preaching of the gospel.

Spurgeon believed that works of charity adorn the gospel and beautify the testimony of Christ in the world. These works not only commend the gospel to the poor and needy who are the recipients of benevolent aid, but they preach to the world at large that the Christian gospel produces real love and compassion in those who put their faith in Jesus Christ. When Christians feed the hungry and clothe the naked, they implicitly say something about the power of God's grace to transform the heart. When Christians meet the needs of the fatherless and the widow, they communicate something about the compassion of Jesus. Christian care and concern for the poor are meant to provide the world with a compelling appeal to the power and beauty of the gospel.

Spurgeon believed that a strong connection exists between Christian social concern and the biblical gospel. He sought to expound this connection when he wrote, "It seems to us that our Lord gave more prominence to cups of cold water, and garments made for the poor, and caring for little ones, than most people do nowadays. We would encourage our friends to attend to those humble unobtrusive ministries which are seldom chronicled, and yet are essential to the success of the more manifest moral and spiritual work."[19] Spurgeon recognized that good deeds of mercy aid the spread of the gospel. Care for the poor is a way of putting hands and feet on the preached word and, under the blessing of God, greatly contributes to its success.

Spurgeon regularly encouraged his church members to engage in various forms of benevolence and social ministry. In an 1883

---

19. Spurgeon, "Lost Children at the Crystal Palace," *Sword and the Trowel*, August 1883, 425.

article, Spurgeon commended those in the church who met practical needs such as escorting blind people to their seats for church services, welcoming strangers into the church, or working in the church kitchen to feed the hungry. He said, "We want more ministries of the practical sort.... The work of the hands is by no means a secondary result of divine grace upon the heart."[20] Spurgeon believed good works to be a direct and primary result of regeneration and an essential element of authentic Christianity. In commenting on Spurgeon's understanding of the importance of Christian benevolence, Tom Nettles writes, "Benevolence was both good in itself, and good as a recommendation of the beauty of the gospel."[21]

Spurgeon promoted benevolence among the members of his church because he saw it as a means of drawing unbelievers into the church where their spiritual needs could be addressed. This represented one very practical way in which care for the poor served the spread of the gospel. He said in an 1862 sermon,

> I would that we who have a purer faith, could remember a little more the intimate connection between the body and the soul. Go to the poor man and tell him of the bread of heaven, but first give him the bread of earth, for how shall he hear you with a starving body? Talk to him of the robe of Jesu's righteousness, but you will do it all the better when you have provided a garment with which he may cover his nakedness. It seems an idle tale to a poor man if you talk to him of spiritual things and cruelly refuse him help as to temporals.... You ask a person to hear your preacher; but he knows that you are crotchety, short-tempered, illiberal, and he is not likely to think much of the Word which, as he thinks, has made you what you are; but if, on the other hand, he sees your compassionate spirit, he will first be attracted to you, then next to what you have to say, and then you may lead him as with a thread, and bring him to listen to the truth as it is in Jesus, and who can tell but thus, through

---

20. Spurgeon, "Lost Children at the Crystal Palace," 425.
21. Tom Nettles, *Living by Revealed Truth: The Life and Pastoral Theology of Charles Haddon Spurgeon* (Scotland: Christian Focus Publications, 2013), 340.

the sympathy of your tender heart, you may be the means of bringing him to Christ.[22]

Spurgeon argued that Christian kindness and compassion toward the poor, the suffering, and the oppressed powerfully drew unbelievers toward such a compelling and generous community and, thus, to the gospel message itself. In an 1866 issue of the *Sword and the Trowel*, he wrote, "We can help the poor, the needy, the fatherless, and widow. It is wonderful how well a tract is read when it is wrapped up with a loaf of bread. It is really marvellous how much better you find a word about Jesus Christ go down when there is a little soup with it."[23]

Spurgeon believed gospel proclamation and social ministry ought to be inseparable in the work of the church. Good works of love and mercy toward the poor are the hands and feet of the gospel message. The Christian community should be marked by compassion for the poor, and this compassion should adorn the proclamation of the gospel. Thus, the ministry of the church encompasses social action but primarily as a means of supporting and enhancing gospel witness. Spurgeon said, "We think good works are the witnesses or testimony to other people of the truth of what we believe.... The use of good works is, that they are a Christian's sermon.... There is nothing like faithful practice and holy living, if we would preach to the world."[24]

The Gospel and Good Works

Spurgeon helps to bring some much-needed clarity to an issue that has become shrouded in a haze of poor teaching and misguided practice. Christians today require faithful models to help them properly understand the place of social ministry in the overall mission

---

22. Spurgeon, "Christian Sympathy," in *Metropolitan Tabernacle Pulpit*, 8:630.
23. Spurgeon, "A Spur for a Free Horse," *Sword and the Trowel*, February 1866, 55.
24. C. H. Spurgeon, "Good Works," in *The New Park Street Pulpit: Containing Sermons Preached and Revised by the Rev. C. H. Spurgeon, Minister of the Chapel* (Grand Rapids: Baker Book House, 2007), 2:133.

and ministry of the church. In Spurgeon, we have a way forward that maintains steadfast devotion to the priority of the church's spiritual work of preaching the gospel and ministering the Word while reserving an important place for social concern, benevolence, and mercy ministry. Before leaving this chapter, let's consider a few important lessons for our contemporary context.

The Centrality of Gospel Proclamation

Spurgeon clearly taught that the principal work of the church is the preaching of the gospel unto the saving of souls and the advancement of Christ's kingdom. To put it another way: the church's mission is to make disciples and to build up healthy churches through the proclamation of truth. This has been understood as the central mission of the church from its beginning. It is an ancient mission, originally given by Christ to his disciples in the form of the Great Commission in Matthew 28:16–20. It is the mission that was executed in the book of Acts and in the early days of the primitive church. The mission has not changed.

Spurgeon would exhort us today to keep the main thing the main thing and not to allow ourselves to drift in our understanding of the church's mission. The church is not called to make heaven on earth or to transform the culture. The church is not called to follow a social gospel or to make widespread social change its primary aim. The church is called to preach the gospel in the power of the Holy Spirit unto the salvation of souls for the glory of Christ. The church's work is, in the first place, spiritual in nature. It aims at the heart, not at one's physical circumstances—at spiritual transformation, not at social renewal.

It is noteworthy that among the dozens of benevolent ministries that operated out of the Metropolitan Tabernacle, almost all of them featured gospel proclamation in some form. Whether it was the church's many street missions, children's ministries, or benevolent societies, all of them promoted Bible teaching to varying degrees. Spurgeon was earnest about doing good to others, but he knew the best good he could do was to bring people the truth concerning the salvation offered in Christ. Any material or physical benefits, though valuable in themselves, were of secondary worth.

Missional drift is an ever-present threat to the church. Christians can too easily become preoccupied with political activism and social reform and can slowly begin to see such causes as their primary work. Spurgeon would urge local churches to remain committed to the ministry of the Word and the proclamation of the truth as its central task. He believed that the church's chief mission was to preach the gospel. He would remind churches today, as he did in his own day, "Surely the winning of hearts for Jesus is our work."[25]

The Indispensability of Good Works

Spurgeon believed that gospel proclamation and good works—word and deed—are inseparable in the ministry of the local church. Social ministry was not detached from Spurgeon's burden for soul winning. He held that mercy ministry among the needy, the afflicted, and the disenfranchised plays a pivotal part in the church's witness to the world. The benevolent ministry of the church has evangelistic appeal and apologetic power. Thus, Spurgeon sought to organize his church for all sorts of ministries designed to meet the material and physical needs of the surrounding community, such as the Stockwell Orphanage, the Tabernacle Almshouses for poor widows, and a number of "ragged schools" for the education of poor children. These ministries had the effect of bearing witness to the character of God and the power of the gospel and were often the means of drawing men and women into the life of the church.

Some in our day may feel that involvement in social ministry is simply optional for local churches or that only those who feel especially burdened should get involved in various forms of outreach and

---

25. Spurgeon, "Notes," July 1878, 364. See also Spurgeon, *An All-Round Ministry: Direction, Wisdom, and Encouragement for Preachers and Pastors* (Edinburgh: Banner of Truth, 2018), 213.

service in the community. Such people would not have felt at home in Spurgeon's church. For Spurgeon and his members at the Metropolitan Tabernacle, social ministry was not seen as optional but as indispensable to the church's work. A pastor today might think his church's involvement in benevolence work in the community is optional or a matter of preference, based largely on the church's calendar, location, or the breakdown of its membership. But Spurgeon would hold him to be misguided, failing to understand that the Bible plainly calls all Christians to engage in this kind of ministry. Whether it's Paul calling the Cretan Christians in Titus 2:14 to be a people "zealous of good works," Peter urging the Christians in Asia minor in 1 Peter 2:12 to be known for their "good works," or Jesus calling his disciples in Matthew 5:16 to "let your light so shine before men, that they may see your good works, and glorify your Father which is in heaven," the Bible is replete with exhortations to carry on good works as part of the church's ministry in the world.

It is important to recognize that though social ministry is essential, the precise course this kind of ministry should take in a particular local church may vary considerably. What is important is that the congregation understands the broad principle that social ministry in the community is a vital part of church work. Pastors ought to preach on these principles from texts such as the ones mentioned above in order to convince the congregation of the importance of this work. The church can then exercise a great degree of freedom in terms of how this type of ministry is carried out, with sensitivity to God's providence and one's own context. This command of Scripture can find all kinds of practical expressions in a local church, from informal ministries among the members of the church to more formal church-sponsored ministries such as food pantries, mentoring programs, adoption fairs, ESL classes, and ministries among refugees. The important thing is that the work of addressing material and physical burdens among needy people is seen as indispensable, not optional, for the church.

A Note of Caution

Christians have adopted varying approaches to integrating gospel proclamation and social ministry in their overall understanding of the church's mission. It might be tempting to categorize various approaches into three broad camps. The first camp would be those who see social ministry as central to the mission of the church, an approach perhaps embodied by a figure such as Walter Rauschenbusch and the social gospel movement. A second category would be those who view social ministry as an important part of the church's mission but subordinate in importance to preaching the gospel. The final group would then be those who view the church's work as entirely, even exclusively, spiritual and then relegate social ministry to a matter of minor or tangential importance to the church's mission—or, in some cases, even of no importance at all.

Though Spurgeon would probably fit best within the second group, he would likely object to the kind of scheme outlined above, finding it too reductionistic and inclined to obscure or relativize the significance of social ministry. If Scripture requires social ministry, then it is essential and must be a matter of urgent importance for the church. Integrating social ministry in terms of a scheme of priorities would probably have felt somewhat artificial to Spurgeon. The issue for him was always faithfulness to the revealed will of God. Attempting to construct a hierarchy of priorities for Christian obedience would have been intolerable to Spurgeon. There is no question that gospel proclamation was primary for him, yet he viewed social ministry as inextricably linked with that work. Attempts to bifurcate the two will inevitably have the effect of weakening both. They must be seen as mutually reinforcing. Yes, gospel proclamation is the main thing, but, as Spurgeon said, social ministry must always "keep pace with the preaching of faith."

The Church:
A City on a Hill

To this point, we have seen that Spurgeon viewed benevolence and social concern not as optional or even preferable but as essential to the Christian life and the ministry of the church. Christians are called to good works of charity and mercy as a matter of basic Christian faithfulness. Spurgeon believed engagement in works of benevolence is the inevitable result of the new birth and a necessary part of following Jesus's teaching and example in basic discipleship. Moreover, Spurgeon understood social ministry to form an important part of the church's work in the world, particularly in strengthening the church's witness and lending credence to the gospel message. For Spurgeon, gospel proclamation and social concern belong together. Wherever faithful preaching of the truth takes place, good works are meant to follow. Thus, Spurgeon held that practical concern for the poor and needy should be one of the hallmarks of local church ministry.

This chapter will explore Spurgeon's understanding of the priority of the local church as the primary channel for the promotion of benevolence and good works in the community. When it came to Christian ministry and mission, Spurgeon believed the church always has pride of place. This chapter will further explore Spurgeon's view of the relationship between the local church and the surrounding community, particularly highlighting his view of the church's responsibility in ministering to the community's material needs. Spurgeon believed each local church has a special responsibility to reach its community through gospel preaching and ministries of mercy. Word and deed belong together in the ministry of the church.

The Priority of the Local Church

Spurgeon understood the church to be God's special agent in the world. He wrote, "The world is all scaffolding; the church of Christ is the true building."[1] The church occupies a place of priority that is altogether unparalleled in God's purposes and plans. No other organization can claim the same divine sanction and commission. On this point, Spurgeon said, "We have been wondering why our societies have not greater success. I believe the reason is because there is not a single word in the Book of God about anything of the kind. The Church of God is the pillar and ground of the truth, not a society. The Church of God never ought to have delegated to any society whatever, a work which it behoved her to have done herself."[2]

Victorian evangelicalism teemed with all kinds of organizational activity.[3] Spurgeon did not view all parachurch associations, societies, and agencies as undesirable or unnecessary; in fact, he founded and promoted many himself. However, he sharply distinguished between such parachurch groups and the church itself. He saw the church as unique and preeminent in God's purposes. No other organization can claim its special privileges, promises, and calling. This perspective manifested itself in Spurgeon's clear preference for church-led ministry over ministry conducted outside the auspices of the local church. Baptist historian J. H. Y. Briggs highlights one such example of this preference with respect to evangelism. He writes, "Spurgeon's

---

1. Spurgeon, "The Church Encouraged and Exhorted," in *The Metropolitan Tabernacle Pulpit: Sermons Preached and Revised by C. H. Spurgeon* (Pasadena, Tex.: Pilgrim Publications, 1977), 48:473.

2. Spurgeon, "The Church—Conservative and Aggressive," in *Metropolitan Tabernacle Pulpit*, 7:363.

3. David W. Bebbington, *Evangelicalism in Modern Britain: A History from the 1730s to the 1980s* (New York: Routledge, 1989), 12; David W. Bebbington, "Response," in *The Emergence of Evangelicalism: Exploring Historical Continuities*, ed. M. A. G. Haykin and K. J. Stewart (Nottingham, U.K.: Apollos, 2008), 419.

commitment, for example, like that of so many, was to evangelism through the local church, though he admitted that the Home Missionary Society was a good second best.... But ideally the churches should make the society redundant and by the excellence of their own work provoke its demise."[4] Certainly parachurch organizations have their place, but that place is always second behind the church.

For Spurgeon, the church's place of priority in the purposes and plans of God was indisputable. Thus, the church was central to Spurgeon's thoughts about ministry and mission. "The church is the world's hope," he said. "As Christ is the hope of the Church, so the Church is the hope of the world."[5] In an 1886 article in the *Sword and the Trowel*, he wrote, "Under God we have in the Church all that is needful for her great work; it only needs bringing out and setting in order—perhaps we ought to say arousing and quickening. The world is full of stir, social, political, scientific, selfish; and shall the Saviour's household be given to slumber?"[6] The church is called to engage in active labor for the Lord as His divinely appointed agency in the world. The church has been given a task and mission to carry out in service to Christ. Spurgeon, therefore, understood the church to be Christ's official embassy, conducting her work on behalf of the kingdom of God. Spurgeon said, "Christ ordained his church to be his great aggressive agency in combating with sin, and with the world that lieth in the wicked one. It is to be a light, not to itself, as a candle in a dark lantern, but a light unto that which is without."[7] Christ commissioned the church to be a light to the world. There is to be something outward about the orientation of the church, inclining it

---

4. J. H. Y. Briggs, *The English Baptists of the Nineteenth Century* (Didcot, U.K.: Baptist Historical Society, 1994), 3:302–3.

5. C. H. Spurgeon, *Trumpet Calls to Christian Energy: A Collection of Sermons Preached on Sunday and Thursday Evenings at the Metropolitan Tabernacle* (London: Passmore and Alabaster, 1875), 45.

6. C. H. Spurgeon, "Concerning Doing Nothing," *Sword and the Trowel*, May 1886, 208.

7. Spurgeon, *Trumpet Calls*, 133.

toward mission. "Churches do not exist for themselves," Spurgeon said, "but for the world at large."[8]

The Church and the City

Spurgeon believed each local church is called to represent Christ in its own community. No church ministers in a vacuum, but in a particular place on behalf of a particular people. Spurgeon held that wherever a church is called to minister, it is to be a beacon of light through the proclamation of the truth and the carrying on of good works. Each church is to radiate to the surrounding community a faithful witness through word and deed.

Spurgeon pastored in the largest city in the world in his day, a city that could at times overwhelm him.[9] In an 1875 article titled "London: A Plea," he wrote, "Traversing all parts of London very frequently, we are nevertheless lost in it. Has any living man any idea of the vastness of our metropolitan world? It is not a city, but a province, nay, a nation. Every now and then we find ourselves quite at sea in a locality which we thought we knew as well as our own garden."[10] Throughout his career, Spurgeon would never quite shake the sense of feeling somewhat lost and adrift in the metropolis. Though he was by nature and nurture a lover of the country, especially his beloved Essex, he found himself for most of his life in the heart of the city. In general, Spurgeon had a negative view of London. He referred to it as "this wicked, wretched City of London"[11] and compared it to ancient Corinth.[12] At times he even spoke of London as a modern-day Sodom and Gomorrah. He said, "Oh, this London of ours! It is a horrible place for Christian people to live in! Round about this

---

8. Spurgeon, "The Candle," in *Metropolitan Tabernacle Pulpit*, 27:228.

9. London was the largest city in the world for a century, from roughly 1825 to 1925. See Tertius Chandler and Gerald Fox, *3000 Years of Urban Growth* (New York: Academic Press, 1974), 364.

10. Spurgeon, "London," *Sword and the Trowel*, April 1875, 145.

11. Spurgeon, "The Blind Man's Eyes Opened; or, Practical Christianity," in *Metropolitan Tabernacle Pulpit*, 29:675.

12. Spurgeon, "A Prophetic Warning," *Sword and the Trowel*, October 1883, 522.

neighborhood scarcely can a decent person remain by reason of the vice that abounds, and the language that is heard on every side. Many of you are as much vexed today as Lot was when he was in Sodom."[13]

Spurgeon described in detail his earliest impressions of London from his visit in late 1853 to preach for the first time at New Park Street Chapel. Though this was not Spurgeon's first visit to London, he nonetheless described feeling overwhelmed and misplaced in the city. He painted the picture of a timid country boy lost in the dark alleys and crowded scenes of the sprawling metropolis.[14] This initial impression steadily gave way to a sort of lukewarm acceptance of life in London, though Spurgeon regularly expressed some measure of revulsion at the various expressions of worldliness and immorality in the city. Furthermore, he took every opportunity he could to retreat from the congestion and clamor of London to the dreamy scenes of Mentone, France, for rest and recovery. By the end of his life, Spurgeon said of London, "I confess I can never go through this huge city without feeling unhappy. I never pass from end to end of London without feeling a black and dark cloud, hanging like a pall over my spirit. How my heart breaks for thee, O sinful city of London! Is it not so with you, my brethren? Think of its slums, its sins, its poverty, its ungodliness, its drunkenness, its vice! These may well go through a man's heart like sharp swords. How Jesus would have wept in London."[15] Spurgeon saw London as the object of his compassion and pity but never as his home.

Though Spurgeon never felt at home in the city, he nonetheless loved London and gave his life to reaching her with the gospel. In 1875, he wrote, "Our heart has been palpitating with the question,— what is to be done for these millions religiously? Whatever it is, it

---

13. Spurgeon, "Beginning at Jerusalem," in *Metropolitan Tabernacle Pulpit*, 29:381.

14. C. H. *Spurgeon's Autobiography, Compiled from His Diary, Letters, and Records by His Wife and His Private Secretary* (London: Passmore and Alabaster, 1897), 1:318.

15. Spurgeon, "Jesus Wept," in *Metropolitan Tabernacle Pulpit*, 35:342.

ought to be done at once."[16] Moreover, he believed it was also part of the local church's calling to embrace the material and practical needs of the city and to endeavor to provide help and relief wherever possible. In an 1869 sermon, he said, "A church in London, which does not exist to do good in the slums, and dens, and kennels of the city, is a church that has no reason to justify its longer existing. A church that does not exist to reclaim heathenism, to fight with evil, to destroy error, to put down falsehood, a church that does not exist to take the side of the poor, to denounce injustice and to hold up righteousness, is a church that has no right to be."[17]

Spurgeon studied London's many distresses and developed plans to minister to various areas of need. He encouraged his congregation to cultivate sympathy for the city and to consider ways in which they might minister to needy people in their neighborhoods and local communities. Just a few years into his ministry in London, in a sermon titled "India's Ills and England's Sorrows," Spurgeon urged his members, saying,

> Go ye now your ways, and as ye stand on any of the hills around, and behold this Behemoth city! lying in the valley, say; "O London, London! how great thy guilt. Oh! that the Master would gather thee under his wing, and make thee his city, the joy of the whole earth! O London, London! full of privileges, and full of sin, exalted to heaven by the gospel, thou shalt be cast down to hell by thy rejection of it!" And then, when ye have wept over London, go and weep over the street in which you live, as you see the sabbath broken, and God's laws trampled upon, and men's bodies profaned—go ye and weep! Weep, for the court in which you live in your humble poverty, weep for the square in which you live in your magnificent wealth; weep for the humbler street in which you live in competence, weep for

---

16. Spurgeon, "London," 147.
17. Spurgeon, "The First Cry from the Cross," in *Metropolitan Tabernacle Pulpit*, 15:597.

your neighbors and your friends, lest any of them, having lived godless, may die godless![18]

In another message, he said,

> We want to be educated into the knowledge of our national poverty; we want to be taught and trained, to know more of what our fellow-men can and do suffer. Oh! if the Christian Church knew the immorality of London, she would cry aloud to God. If but for one night you could see the harlotry and infamy, if you could but once see the rascality of London gathered into one mass, your hearts would melt with woe and bitterness, and you would bow yourselves before God and cry unto him for this city as one that mourneth for his only son, even for his firstborn.[19]

Spurgeon believed local churches had the responsibility to minister to the city and to take on her sorrows and burdens. He always hoped that his church and the churches within his network would truly make a difference in London for good. Spurgeon framed the question in this way, "There is the city with its sorrows, and here is the church with its heaven-born love; the question is, how shall these be brought into contact so that the evil shall find its remedy and the medicine shall reach the disease?"[20]

Through gospel proclamation and social ministry, the church would address the needs of London. Preeminent in Spurgeon's mind were always the spiritual needs of London's citizens, but he did not neglect their physical needs either. Churches that were faithful to their mission in both word and deed would always have the potential to impact the city greatly. Spurgeon said, "And now, could we only get the church of God to awake, we should soon have the whole city moved. Let our ministers preach the gospel, or let them preach it

---

18. C. H. Spurgeon, "India's Ills and England's Sorrows," in *The New Park Street Pulpit: Containing Sermons Preached and Revised by the Rev. C. H. Spurgeon, Minister of the Chapel* (Grand Rapids: Baker Book House, 2007), 3:348.

19. Spurgeon, "Christian Sympathy," in *Metropolitan Tabernacle Pulpit*, 8:632.

20. Spurgeon, "Visiting the Poor," *Sword and the Trowel*, January 1880, 18.

with something like force.... Let the members of the church back them up by vehement zeal, earnest prayer, and incessant labours; we should want nothing else to stir this city from end to end.... Let the church, then, awake; and that influence shall be had whereby the city shall be moved."[21] Spurgeon urged his members to open their eyes and their hearts to the needs of the city. He said, "There are sights in this metropolis that might melt a heart of steel, and make a Nabal generous. But it is an easy way of escaping from the exercise of benevolence to shut your eyes and see nothing of the abject misery, which is groveling at your feet."[22] Spurgeon wanted his church to have their eyes open to the real and urgent needs of London and to apply aid and relief, both spiritually and physically. He said, "I want you to help the heathen world, but I want you to begin with caring for this great heathen world of London."[23]

The Metropolitan Tabernacle

Of all the organizations and groups with which Spurgeon was connected, his own local church was preeminent. The Tabernacle represented not only the biblical context for Spurgeon's preaching and pastoral ministry, but it was also his plan A for reaching the city of London. Though he founded and participated in several other ministries, agencies, and parachurch groups, the local church was always at the center of his ministry. This was because Spurgeon believed, as noted above, that Christ's kingdom advances primarily through the ministry of the local church. Thus, Spurgeon ensured that his own local church embodied his vision for the church's unique calling and mission in the world.

Throughout Spurgeon's tenure, the Metropolitan Tabernacle was a dynamic and pulsating center for ministry in the heart of London. Strategically located just south of the Thames, the Tabernacle became

---

21. Spurgeon, *Trumpet Calls*, 5.
22. Spurgeon, "Blind Man's Eyes Opened," 29:675.
23. Spurgeon, *Trumpet Calls*, 24.

Spurgeon's headquarters for ministry in the surrounding neighborhoods and boroughs. From the day he accepted the call to pastor in London, he was determined to reach the city, and reach the city he did. He endeavored to reach London, first and foremost, through the preaching of the Word. By the proclamation of truth, he sought to win men and women to salvation in Christ and disciple them in the faith. Moreover, Spurgeon maintained his belief that "works of charity must keep pace with the preaching of faith." Therefore, he also attended to the material and physical needs of the city through the church's various benevolence ministries.

These ministries of the Tabernacle not only provided genuine aid and relief for needy people, but they also adorned the church's witness in the community. Spurgeon eagerly studied the peculiar needs of his community and sought to lead his church in addressing them. The Metropolitan Tabernacle, under Spurgeon's leadership, fed London's hungry, adopted her orphans, cared for her widows, ministered to her fallen women, comforted her sick and bereaved, and housed her poor. Through these efforts, the church embraced the city of London and sought to address her many and diverse needs, both spiritual and physical. The Metropolitan Tabernacle was truly a church for the city.

The Church in the City Today

In Matthew 5:14–16, Jesus said His disciples were to be the salt of the earth, the light of the world, a city on a hill, and a lamp in a dark room. Jesus emphasized the power of the good works of the Lord's people in drawing men and women into a proper relationship with God. This passage teaches that the Christian community is meant to radiate light to the world through works of benevolence, mercy, and kindness toward others. These works are meant to be visible, like a lighthouse directing weatherworn ships to the shore. Of course, the lighthouse itself is not the shore, but it shines brightly, signaling to ships at sea where the shore can be found. This is how the good works of Christians function, directing outsiders by the light of their good works to the shore that is Christ.

Spurgeon sought to create such a community in his own local church. The Metropolitan Tabernacle was a bustling hub for gospel ministry and good works that issued forth in a host of different ministries throughout the metropolis of London. Spurgeon set up the Tabernacle to be a center for good in the city, where people could come to find both temporal help and relief through its mercy ministries, as well as everlasting life through the preaching of the gospel. Though times have changed, and every town, city, and region is different, Spurgeon's teaching and example still provide us with several timeless lessons for ministry today.

The Unique Role of the Local Church
As noted above, Spurgeon was by no means negative about parachurch ministries. He was involved in parachurch ministry on many levels. However, he believed that God has special plans and purposes for the church. The church is, in a sense, God's plan A for reaching the world, and there is no plan B. This is true with respect to the preaching of the gospel but also true with respect to mercy ministry among the poor and the needy. Almost all of Spurgeon's benevolent ministries originated within the local church, and even those that didn't were still in some way connected to it. He preferred the local church to be the main platform for social ministry in the community. He believed it was incumbent upon London's churches to be engaged in doing good "in the slums, and dens, and kennels of the city." The poor and the needy were not to be left only to parachurch groups. Spurgeon understood mercy ministry to be the province of the local church as well.

Though it is certainly beneficial to partner with parachurch organizations, Christians should also endeavor to address material needs through the ministry of the local church. The local church should have a place of priority when it comes to carrying on mercy ministry. After all, in the New Testament, it was the local churches in particular that provided for the material needs of the saints. It was the local churches that were called to minister aid and carry out good works in needy communities. There are special promises and privileges that belong uniquely to the local church. When Christians carry out works of mercy and charity through their local churches, they are creating the best possible environment to testify to the grace of God and to draw needy people into the life of the church where they can be discipled. The church alone brings together a community of saints covenanted around the truth, accountable to one another, committed to proclaiming the gospel, and devoted to displaying God's character to the world through good works. Thus, in the context of the local church, there exists the optimal setting for integrating word, deed, and community in service to the church's biblically defined calling and mission. Within this context, social ministry has its most potent effect for good. Spurgeon understood this, which is why he sought to tether his social ministries as much as possible to his local church.

Churches today should view mercy ministry as a vital part of their calling. Governments may organize systems and programs for social relief, and so may numerous nonprofits and philanthropic organizations. However, it ought to be true that, regardless of whatever other social arrangements have been made, the church sees itself as having a special part to play in caring for the poor, the afflicted, and the oppressed. The church must be a community that makes significant efforts to care for the material and temporal needs of people through good works. Such works reflect the character and compassion of Christ, testify to the power of grace, and attract outsiders to the church community. Properly understood, philanthropic work is church work, mercy ministry is church ministry, and social concern is the church's concern.

Knowing the Needs
Spurgeon's commitment to the vital importance of social ministry caused him to labor to make himself intelligently aware of the various needs in his community. Part 2 of this book will document the

history of many of the Metropolitan Tabernacle's ministries and benevolent efforts in the city of London and will highlight Spurgeon's example in leading his church to engage in good works of benevolence. For now, it should simply be noted that Spurgeon and others in leadership at the Tabernacle took a genuine interest in learning the peculiar needs of London. They wanted to know the aches and pains of their community. Moreover, they especially wanted to know how they were uniquely fitted as the church to provide help and support.

Churches today should take a similar interest in their communities, whether they find themselves in a small town or a big city. Churches should ask, What are some of the material challenges facing our community? Where are some of the unique areas of deprivation and need in our own town or city? In what ways can our local church begin to address pressing material needs in our community as a means of showing forth the power of grace and the love of Christ? The point is to know the needs of your community and to consider practical ways in which the church could be organized to meet such needs. In so doing, the church will strengthen its reputation for being a friend of the community and may also enhance the church's witness among outsiders.

The Church as a Center for Community Benevolence
A final lesson for Christians today has to do with Spurgeon's basic vision for how churches should relate to the needs present in their surrounding communities. Spurgeon wanted to see churches become hubs for benevolent ministry in their particular neighborhoods. He believed local churches should position themselves as centers for ministry in their communities. The establishment of any church in a city should be good news for that city's poor and needy citizens. Such should be the case, first of all, because the members of the church ought to be full of compassion and zealous for doing good. Christians ought to be good neighbors. They ought to care for others and should be eager to provide help and support where they can. Second, if the church understands care for the afflicted and the needy as

constituting part of its mission, then the community only stands to benefit from the church's presence.

The Metropolitan Tabernacle was well-known in London as a haven for those in need. There the oppressed would find helpers, and the outcast would discover friends; the weak would find sympathy, and the poor would obtain relief. The Tabernacle was essentially one massive dispensary of benevolent aid. Churches today can emulate this model by equipping their members to care for the needs of others and by preparing them for various forms of mercy ministry in the community. Spurgeon believed local churches ought to be vibrant centers for doing good in the community. As such, they fulfill not only Spurgeon's vision but the Lord's, who said that His disciples were to let their light shine before others "that they may see your good works, and glorify your Father which is in heaven." Spurgeon saw this as part of the church's calling in his own day and age, and so it remains today.

Political Preaching?

Charles Spurgeon ministered in a climate of political change in Victorian Britain. The nineteenth century saw, through a series of reform acts, the enfranchisement of millions of new voters. Voting privileges extended down the social ladder to many laborers and workers and gave a voice to the lower classes of England and Wales for the first time. The two main political parties in England in that period, the Conservatives (usually called Tories) and the Liberals (sometimes called Whigs), were led by political rivals Benjamin Disraeli and William Gladstone, respectively. Spurgeon, in keeping with most Nonconformists (non-Anglicans) of his day, supported the Liberal party.[1] He even counted Gladstone among his personal

---

1. Many in nineteenth-century Britain viewed the Liberal Party as the champion of the Nonconformist's cause. For over two centuries, Nonconformists groaned under various laws restricting their freedoms. In Spurgeon's day, Nonconformists were still treated as second-class citizens in a number of significant ways. The Test and Corporations Acts were only repealed in 1828, just six years before Spurgeon's birth in 1834, finally making it legal for non-Anglicans to serve in Parliament. Not surprisingly, there was a lag in Nonconformist parliamentary representation after the passing of this important reform. The compulsory church rate requiring English citizens to pay taxes to repair Anglican parish churches remained until 1868. England's graveyards belonged to the Church of England, which meant that for most of Spurgeon's life, Nonconformists were not permitted to have their own funeral rites but rather had to endure the Anglican rites or a burial in silence. This was finally amended by the Burial Act of 1880. When Spurgeon was deliberating whether he would attend university in the early 1850s, Oxford and Cambridge were still closed to Nonconformists, a legal form of discrimination that was not fully addressed until the passing of the Universities Test Act in 1871. These disabilities perpetually fueled ani-

friends and occasionally welcomed the prime minister to his vestry at the Metropolitan Tabernacle after services.

It is important for American readers to appreciate, as a matter of context, that the divides between conservatives and liberals in the United States in the twenty-first century do not mirror those between the Conservative and Liberal parties in Britain in the nineteenth century. The differences between Conservative and Liberal agendas in Victorian Britain are captured well by considering the rival visions of Disraeli and Gladstone. The Conservative Disraeli advocated for what came to be known as "one-nation conservatism" or "Tory democracy," which promoted state paternalism in domestic policy and generally favored the preservation of established institutions and traditions. Disraeli also endorsed the idea of British imperialism, and his two premierships were marked by an aggressive foreign policy. The Liberal Gladstone, for his part, promoted a vision for liberalism that consisted of limited government, low taxation, laissez-faire economics, balanced budgets, and anti-interventionist foreign policy. Gladstone was also a persistent advocate for Irish Home Rule (a point on which Spurgeon, along with many other Liberals, departed from Gladstone) and eventually saw his Second Home Rule Bill passed through the House of Commons in 1893 but ultimately defeated in the House of Lords.

As a Liberal, Spurgeon was not at all shy about making his vote public, and he even occasionally sought to influence the votes of others. As the most popular preacher of his day, Spurgeon's political support was of no small value. He commanded not only the power of the pulpit but the power of the press as well. As such, he could potentially influence the votes of many thousands. It is of interest, therefore, to consider how Spurgeon thought about political involvement, particularly as it related to his own preaching. Chapter 12 will

---

mosity between Nonconformists and the Established Church. Spurgeon identified with the Liberals, in part, because he believed they were prepared "to grant at least a portion of those concessions which are due to Nonconformists." C. H. Spurgeon, "Notes," *Sword and the Trowel*, March 1874, 142.

highlight and examine many of Spurgeon's political positions on select issues and how he engaged in social and political activism on a practical level. The present chapter is more theoretical in nature and explores how Spurgeon thought about the place of politics with respect to preaching and the overall ministry of the church.

A Political Preacher?

When it comes to the subject of Spurgeon's political engagement, misunderstandings and misrepresentations abound. However, to date, very little in the way of significant scholarly research has been published on Spurgeon's politics. The most significant treatment of the subject is found in a rather long chapter in Patricia Kruppa's 1982 biography, *Charles Haddon Spurgeon: A Preacher's Progress*.[2] Kruppa's work was groundbreaking in that it provided scholars and historians with one of the first truly academic biographies of Spurgeon. Prior to Kruppa, few studies of Spurgeon went beyond basic hagiography. However, though Kruppa's work represents a significant contribution to Spurgeon studies, the book contains a number of notable flaws.

Most significantly among them is its problematic thesis, which appears to contradict itself, suggesting that Spurgeon was at the same time a "representative Victorian" as well as an "intellectual captive of the past."[3] Another significant shortcoming of the book is Kruppa's treatment of Spurgeon's political activism. In her chapter titled "A Political Dissenter," Kruppa makes the indefensible claim that "Spurgeon, like [Henry Ward] Beecher, was a 'political preacher,' and, inevitably, a subject of controversy as a result of his political

---

2. Patricia Stallings Kruppa, *Charles Haddon Spurgeon: A Preacher's Progress* (New York: Garland, 1982), 282–361. See also Alex DiPrima, "'An Eagerness to Be Up and Doing': The Evangelical Activism of Charles Haddon Spurgeon" (PhD diss., Southeastern Baptist Theological Seminary, 2020), 126–42; and Albert R. Meredith, "The Social and Political Views of Charles Haddon Spurgeon, 1834–1892" (PhD diss., Michigan State University, 1973).

3. Kruppa, *Charles Haddon Spurgeon*, 6.

activism."[4] Though Kruppa labels Spurgeon a "political preacher," she never provides any evidence for such an assertion. It is telling that in an eighty-page chapter, which begins with the thesis that Spurgeon was a political preacher, Kruppa does not cite a single one of Spurgeon's sermons.[5]

Other scholars such as David Bebbington, Horton Davies, Peter Morden, and R. J. Helmstadter have all argued that Spurgeon was not particularly political in his preaching. "Spurgeon," writes Davies, "took the pietistical view that preachers should keep politics out of the pulpit."[6] Helmstadter makes a similar statement, writing, "His political involvement had never been significant. The sermons contain almost no reference to political affairs."[7] Morden, a leading Spurgeon scholar, is even more candid, writing,

> Spurgeon was not as active politically as many other nineteenth-century Dissenters, such as John Clifford. He was not a significant figure shaping the politics of Nonconformity or, indeed, more narrowly, of Baptists. Rather, he shared the political views held by the majority of Dissenters and Baptists from the middle of the century onwards, which were, of course, staunchly Liberal. He shied away from making party political comments from the pulpit and did not want the Tabernacle to be used for political meetings in support of Liberal candidates. When compared to Spurgeon's other activities, the political dimension, although certainly present, does not loom large.[8]

---

4. Kruppa, *Charles Haddon Spurgeon*, 283.
5. Kruppa, *Charles Haddon Spurgeon*, 282–361.
6. Horton Davies, *Worship and Theology in England*, vol. 4, *From Newman to Martineau, 1850–1900* (Grand Rapids: Eerdmans, 1996), 345.
7. R. J. Helmstadter, "Spurgeon in Outcast London," in *The View from the Pulpit: Victorian Ministers and Society*, ed. P. T. Phillips (Toronto, Ont.: Macmillan of Canada, 1978), 180. Helmstadter acknowledges that Spurgeon opened the Tabernacle to the annual meetings of the Liberation Society but suggests that his support for that cause diminished over the years.
8. Peter J. Morden, *Communion with Christ and His People: The Spirituality of C. H. Spurgeon* (Eugene, Ore.: Pickwick Publications, 2013), 196–97.

Kruppa's assertion that Spurgeon was a political preacher is an overstatement at best. The evidence simply does not support the claim that political concerns occupied a large place in Spurgeon's preaching. Any remarks Spurgeon made in his sermons concerning politics were fairly obscure and were usually either tangential to his main burden or were connected to some extraordinary national event. Bebbington's comment is nearer the mark when he writes, "Although politically partisan statements occasionally crept into his sermons, they were always defensible as pronouncements on moral issues that had caught the public eye."[9]

How then did Spurgeon think about politics and the role it should play in preaching and in the ministry of the church? Below it will be argued that Spurgeon was not a political preacher but, at the same time, felt it his duty to occasionally address particular political subjects that he believed intersected with biblical concerns, such as slavery, concern for the poor, and the disestablishment of the state church. Though he rarely made use of the pulpit to address political matters, Spurgeon was less reticent about doing so through other channels, such as his monthly magazine, the *Sword and the Trowel*, where he addressed political subjects with greater freedom. A political preacher he most certainly was not, yet he took an interest in politics, particularly when politics collided with religious concerns.

Guarding the Pulpit

As a rule, Spurgeon avoided politics in his sermons. He did not believe that the pulpit was the place for political commentary or partisan wrangling. After several years of publishing his sermons, he challenged his readers in an 1873 article, "Take the eighteen volumes of the Metropolitan Tabernacle Pulpit, and see if you can find eighteen pages of matter which even look towards politics; nay, more, see if there be one solitary sentence concerning politics, which did not,

---

9. David W. Bebbington, "The Political Force," *Christian History* 10, no. 1 (1991): 38.

to the preacher's mind, appear to arise out of his text, or to flow from the natural run of his subject."[10] A survey of Spurgeon's preaching in any volume of his sermons would tend to vindicate this claim. One can read hundreds of pages of his sermons without finding any references to politics.

Spurgeon encouraged pastors to avoid introducing political subjects into their sermons, and he often criticized the "minister absorbed in politics."[11] In 1876, he said, "In proportion as the preaching becomes political, and the pastor sinks the spiritual in the temporal, strength is lost, and not gained."[12] Thus, Spurgeon also urged the many students in his Pastors' College to avoid politics in their sermons as well.[13] His desire was that they be known for gospel preaching and not political partisanship.

Spurgeon could easily have echoed the sentiments expressed by a prominent Baptist preacher from a generation earlier and a man whom Spurgeon greatly admired, Robert Hall Jr., who wrote in an open letter to the famous Anglican minister Charles Simeon, "For myself, all who have ever heard me are witnesses that I never introduced a political topic into the pulpit on any occasion."[14] This was,

---

10. Spurgeon, "A Political Dissenter," *Sword and the Trowel*, March 1873, 108.

11. Spurgeon, "The Ministry Needed by the Churches, and Measures for Providing It," *Sword and the Trowel*, May 1871, 215.

12. Spurgeon, "The Power of Nonconformity," *Sword and the Trowel*, July 1876, 304.

13. See Spurgeon, "Ministry Needed," 215, 219–20; Spurgeon, *An All-Round Ministry: Direction, Wisdom, and Encouragement for Preachers and Pastors* (Edinburgh: Banner of Truth, 2018), 213, 253.

14. Robert Hall, in a letter to Charles Simeon, cited in Charles Smyth, *Simeon and Church Order: A Study of the Origins of the Evangelical Revival in Cambridge in the Eighteenth Century* (Cambridge: Cambridge University Press, 1940), 296. Robert Hall Jr. was the minister of St. Andrews Street Baptist Chapel in Cambridge from 1791 to 1826. Spurgeon became a member of this same congregation roughly twenty-five years after Hall's ministry had ended, though his influence was still alive in Cambridge when Spurgeon was there. Spurgeon held Hall in the highest esteem; see C. H. Spurgeon, "A Safe Prospective," in *The Metropolitan Tabernacle Pulpit: Sermons Preached and Revised by C. H. Spurgeon* (Pasadena, Tex.: Pilgrim Publications, 1970), 15:465; Spurgeon, "St. Brelade's Bay," *Sword and the Trowel*, November 1871, 510; and

in essence, Spurgeon's claim if accused of being a political preacher. Simply put, Spurgeon believed the pulpit was the place for gospel preaching, not politics.

The "Collision" of Politics and Faith

"As Christians we take small interest in party politics," Spurgeon wrote, "and were it not for the religious questions involved we should not concern ourselves to any great extent with the doings of the polling booths."[15] Though Spurgeon was averse to introducing political rhetoric into his sermons, it should not be imagined that this aversion was absolute. On the contrary, Spurgeon was quite willing to speak to political issues that he believed intersected with biblical concerns. Thus, Spurgeon did address subjects such as the various forms of legal discrimination against Nonconformists, Irish Home Rule, and certain matters related to British imperialism. He addressed these subjects primarily because he believed them to be closely related to biblical concerns. He never addressed politics for politics' sake in his preaching but only took up such subjects as they came in contact with scriptural matters—which, at times, they inevitably did.

In an 1873 article, Spurgeon wrote,

> For a Christian minister to be an active partisan of Whigs or Tories, busy in canvassing, and eloquent at public meetings for rival factions, would be of ill repute. For the Christian to forget his heavenly citizenship, and occupy himself about the objects of place-hunters, would be degrading to his high calling: but there are points of inevitable contact between the higher and lower spheres, points where politics persist in coming into collision with our faith, and there we shall be traitors both to heaven and earth if we consult our comfort by sinking into the rear.[16]

C. H. Spurgeon's Autobiography, Compiled from His Diary, Letters, and Records by His Wife and His Private Secretary (London: Passmore and Alabaster, 1898), 2:72.
  15. Spurgeon, "Notes," March 1874, 142.
  16. Spurgeon, "Political Dissenter," 108.

Thus, Spurgeon did not entirely avoid political topics in his preaching but chose to address select issues insofar as they came into contact with the Bible and what he viewed as matters of Christian faithfulness. Even in such instances, Spurgeon was often temperate and restrained in his remarks, always seeking to preserve the pulpit for gospel preaching above all else.

While Spurgeon was quite cautious about addressing politics in his preaching, he was generally more willing to speak to political subjects through other mediums. The most significant channel for his political commentary was the *Sword and the Trowel*. This periodical drew a monthly readership of fifteen thousand and contained diverse content, including sermons, reports on various ministries and institutions, book reviews, and articles on wide-ranging subjects of interest to his readers. Occasionally, Spurgeon included articles that addressed contemporary social and political issues. For example, in an 1873 article, Spurgeon spoke out against various forms of animal cruelty taking place in London.[17] In an 1877 article, he addressed the local school board's policies with respect to religious instruction.[18] And in 1880, he commented on the famous Burials Bill which granted Nonconformists the right to bury their dead without the traditional Anglican burial rites.[19] In each of these cases, Spurgeon understood himself to be addressing political issues that clearly intersected with religious concerns. He saw himself contributing biblical perspectives to national issues that were of interest to Christians.

Even with the *Sword and the Trowel*, it must be noted that Spurgeon's political commentary was still occasional and limited. Nonetheless, it is true that Spurgeon felt far fewer reservations about addressing politics within the pages of his magazine as opposed to his preaching. An important principle lay at the heart of this approach.

---

17. Spurgeon, "A Word for Brutes against Brutes," *Sword and the Trowel*, June 1873, 241–46.

18. Spurgeon, "The School Board Victory," *Sword and the Trowel*, January 1877, 36–38.

19. Spurgeon, "The Burials' Bill," *Sword and the Trowel*, October 1880, 506.

Spurgeon believed the preaching of the Word of God in the context of the gathered church requires a narrower focus. Preaching is for the worship of God, the edification of the saints, and the evangelism of the lost, not for political commentary. Simply put, the pulpit is not the venue for politics.

Though Spurgeon clearly exercised some measure of restraint in his public political commentary, he nonetheless believed Christians should give thoughtful attention to politics and allow their Christian faith to shape their political perspectives. He said, "Every God-fearing man should give his vote with as much devotion as he prays."[20] Christians are called to heavenly-mindedness and to live for Christ's kingdom, but this should not lead them to ignore the world around them. Spurgeon believed Christians should endeavor to steward their earthly citizenship for good and should desire to see the will of God prevail in the public square. In an 1881 sermon, he said,

> I long for the day when the precepts of the Christian religion shall be the rule among all classes of men, in all transactions. I often hear it said 'Do not bring religion into politics.' This is precisely where it ought to be brought, and set there in the face of all men as on a candlestick. I would have the Cabinet and the Members of Parliament do the work of the nation as before the Lord, and I would have the nation, either in making war or peace, consider the matter by the light of righteousness. We are to deal with other nations about this or that upon the principles of the New Testament.[21]

Insofar as Christians have the ability to influence the political arena, they should do so according to the light of Scripture and the revealed will of God. Spurgeon went on to say, "Godliness should as much influence the House of Commons as the Assembly of Divines. God grant that the day may come when the mischievous division between secular and religious things shall no more be heard of, for in all things

---

20. Spurgeon, "Notes," April 1880, 191.
21. Spurgeon, "The Candle," in *Metropolitan Tabernacle Pulpit*, 27:225.

Christians are to glorify God, according to the precept, 'Whether ye eat or drink or whatsoever ye do, do all to the glory of God.'"[22]

Individual Regeneration and Social Change

To grasp Spurgeon's approach to politics fully, one must appreciate another important principle that regulated his thinking. Simply put, Spurgeon believed the principal means of changing the world and building the church would not be political policy or systemic reform but individual regeneration and widespread revival. Spurgeon's approach to social change was largely individualistic and focused on the necessity of the new birth. He placed little faith in politics to achieve significant social transformation. However, he placed great faith in the power of the gospel to change hearts and thus change people within society.

Spurgeon's career in London coincided with the rise of the Christian socialist movement. His contemporaries F. D. Maurice, J. M. Ludlow, and Charles Kingsley were all major players in the movement. In the latter decades of the nineteenth century, the Baptist John Clifford and the Methodist Hugh Price Hughes embraced Christian socialism as well. The movement promoted the merging of Christian ethics with socialist economic and political thought. Thinkers within Christian socialism focused on systemic reforms in order to address far-reaching societal problems.[23]

Though there is little evidence to suggest that Spurgeon interacted extensively with the Christian socialist thought of his day, it is nonetheless plain that Spurgeon was not at home within the movement. Every single reference to socialism in Spurgeon's writings is negative. He told his congregation in 1889, "I would not have you

---

22. Spurgeon, "The Candle," 27:226.
23. For an introduction to the historical context surrounding Christian socialism in the latter half of nineteenth-century Britain, see Owen Chadwick, *The Victorian Church*, vol. 1, *1829–1859* (London: SCM, 1971), 269–86; Gary Dorrien, *Social Democracy in the Making: Political and Religious Roots of European Socialism* (New Haven, Conn.: Yale University Press, 2019), 27–113; and Edward R. Norman, *The Victorian Christian Socialists* (Cambridge: Cambridge University Press, 2002).

exchange the gold of individual Christianity for the base metal of Christian Socialism."[24] In 1891, he said, "Great schemes of socialism have been tried and found wanting; let us look to regeneration by the Son of God, and we shall not look in vain."[25] From what little evidence we have, it would appear that Spurgeon was opposed to the emerging Christian socialist movement that dawned in Britain toward the latter part of his life. Spurgeon rejected socialism and believed a preoccupation with seeking to address the world's needs through large-scale social and structural engineering was mostly futile.

Kruppa's suggestion that Spurgeon labored "for a kingdom of heaven on earth" is, therefore, profoundly inaccurate and unhelpful.[26] Spurgeon did not entertain delusions of what he called "a certain imaginary kingdom of God" on earth.[27] Albert Meredith's conclusion is nearer the mark: "He was convinced that the world would be reformed, not by changing the system, but by changing the individuals who comprised that system. Thus, individualistic evangelism was the means whereby one might reform society as a whole."[28] Spurgeon's thoughts on social reform were regulated by an individualist ethic. Society would be reformed, not through systemic changes, but through individuals submitting their lives to Christ and the precepts of his kingdom. Even as Spurgeon believed these individuals ought to be gathered into local churches where corporately they would engage in social ministry, such ministry focused on performing individual good to others rather than enacting systemic social change.

Spurgeon's individualism was overt and could, at times, seem simplistic. As he contemplated many of the great social problems facing London, he wrote in an 1872 article, "We believe that national

---

24. Spurgeon, "One Lost Sheep," in *Metropolitan Tabernacle Pulpit*, 35:241–42.
25. Spurgeon, "Jesus—'All Blessing and All Blest,'" in *Metropolitan Tabernacle Pulpit*, 37:71.
26. Kruppa, *Charles Haddon Spurgeon*, 287.
27. Spurgeon, *All-Round Ministry*, 253.
28. Meredith, "Social and Political Views," 124. See also David Nelson Duke, "Charles Haddon Spurgeon: Social Concern Exceeding an Individualistic, Self-Help Ideology," *Baptist History and Heritage* 22, no. 4 (October 1987): 47–56.

peace, and the security of our great cities, can only be guaranteed for a long future, by the recognition of the religion of Jesus Christ, and the wider spread of its principles.... Let the spirit, the essence, the governing power of our holy faith predominate, and the work is done."[29] Spurgeon then went on to illustrate this principle with practical examples:

> It would greatly tend to allay all feeling of popular discontent, if all employers acted as true Christians should in the matter of wages. Political economy gives the workman what it must, but Christianity commands that we give him what we should. "Masters, give unto your servants that which is just and equal," is a plain command of the Christian's law-book.... When the artisan or labourer becomes a Christian, he is at once removed from the ignorance and excess which are so damaging to social order, and he becomes at the same time an advocate for justice between man and man. If true to his profession, he gives a fair day's work for his wage, which, begging the pardon of thousands, is by no means a common thing. He is no eye-server, but labours diligently, doing in his sphere as he would have others do to him, were he their employer.... The Christian workman is the hope of the age.... It is plain, then, that the religion of Jesus, when it creates obedience to its golden rule, becomes the Saviour of Society.... Not empty profession, but genuine godliness, is the cement of our social fabric. England will suffer nothing, whether her government be of one form or another, so long as her people love God, and, therefore, love righteousness. Wrong-doing in any quarter divides, distracts, and incites to rebellion; but when all seek the right for all, mutual confidence creates union, union strength, and strength prosperity.[30]

What was needed was not principally the passage of new laws or the reformation of existing systems. The great need of society, according to Spurgeon, was the spread of the gospel and the promotion of

---

29. Spurgeon, "Paris and London," *Sword and the Trowel*, January 1872, 7.
30. Spurgeon, "Paris and London," 8–10.

Christian principles. People needed to be changed at the heart level through new birth, and only then could society be lastingly changed. In one of his Pastors' College conference addresses to current and former students, Spurgeon conveyed a similar perspective, saying,

> The gospel, if it were fully received through the whole earth, would purge away all slavery and all war, and put down all drunkenness and all social evils; in fact, you cannot conceive a moral curse which it would not remove; and even physical evils, since many of them arise incidentally from sin, would be greatly mitigated, and some of them for ever abolished. The spirit of the gospel, causing attention to be given to all that concerns our neighbours' welfare, would promote sanitary and social reforms, and so the leaves of the tree which are for the healing of the nations would work their beneficial purpose.[31]

Simply put, Spurgeon believed that individual Christians, changed by the grace of God and living just, compassionate, and benevolent lives, are the greatest hope for society's ills. He placed no trust in what he termed an "imaginary kingdom" built on "sanitary regulations, social arrangements, scientific accommodations, and legislative enactments."[32] Carlile's summation of Spurgeon's views fifty years after his death is still accurate: "Spurgeon believed in doing what he could to change conditions by changing individuals. His theory was that the changed life transformed the circumstances."[33]

To many, Spurgeon's perspectives can appear simplistic and naive, lacking in sophistication and an appreciation for the role of systematic forces in societal change. However, we must remember that, in general, Spurgeon's thoughts on social reform were in keeping with those of the majority of Victorian society, at least in the mid-nineteenth century.[34] Individual activism and personal philanthropy

---

31. Spurgeon, *All-Round Ministry*, 253.
32. Spurgeon, *All-Round Ministry*, 253.
33. J. C. Carlile, *C. H. Spurgeon: An Interpretive Biography* (London: Kingsgate, 1933), 228.
34. Sarah Förster, *Philanthropic Foundations and Social Welfare: A Comparative*

were the primary tools for improving the world around them. Those who labored for large-scale systemic reforms without regard to changing the hearts of the individuals those systems comprised were far rarer, and they could often be viewed as innovators and progressives.

Spurgeon thought little about impersonal systemic reform. To him, social change would come about primarily as the gospel changed people's hearts and reformed their natures. In this, Spurgeon was much like the typical Victorian evangelicals of his day, as Meredith argues: "To them, each individual was of infinite worth; their concern was centered upon the individual and his family, and rare was the philanthropist who stopped to consider whether there were any basic principles underlying the conditions which they were trying to ease. Spurgeon placed little value on grand schemes which proposed to end poverty, sickness, and despair by restructuring the social system. In typical Victorian style, he was convinced that the problems of society lay with the individuals of that society."[35] As simple as such a perspective might seem to many by today's standards, Spurgeon felt certain that individual heart change was indeed the heart of the matter itself.

Preachers and Politics

I have endeavored to provide a sketch of Spurgeon's approach to politics, particularly from the standpoint of his public ministry. There is much more that can be said about Spurgeon's approach to politics, and there is room for some eager scholar to prepare such a study in the future. Here, I will only briefly note a few very basic lessons that Christians, especially pastors, should learn from Spurgeon's example.

Study of Germany, Sweden and the United Kingdom (England) (München, Germany: Springer VS, 2018), 125–56; Alan J. Kidd, *State, Society and the Poor in Nineteenth-Century England* (New York: St. Martin's, 1999), 1–7, 65–108; Chadwick, *Victorian Church*, 2:269–71.

35. Meredith, "Social and Political Views," 165–66. See also Kathleen Heasman, *Evangelicals in Action: An Appraisal of Their Social Work in the Victorian Era* (London: Geoffrey Bles, 1962), 20.

The first lesson one should learn from Spurgeon's approach to politics is that *the pulpit is the venue for Bible preaching, not political commentary.* Spurgeon jealously guarded the pulpit against all extraneous intrusions and carefully stewarded the preaching ministry of his local church. Spurgeon held that when believers gather on the Lord's Day to worship God, the errand of the preacher is clear—"Preach the Word" (2 Tim. 4:2). The preacher is called to appear as God's ambassador on behalf of the people and is obliged to expound the Bible in order to feed the flock and evangelize the lost. The preaching ministry of the church is not the proper context for political commentary, social analysis, and cultural critique. The pulpit is designed for the preaching of the Word of God. As Peter said in 1 Peter 4:11, "If any man speak, let him speak as the oracles of God." For Spurgeon, this meant that he had to exercise self-control and restraint and had to commit himself to stay on task. He was not at liberty to say whatever he might think or wish about contemporary events or political developments. He was in that pulpit to preach the Bible and to proclaim the truth. For pastors today, the assignment has not changed. The work of the preacher is to proclaim the Word of God for the sake of God's people. Preaching is a thus-saith-the-Lord enterprise.

Of course, the regular preaching of the Bible will provide occasional opportunities to address political issues and current events by way of applying the Scriptures faithfully in one's particular historical and social context. Furthermore, there may be significant national tragedies, spontaneous events, or providential occurrences that periodically require the preacher to provide biblical perspective for the benefit of the congregation. Spurgeon occasionally endeavored to do this in response to contemporary events, but he always did so from the standpoint of Scripture. This leads to a second lesson: *if ever political subjects or contemporary events are to be addressed from the pulpit, they should generally flow out of the text under consideration.* Spurgeon periodically addressed political questions and matters of public interest. However, in such rare instances, he did so by bringing the Scriptures to bear on the matter at hand. When addressing issues that touched on politics from the pulpit, Spurgeon endeavored to do so by expounding God's revealed will and manifesting its connection to the subject at hand. He did not view the sermon as his opportunity to provide his unique analysis and perspective on the headlines of the day. If he was to address a contemporary event or issue from the pulpit, he did so within the framework of his broader exposition of Scripture.

One of the reasons Spurgeon did not invest much of his energy and attention in political and social activism had to do with his understanding of the kingdom of God and the mission of the church. Spurgeon would wish to teach preachers today a third lesson: *the primary work of the church is the proclamation of truth unto the salvation of souls and the building up of the church, not political activism.* Many will perhaps object at this point. Shouldn't the church be concerned about culture? Shouldn't Christians try to influence the political realm? Shouldn't believers steward their opportunities to voice their perspectives in the public square? Spurgeon would not object to any of these concerns. He occasionally spoke to cultural issues, participated in the political process, and lent his voice on certain matters of public interest. Nonetheless, he did not believe the church should view the political arena as its primary theater of action. Spurgeon saw the principal work of the church as proclaiming the gospel, making disciples, and building healthy churches. Spurgeon wanted to win souls and to see men and women come to faith in Christ through the new birth. The work of the church is primarily a spiritual work of drawing men and women out of the darkness of sin and into the light of Christ and gathering these redeemed sinners into churches that show forth the glory of God to the world through word and deed. Spurgeon could be quite pessimistic about the wider world, but the church was ever the cause for optimism and hope. Spurgeon trusted what Christ had promised: "I will build my church; and the gates of hell shall not prevail against it" (Matt. 16:18). This glorious vision would not be accomplished primarily through political and social activism, but through gospel preaching and new birth.

PART 2

Spurgeon's Practice

The Priority of Soul Winning

In part 2 of this book, we turn from Spurgeon's teaching to his practice. What did Spurgeon actually do in the arenas of benevolence, philanthropy, and social concern, and how did he do it? As we consider these subjects, it is important to situate Spurgeon's approach to mercy ministry in the context of his broader pastoral work, which had as its focal point a prolific pulpit ministry. His emphasis on benevolence and good works flowed out of his preaching of the gospel and his passion for soul winning. Spurgeon always considered preaching unto the salvation of souls to be his primary work. One potential danger when focusing on a single aspect of a man's theology and teaching is that one can inadvertently exaggerate the significance of that particular subject in his overall life and ministry. One of the ways to avoid this danger is to endeavor to situate the particular issue under consideration in the larger context of his entire ministry. In the case of Spurgeon's view of benevolence and mercy ministry, it is important to appreciate that these concerns, though certainly biblical, were downstream of the larger burden of preaching the gospel. Spurgeon's interest in social ministry grew out of his more prominent concern to see men and women won to faith in Christ.

Therefore, this chapter will survey Spurgeon's extraordinary preaching ministry, as well as his labors in evangelism and church planting, in order to create the proper context for considering his efforts in social ministry in the chapters that follow. We must first see what was primary for Spurgeon—namely, proclaiming the truth—in order to appreciate how benevolence ministry interacted and intersected with this larger concern. What follows is a survey of Spurgeon's extraordinary efforts in evangelism, preaching, and soul winning, beginning with his earliest days as a new Christian in Cambridgeshire and continuing through his exceptional career in London.

Early Evangelism, Tract Distribution, and Visitation

Spurgeon was born again in January 1850 at the age of fifteen, upon hearing an evangelistic sermon from Isaiah 45:22. This experience came after what Spurgeon described as a long and protracted struggle with spiritual doubt and depression.[1] The significance of Spurgeon's conversion and its impact on the immediate trajectory of his life is hard to overstate. He would, for the rest of his life, understand his conversion to be the defining moment of his biography. Spurgeon emerged from this experience with a robust assurance of salvation and an eagerness to throw himself energetically into work for Christ. Prior to his conversion, Spurgeon, though at times boyish and playful, could be pensive, bookish, and retiring. However, after he came to faith, he began to display an unprecedented zeal and passion for ministering among needy people. From distributing tracts to teaching Sunday school, Spurgeon eagerly pursued every opportunity to engage in Christian work. These early blossoms of evangelical activity would eventually come into full bloom in a thriving preaching ministry in the surrounding region of Cambridgeshire.

Spurgeon's letters from this period, written shortly after his conversion, provide a window into his early evangelical activism. The portrait that emerges from these letters is of a devoted young man who gave himself to evangelical activism with youthful energy and fervor. From the ages of fifteen to seventeen, Spurgeon regularly engaged in evangelism, tract distribution, prayer meetings, min-

---

1. C. H. *Spurgeon's Autobiography, Compiled from His Diary, Letters, and Records by His Wife and His Private Secretary* (London: Passmore and Alabaster, 1897), 1:75–96.

istry to the poor, home visitation, Sunday school ministry, and lay preaching. Mark Hopkins documents Spurgeon's spiritual progress during his first year as a new convert, saying, "Spurgeon lost no time in channelling this rush of spiritual life into practical Christian commitment and work. By February 1850 he was distributing tracts, in April he was admitted to church membership, in May he was baptized by immersion (in accordance with convictions arrived at before his conversion) and began teaching a Sunday school class, and by June he was visiting seventy people regularly on Saturdays to converse on spiritual things. He started lay preaching soon after moving to Cambridge in September 1850, and began his first ministry a year later in the nearby village of Waterbeach when only seventeen."[2]

Spurgeon's early letters include statements such as, "I feel now as if I could do everything for Christ,"[3] "Oh how I wish I could do something for Christ,"[4] and "I have more than sufficient to induce me to give up myself entirely to Him who has bought me and purchased me with an everlasting redemption."[5] As a new Christian, Spurgeon understood it to be his privilege and responsibility to serve Christ with all of his energy, which is why he immediately gave himself to Christian work after his conversion. George Needham writes, "Having thus publicly devoted himself to the service of God, he was more earnest than ever in his efforts to do good.... He was instant in season, and, indeed, seldom out of season, in his efforts to do good."[6]

Tract distribution was perhaps the most obvious avenue of Christian service available to Spurgeon as a young convert. He referred to it as his "little effort."[7] Within just a few weeks of his conversion,

---

2. Mark Hopkins, *Nonconformity's Romantic Generation: Evangelical and Liberal Theologies in Victorian England* (Eugene, Ore.: Wipf and Stock, 2006), 127.
3. *C. H. Spurgeon's Autobiography*, 1:117.
4. *C. H. Spurgeon's Autobiography*, 1:118.
5. *C. H. Spurgeon's Autobiography*, 1:124.
6. George Needham, *The Life and Labors of Charles H. Spurgeon: The Faithful Preacher, the Devoted Pastor, the Noble Philanthropist, the Beloved College President, and the Voluminous Writer, Author, Etc., Etc.*, (Boston: D. L. Guernsey, 1887), 41.
7. Needham, *The Life and Labors of Charles H. Spurgeon*, 121.

Spurgeon took over a district in Newmarket containing thirty-three homes that had previously been under the oversight of two women in the town. His visits to these homes involved more than simply dropping a tract by the front door. He approached the people he visited almost like a pastor would members of his parish, seeking to provoke spiritual conversation with those he visited and minister to their practical needs.[8] His descriptions of these home visits in his early letters are redolent of some passages in Richard Baxter's writings, especially *The Reformed Pastor*,[9] which Spurgeon had most likely read by this time in his life.[10] Though Spurgeon was not yet a recognized minister, he began to behave like one at the outset of his Christian life, informally carrying on many of the types of activities that would mark his ministry at Waterbeach just two years later.

Spurgeon's passion for soul winning was evident in these early stages of his Christian life. Speaking of his "tract people," he said, "Oh, that I could see but one sinner constrained to come to Jesus!"[11] One of the foremost marks of Spurgeon's young faith was a pronounced burden for the lost and an almost all-consuming desire to proclaim the good news to them. He desired to follow in the footsteps of his father and his grandfather as preachers of the gospel. There is little indication that Spurgeon ever doubted his calling to

---

8. Needham, *The Life and Labors of Charles H. Spurgeon*, 121.

9. Richard Baxter, *The Reformed Pastor* (Grand Rapids: Sovereign Grace, 1971).

10. For examples, see Spurgeon's comment that he endeavored to address Sunday school children "as a dying being to dying beings" in *C. H. Spurgeon's Autobiography* (1:124) and compare with Richard Baxter's famous remark that he "preach'd, as never sure to preach again, and as a dying man to dying men!" in *The Poetical Fragments of Richard Baxter*, 4th ed. (London: Samuel and Richard Bentley, 1821), 35; see also Spurgeon's descriptions of how he approached the people of the homes he visited in *C. H. Spurgeon's Autobiography* (1:121, 124), compared with Baxter's comments in *The Reformed Pastor* (67–75); and later Spurgeon's description of the revival he witnessed at Waterbeach in *C. H. Spurgeon's Autobiography* (1:227–28), compared with Baxter's comments in *Reliquiae Baxterianae: or Mr. Richard Baxter's Narrative of the Most Memorable Passages of His Life and Times* (London: printed for T. Parkhurst, J. Robinson, J. Lawrence, and J. Dunton, 1696), 1:84–86.

11. *C. H. Spurgeon's Autobiography*, 1:121.

preach. Even as a young boy, Spurgeon exhibited gifts that led some to predict that he would be a great preacher.[12] It appears from a survey of Spurgeon's early letters almost as though his conversion was the last puzzle piece to fall into place in completing his call to preach. Having closed with Christ and committed his life to Christian service, Spurgeon was perfectly poised to become a gospel preacher.

Preaching

The lifeblood of Spurgeon's ministry was his preaching. Hopkins notes, "Preaching never strayed from its central place in Spurgeon's life and work: it must be the starting point for an examination of the various means by which his influence made itself felt."[13] R. J. Helmstadter writes, "His was a preaching ministry; his sermons, above all else, were the central feature of the religious life of the Tabernacle."[14] More than anything else, Spurgeon was a preacher, and he gave himself to this work with an almost fervid obsession. His interest in preaching began before he was converted, but afterward, it became an all-consuming passion, such that before he reached the age of twenty, he had already preached over six hundred sermons.[15] He often preached seven times per week and occasionally more than ten times per week.[16] He once remarked, "People said to me years ago, 'You will break your constitution down with preaching ten times a week,' and the like. Well, if I have done so, I am glad of it. I would do the same again. If I had fifty constitutions I would rejoice to break them down in the service of the Lord Jesus Christ."[17] When it came

---

12. C. H. Spurgeon's Autobiography, 1:33–38.
13. Hopkins, Nonconformity's Romantic Generation, 152.
14. R. J. Helmstadter, "Spurgeon in Outcast London," in The View from the Pulpit: Victorian Ministers and Society, ed. P. T. Phillips (Toronto, Ont.: Macmillan of Canada, 1978), 165.
15. Eric W. Hayden, "Did You Know?" Christian History 29, no. 1 (1991): 2.
16. Eric W. Hayden, Highlights in the Life of C. H. Spurgeon (Pasadena, Tex.: Pilgrim Publications, 1990), 12; Needham, Life and Labors, 65; C. H. Spurgeon's Autobiography, 1:38.
17. C. H. Spurgeon, "For the Sick and Afflicted," in The Metropolitan Tabernacle

time to erect the Metropolitan Tabernacle in order to accommodate the enormous crowds who came to hear him, Spurgeon embarked on a grueling preaching tour across Britain to raise funds for the project. Spurgeon gave himself, with unusual drive and devotion, to preach as much as possible. He did this because soul winning was at the heart of Spurgeon's mission in life, and preaching was the God-ordained means of soul winning.

There were few places where Spurgeon would not preach. In his early days, he preached in cottages, barns, and the open air as part of the St. Andrew's Street Baptist Lay-Preachers Association. When he came to London, he preached in the Crystal Palace, Exeter Hall, and the Surrey Gardens Music Hall as efforts were made to enlarge the New Park Street Chapel and eventually to construct a larger building—the Metropolitan Tabernacle. As was mentioned earlier, Spurgeon's decision to use the Surrey Gardens Music Hall for his services drew criticism from many, including some of the members of New Park Street, who viewed the use of a secular venue for such services as inappropriate.[18] Yet, Spurgeon was undismayed and preached some of his most storied sermons in that place, only abandoning the venue after it began to host secular events on Sabbath evenings, which violated his scruples.[19] By the end of his life, Spurgeon was even preaching sermons from his sickbed in Mentone, France.[20]

The primary venue for Spurgeon's preaching for most of his life was the Metropolitan Tabernacle, erected seven years after his arrival in London. Beginning in 1861 and continuing for three decades thereafter, Spurgeon preached on Sundays to gatherings of over six thousand in both the morning and the evening. In his very first Sunday sermon delivered there, Spurgeon said, "I would propose that

---

Pulpit: Sermons Preached and Revised by C. H. Spurgeon (Pasadena, Tex.: Pilgrim Publications, 1971), 22:45.

18. Morden, *C. H. Spurgeon: The People's Preacher* (Farnham, U.K.: CWR, 2009), 67–68.

19. Robert Shindler, *From the Usher's Desk to the Tabernacle Pulpit: Pastor C. H Spurgeon, His Life and Work* (London: Passmore and Alabaster, 1892), 104.

20. *C. H. Spurgeon's Autobiography*, 4:370.

the subject of the ministry of this house, as long as this platform shall stand, and as long as this house shall be frequented by worshippers, shall be the person of Jesus Christ. I am never ashamed to avow myself a Calvinist.... I do not hesitate to take the name of Baptist.... But if I am asked to say what is my creed, I think I must reply—'It is Jesus Christ.'"[21] Jesus Christ—His person and work—was indeed the central theme of his preaching. Spurgeon's message was not one of moralism, religious formalism, or political revolution but of Jesus Christ and Him crucified.[22]

One factor that greatly expanded the reach of Spurgeon's preaching was his decision to print his sermons on a weekly basis. With the help of the publishers Joseph Passmore and James Alabaster, Spurgeon began printing his sermons in 1855. This effort would continue throughout the rest of his life and after his death in 1892 until 1917 when World War I precipitated a national paper shortage and brought the project to a grinding halt. Altogether, Passmore and Alabaster oversaw the publication of sixty-three volumes of sermons between *The New Park Street Pulpit* (six volumes) and *The Metropolitan Tabernacle Pulpit* (fifty-seven volumes). In recent days, seven volumes of Spurgeon's *Lost Sermons*[23] (sermons from his pre-London days) have been published, adding roughly 10 percent to the overall corpus of Spurgeon's published sermons.

Spurgeon made small attempts at publishing his sermons before committing to the far more substantial publishing effort with Passmore and Alabaster.[24] Once he did begin working with them, he published a sermon every week for the rest of his life, an effort

---

21. Spurgeon, "The First Sermon in the Tabernacle," in *Metropolitan Tabernacle Pulpit*, 7:169.
22. Thomas Breimaier, *Tethered to the Cross: The Life and Preaching of Charles H. Spurgeon* (Downers Grove, Ill.: IVP Academic, 2020) explores the dynamic christocentrism of Spurgeon's preaching and hermeneutics in greater detail.
23. *The Lost Sermons of C. H. Spurgeon: His Earliest Outlines and Sermons Between 1851 and 1854*, ed. Christian T. George, 7 vols. (Nashville: B&H Academic, 2016–2022).
24. W. Y. Fullerton, *C. H. Spurgeon: A Biography* (London: William and Norgate, 1920), 212.

that required a great deal of exertion on his part. Spurgeon wrote, "The labour has been far greater than some suppose, and has usually occupied the best hours of Monday, and involved the burning of no inconsiderable portion of midnight oil. Feeling that I had a constituency well deserving of my best efforts, I have never grudged the hours, though often the brain has been wearied, and the pleasure has hardened into a task."[25] As time went on, Spurgeon gave increased attention to the work of editing his sermons after they had been preached, partly to enhance his own abilities as a preacher and a writer, and partly because he recognized how significant the sales of his sermons were to his wider ministry. By 1870, Spurgeon's sermons were selling at a rate of twenty-five thousand copies per week.[26] One of Spurgeon's friends purchased over one million copies of one sermon and distributed them to all the crowned heads of Europe, every university student in Britain, and every member of Parliament.[27]

The preparation of Spurgeon's sermons for publishing involved the work of several others in addition to the preacher. Peter Morden describes the typical process by which the sermons went from Spurgeon's few scribbled notes on a small piece of paper to final publication:

> Each week someone sat in the Tabernacle congregation and took down Spurgeon's message, word for word, in longhand. The many people who have enjoyed reading Spurgeon's sermons down the years owe them a significant debt. The preacher would be given these longhand notes on the Monday. These he would proceed to edit, usually quite lightly. The edited notes would then be typeset by his publishers.... The next phase involved returning the draft printed pages to Spurgeon. Spurgeon would work from these galley proofs, doing any further editing he thought was required. It was the corrected galley

---

25. C. H. Spurgeon, "Twenty Years of Published Sermons," *Sword and the Trowel*, January 1875, 5.

26. Christian T. George, "Timeline 1800–1910," in *Lost Sermons of C. H. Spurgeon*, 1:xliv.

27. Hayden, *Highlights*, 75.

proof that was the basis of the final published message.... The process by which the preached sermon became the printed text was so well honed that Sunday's sermon could be available to buy and read before the week was out.[28]

The printing of his sermons week by week involved no small amount of work on Spurgeon's part and required the assistance of many helpers. But the effort was not in vain, as millions over the years have read these sermons to their personal edification and, in some cases, to their own conversion.

It is impossible to assess the overall impact of Spurgeon's printed sermons. They sold over fifty-six million copies in Spurgeon's lifetime.[29] J. C. Carlile estimates that over one hundred million copies of Spurgeon's sermons had been sold by 1899.[30] In Spurgeon's day, his sermons were translated into more than forty languages, including Arabic, Chinese, German, Russian, and Syriac.[31] Christian George notes that Spurgeon's sermons "were found in the hands of fishermen in the Mediterranean, coffee farmers in Sri Lanka, sailors in San Francisco, and even Catholics on pilgrimage."[32] One of Spurgeon's good friends, D. L. Moody, famously said, "It is a sight in Colorado on Sunday to see the miners come out of the bowels of the hills and gather in the schoolhouses or under the trees while some old English miner stands up and reads one of Charles Spurgeon's sermons."[33] Spurgeon recognized the impact that his sermons were having globally, and this fueled his preaching output. Most gratifying to him was the knowledge that the sermons were conducive to his mission

---

28. Morden, *C. H. Spurgeon*, 112.
29. Jason K. Allen, foreword to *Lost Sermons of C. H. Spurgeon*, 2:xiv.
30. J. C. Carlile, *C. H. Spurgeon: An Interpretive Biography* (London: Kingsgate, 1933), 236–37; Ian M. Randall, *A School of the Prophets: 150 Years of Spurgeon's College* (London: Spurgeon's College, 2005), 1.
31. *C. H. Spurgeon's Autobiography*, 4:291.
32. Christian T. George, "A Man of His Time," in *Lost Sermons of C. H. Spurgeon*, 1:14.
33. William R. Moody, *The Life of Dwight L. Moody* (New York: Fleming H. Revell, 1900), 456.

of soul winning. He wrote, "Seldom does a day pass, and certainly never a week, for some years past, without letters from all sorts of places, even at the utmost ends of the earth, declaring the salvation of souls by the means of one or other of the sermons."[34]

In 1875, Spurgeon wrote an article in the *Sword and the Trowel* marking twenty years of the weekly printed sermons. He reflected on the preeminence that preaching played in his overall ministry—a ministry, it should be noted, that was filled with many other significant endeavors. He said,

> Chief of all is the responsibility which the preaching of the Word involves; I do not wish to feel this less heavily, rather would I fain feel it more, but it enters largely into the account of a minister's life-work, and tells upon him more than any other part of his mission. Let those preach lightly who dare do so, to me it is the burden of the Lord.... However let no man mistake me, I would sooner have my work to do than any other under the sun. Preaching Jesus Christ is sweet work, joyful work, heavenly work.... It is a bath in the waters of Paradise to preach with the Holy Ghost sent down from heaven. Scarcely is it possible for a man, this side the grave, to be nearer heaven than is a preacher when his Master's presence bears him right away from every care and thought, save the one business in hand, and that the greatest that ever occupied a creature's mind and heart.[35]

Nothing else in Spurgeon's ministry rose to the same level of importance to him as his preaching. It constituted the most significant aspect of his life's work in terms of time spent, energy exerted, and influence achieved. Thus, he is rightly remembered as "the Prince of Preachers."

Church Planting and Missions

Spurgeon's commitment to soul winning led to the rapid multiplication of churches on a wholly unprecedented scale in the religious

---

34. Spurgeon, "Twenty Years," 6.
35. Spurgeon, "Twenty Years," 7.

life of Britain. Spurgeon planted 187 churches in Britain alone.[36] It has been estimated that between 1865 and 1887, Spurgeon and his students founded over half of the new Baptist churches in England.[37] Spurgeon's influence in London, in particular, was extraordinary. He believed that churches should give special attention to London, with its sprawling boroughs, crowded neighborhoods, and overflowing population. He said, "Every Christian denomination should be on the alert for London.... London is in some respects the very heart of the world; it influences every land, its vice is a plague to the whole human race, and its religion may be a balm to the remotest lands. London must be the Lord's; we long to see it set as a gem in the diadem of Jesus, as the Kohinoor among his crown jewels."[38] Between 1865 and 1876, he helped to found fifty-three of the sixty-two new Baptist churches in London.[39] Mike Nicholls states that by Spurgeon's death, "nearly half the Baptist membership in London was found in Spurgeon churches."[40]

Nonetheless, Spurgeon's church planting efforts went far beyond the capital city. He was ever mindful that "hundreds of towns and large villages are yet without the pure gospel ministry."[41] Spurgeon planted dozens upon dozens of churches in such places and in other major metropolitan areas such as Birmingham, Liverpool, and Manchester.[42] Perhaps most surprising were the nineteen churches planted in the north of England, furthest from Spurgeon's home base in London.[43]

---

36. Mike Nicholls, *C. H. Spurgeon: The Pastor Evangelist* (Didcot, U.K.: Baptist Historical Society, 1992), 175–77.
37. Morden, *C. H. Spurgeon*, 151.
38. Spurgeon, "London," *Sword and the Trowel*, April 1875, 147.
39. Nicholls, *C. H. Spurgeon*, 98.
40. Nicholls, *C. H. Spurgeon*, 99.
41. Spurgeon, "The Ministry Needed by the Churches, and Measures for Providing It," *Sword and the Trowel*, May 1871, 228.
42. Nicholls, *C. H. Spurgeon*, 99.
43. Nicholls, *C. H. Spurgeon*, 175–77.

Spurgeon's energetic commitment to church planting originated from strongly held convictions concerning the mission of the church and the imperative upon all Christians to be active in spreading the faith. In an April 1865 issue of the *Sword and the Trowel*, Spurgeon wrote, "The Christian church was designed from the first to be aggressive. It was not intended to remain stationary at any period, but to advance onward until its boundaries became commensurate with those of the world. It was to spread from Jerusalem to all Judaea, from Judaea to Samaria, and from Samaria unto the uttermost parts of the earth. It was not intended to radiate from one central point only, but to form numerous centers from which its influence might spread to the surrounding parts."[44] Spurgeon believed that the church ought to be a dynamic force for the spread of the gospel and should be proactive in multiplying new churches.

These convictions shaped and fueled the church planting efforts of Spurgeon's own church. At the laying of the foundation stone of the Metropolitan Tabernacle on August 16, 1859, Spurgeon addressed the gathered crowd that attended this historic ceremony in the life of the church, saying,

> I look on the Tabernacle as only the beginning; within the last six months, we have started two churches,—one in Wandsworth and the other in Greenwich,—and the Lord has prospered them; the pool of baptism has often been stirred with converts. And what we have done in two places, I am about to do in a third, and we will do it, not for the third or the fourth, but for the hundredth time, God being our Helper. I am sure I may make the strongest appeal to my brethren, because we do not mean to build this Tabernacle as our nest, and then to be idle. We must go from strength to strength, and be a missionary church, and never rest until, not only this neighborhood, but

---

44. Spurgeon, "Metropolitan Tabernacle Statistics," *Sword and the Trowel*, April 1865, 174.

our country, of which it is said some parts are as dark as India, shall have been enlightened with the Gospel.[45]

A few years later, Spurgeon founded the *Sword and the Trowel* in part to keep his readers regularly apprised of the progress of his many church plants.[46]

Spurgeon pursued a variety of methods for starting new churches.[47] He commended open-air preaching to his students for the evangelization of the lost and the formation of new congregations. He established various missions all over London, and sometimes these missions terminated in new churches. One of Spurgeon's most common methods of church planting involved gathering together small teams from among the membership of the Tabernacle and sending them out to start new churches.[48] Spurgeon spoke of this method of church planting in a sermon in April 1865, saying, "We have never sought to hinder the uprising of other churches from our midst or in our neighborhood. It is with cheerfulness that we dismiss our twelves, our twenties, our fifties, to form other churches. We encourage our members to leave us to found other churches; nay, we seek to persuade them to do it. We ask them to scatter throughout the land to become the goodly seed which God shall bless. I believe that so long as we do this we shall prosper."[49] These teams were sent to

---

45. *C. H. Spurgeon's Autobiography*, 2:329.

46. Nicholls, *C. H. Spurgeon*, 98.

47. Geoff Change provides a helpful outline of Spurgeon's church planting process; see Geoffrey Chang, "The Militant Ecclesiology and Church Polity of Charles Haddon Spurgeon" (PhD diss., Midwestern Baptist Theological Seminary, 2020), 209–11.

48. Arnold Dallimore, *Spurgeon: A New Biography* (Edinburgh: Banner of Truth, 1985), 157; Dallimore notes, "At [Spurgeon's] suggestion two hundred and fifty members left the Tabernacle to begin a new church at Peckam" (172).

49. Spurgeon, "The Waterer Watered," in *Metropolitan Tabernacle Pulpit*, 11:238. See also Spurgeon, *Trumpet Calls to Christian Energy: A Collection of Sermons Preached on Sunday and Thursday Evenings at the Metropolitan Tabernacle* (London: Passmore and Alabaster, 1875), 134–35.

under-reached areas of London and to other parts of the country that were desperately in need of healthy churches.

In addition to domestic church planting, Spurgeon vigorously promoted international missions as well. Spurgeon was proactive in sending out missionaries from the Pastors' College, encouraging missions in his preaching, and contributing to various missions organizations. Ian Randall observes that Spurgeon became more interested in international missions as time went on, especially on account of his growing involvement with the Baptist Missionary Society.[50] Spurgeon spoke often at the meetings of the Baptist Missionary Society, and some of these addresses were among his most famous sermons, such as the one preached at the society's annual meeting in 1858.[51] As Spurgeon became more involved with the society, so did graduates from the Pastors' College. One such graduate was Thomas Johnson, a former American slave who told his story in his memoir, *Twenty-Eight Years a Slave*.[52] Johnson, along with Calvin Richardson, served as a missionary to West Africa.[53]

The Pastors' College was a tremendously evangelistic institution and emphasized soul winning as part of its mission. "Our aim from the first," Spurgeon said in the 1873–74 annual report of the Pastors' College, "has been to glorify God by the spread of the gospel."[54]

---

50. Ian Randall and Anthony R. Cross, eds., *Baptists and Mission: Papers from the Fourth International Conference on Baptist Studies* (Eugene, Ore.: Wipf and Stock, 2007), 64–65. Spurgeon spoke on a number of occasions at the meetings of the various missionary societies, not only among the Baptists, but also among other groups, such as the Congregationalists and the Methodists; see Hayden, *Highlights*, 9, 28, 55.

51. C. H. Spurgeon, "Christ—The Power and Wisdom of God," in *The New Park Street Pulpit: Containing Sermons Preached and Revised by the Rev. C. H. Spurgeon, Minister of the Chapel* (Grand Rapids: Baker Book House, 2007), 3:201–8.

52. A popular treatment of the relationship between Spurgeon and Thomas Johnson, written in the form of an imaginative narrative, is Matt Carter and Aaron Ivey, *Steal Away Home: Charles Spurgeon and Thomas Johnson, Unlikely Friends on the Passage to Freedom* (Nashville: B&H, 2017).

53. Randall and Cross, *Baptists and Mission*, 65–67.

54. C. H. Spurgeon, *Report of the Pastors' College: 1873–74* (London: Passmore and Alabaster, 1874), 1.

The Priority of Soul Winning 107

Spurgeon wanted to see the school infused with a "missionary spirit," and he longed to see his students sent to preach throughout the world. He went on to write in the same annual report, "Our field is the world. Our heart pleads continually for the missionary spirit to move among our brethren, that very many of them may carry the gospel to the regions beyond, both in our own land, among the churches of America, and the colonies, and, better still, among the heathen. This prayer has begun to receive its answer and will have, in future days, a plentiful reward. The world is all before us, and the more heralds of the cross the better for the dying multitudes."[55] As was noted earlier, a remarkable number of graduates from the institution participated in the work of church planting. Graduates from the college also participated in foreign missions to an unusual degree. By 1876, two decades after the college's inception, nearly 15 percent of the alumni were ministering overseas.[56] The Pastors' College had its own missions society that promoted this work among the student body. In the 1881 president's report of the Pastors' College, Spurgeon said, "The earnest action of the College Missionary Society has been a source of great joy to me, for above all things, I desire to see many students devoting themselves to foreign work."[57]

Spurgeon made a point of keeping these missionaries before the attention of his readers in the *Sword and the Trowel*. For example, in an April 1873 article, Spurgeon profiled the missionary labors of several graduates of the college, including one in Santa Domingo, two in Barcelona, one serving under the direction of Hudson Taylor in China, twenty-one in the United States and Canada, and seven in Australia.[58] Spurgeon occasionally advocated for especially needy

---

55. Spurgeon, *Report of the Pastors' College: 1873–74*, 3.
56. C. H. Spurgeon, *The Metropolitan Tabernacle: Its History and Work, Mr. Spurgeon's Jubilee Sermons, A Memorial Volume* (London: Passmore and Alabaster, 1876), 103.
57. Spurgeon, "Annual Report of the Pastors' College," *Sword and the Trowel*, May 1881, 304–5.
58. Spurgeon, "The Pastors' College," *Sword and the Trowel*, April 1873, 145–50.

parts of the world and encouraged ministers to consider going to such places to spread the gospel. One example is found in a February 1875 article, in which Spurgeon called for missionaries to serve the China Inland Mission. He wrote, "Our present pressing need is for missionaries to lead the way. Will each of you Christian readers at once raise his heart to God, and spend one minute in earnest prayer that God will raise up this year eighteen suitable men to devote themselves to this work?... There are doubtless such *in* the churches of the United Kingdom. May the Lord *thrust many of them out.*"[59] By 1889, estimates suggested that approximately 168 former students of the Pastors' College were serving outside the United Kingdom. In 1892, the year of Spurgeon's death, nearly one-third of the graduating class went overseas to places such as the Congo, Australia, and South Africa.[60] Spurgeon's zeal for soul winning among the nations propelled the students of the college to proclaim the good news far and wide. The missionary endeavors of the Pastors' College were nothing less than the realization of the vision of its founder.

Principles for Pastors and Churches Today

At the heart of Spurgeon's ministry was his commitment to spreading the faith and winning souls through preaching. Early in his Christian life, he gave himself to evangelism, tract distribution, and home visitation; shortly thereafter, he began to preach as a teenager. His preaching ministry would become the central focus of his life and fueled all his other efforts in ministry. After Spurgeon came to London, he gave himself to the work of church planting and missions through the Metropolitan Tabernacle and the Pastors' College. Spurgeon was not content simply to promote his own preaching ministry and build an ever-growing nest at the Metropolitan Tabernacle. His passion for soul winning led him to plant and promote pioneering gospel efforts not only in Britain but across the world.

---

59. Spurgeon, "Notes," *Sword and the Trowel*, February 1875, 92.
60. Randall, *School of the Prophets*, 104.

It has already been stated in this book, but it bears repeating that the heart of the church's mission is the preaching of the truth unto the salvation of sinners and the edification of the saints. As Spurgeon said, the preaching of the Word "enters largely into the account of a minster's life-work and tells upon him more than any other part of his mission."[61] It is possible for a pastor to become so invested in social ministry and so fixated on the immediate physical needs in his congregation and his community that he neglects what ought to be at all times the primary burden of his ministry—namely, the proclamation of the Word of God. The preaching of the truth can never be moved from its central place in the ministry of the pastor. It is like the sun in the center of the universe of all his other labors and concerns.

This commitment to preaching did not diminish the importance of social concern in Spurgeon's ministry. Rather it gave Spurgeon's efforts in mercy ministry their shape and energy. All of Spurgeon's other labors flowed out of the supreme work of the proclamation of the truth. Social ministry will have its proper place and most potent effect for good when situated in the context of a healthy and thriving preaching ministry within the local church. Benevolence, charity, and philanthropy for their own sake will ultimately result in only limited and finite good. But when these efforts are combined with and fueled by the preaching of the truth in the context of the local church, they will accomplish good of the infinite kind, connected with an eternal purpose that will outlive this world.

---

61. Spurgeon, "Twenty Years," 7.

The Pastors' College

"This is my life's work, to which I believe God has called me."[1] Spurgeon said this not of his preaching ministry, his writing ministry, or even his pastoral ministry in his local church. He said this of his ministerial training college, simply known as the Pastors' College. The Pastors' College was one of the focal points of Spurgeon's ministry.[2] Mike Nicholls writes, "The College was his most cherished creation. Its idea, formulation and support were his chief concern."[3] Speaking of the college, Spurgeon once said to J. C. Carlile, "By that I multiply myself."[4] Outside of his church, the Pastors' College received more of his attention than any of his other ministries and institutions. In 1871, Spurgeon published an article titled "The Ministry Needed by the Churches, and Measures for Providing It," which is perhaps the best summation of Spurgeon's vision for the Pastors' College,

---

1. W. Y. Fullerton, *C. H. Spurgeon: A Biography* (London: William and Norgate, 1920), 227.

2. Though many publications on Spurgeon include chapters on the Pastors' College, few rise above the level of general introduction. The most in-depth studies of the Pastors' College are Ian Randall, *A School of the Prophets: 150 Years of Spurgeon's College* (London: Spurgeon's College, 2005); Mike Nicholls, *Lights to the World: A History of Spurgeon's College, 1856–1992* (Harpenden, U.K.: Nuprint, 1994); and David W. Bebbington, "Spurgeon and British Evangelical Theological Education," in *Theological Education in the Evangelical Tradition*, ed. D. G. Hart and R. A. Mohler Jr. (Grand Rapids: Baker Books, 1996), 217–34.

3. Mike Nicholls, *Lights to the World*, 45.

4. J. C. Carlile, *C. H. Spurgeon: An Interpretive Biography* (London: Kingsgate, 1933), 169.

in particular, and pastoral ministry, more generally.[5] In this article, he wrote, "It appears to us that the maintenance of a truly spiritual College is probably the readiest way in which to bless the churches. Granting the possibility of planting such an institution, you are no longer in doubt as to the simplest mode of influencing for good the church and the world."[6]

The work of ministerial training occupied a place of special significance in Spurgeon's view of his life and calling. Thus, the Pastors' College enjoyed a place of prominence among Spurgeon's many institutions and benevolences.

We ought to regard the Pastors' College as one of Spurgeon's benevolences not only because Spurgeon originally funded the cause entirely by himself but also because it provided its students with a free education, along with many other free benefits, such as room, board, books, clothing, healthcare, and occasionally even spending money. David Gracey called the Pastors' College "the first of [Spurgeon's] philanthropic institutions."[7]

Benevolent Origins

Spurgeon's aim in establishing the Pastors' College was to provide an education for qualified students who otherwise would not have been able to pursue training due to a lack of funds or prior education. The official founding of the college occurred in 1857, but its origins date before that time. In 1855, a man named T. W. Medhurst came to faith under Spurgeon's ministry and quickly showed evidence of an ability to preach.[8] Spurgeon offered to support Medhurst financially if he would agree to pursue ministerial training. Medhurst consented and

---

5. C. H. Spurgeon, "The Ministry Needed by the Churches, and Measures for Providing It," *Sword and the Trowel*, May 1871, 215–28.

6. Spurgeon, "Ministry Needed," 215.

7. David Gracey, "Mr. Spurgeon's First Institution," *Sword and the Trowel*, June 1892, 277.

8. *C. H. Spurgeon's Autobiography, Compiled from His Diary, Letters, and Records by His Wife and His Private Secretary* (London: Passmore and Alabaster, 1898), 2:142–47.

went to study with the Reverend C. H. Hosken. Spurgeon held up his end of the bargain and liberally supported Medhurst's training. Spurgeon wrote, "With a limited income, it was no easy thing for a young minister to guarantee £50 a year."[9] In recounting this commitment to support ministerial training in those early days, Spurgeon's wife, Susannah, said, "My dear husband earnestly longed to help young men to preach the gospel, and from our slender resources we had to contribute somewhat largely to the support and education of T. W. Medhurst.... Together, we planned and pinched in order to carry out the purpose of his loving heart."[10]

Throughout Spurgeon's lifetime, the college always managed to offer education at no cost to qualified students. He was utterly committed to preserving this policy. He said, "We determined never to refuse a man on account of absolute poverty, but rather to provide him with needful lodging, board, and raiment, that he might not be hindered on that account."[11] Throughout Spurgeon's tenure as college president, these and other benefits were provided free of charge to all students, with only rare exceptions.[12]

Spurgeon was especially eager to train students who were at an economic or educational disadvantage. He wanted to raise up men from the working class who could, in turn, reach the working class, and he wanted to remove all barriers to their admission to the college. He wrote,

> We had before us but one object, and that was, the glory of God by the preaching of the gospel. To preach with acceptance, men, lacking in education, need to be instructed; and therefore our Institution set itself further to instruct those whom God had evidently called to preach the gospel, but who laboured under early disadvantages.... We proceeded to sweep away

---

9. C. H. *Spurgeon's Autobiography*, 2:148.
10. C. H. *Spurgeon's Autobiography*, 2:183.
11. C. H. *Spurgeon's Autobiography*, 2:149.
12. Spurgeon, "Ministry Needed," 224; Arnold Dallimore, *Spurgeon: A New Biography* (Edinburgh: Banner of Truth, 1985), 105.

every hindrance to the admission of fit men. We determined never to refuse a man on account of absolute poverty, but rather to provide him with needful lodging, board, and raiment, that he might not be hindered on that account. We also placed the literary qualifications of admission so low that even brethren who could not read have been able to enter and have been among the most useful of our students in after days. A man of real ability as a speaker, of deep piety, and genuine faith, may be by force of birth and circumstances, deprived of educational advantages, and yet, when helped a little, he may develop into a mighty worker for Christ.[13]

Through the Pastors' College, Spurgeon made it his goal to remove as many obstacles as possible to the effective training of these sorts of men. Arnold Dallimore writes of the college, "Except in the case of a few who could afford to pay, the tuition and board were free, and clothing, books, and even pocket money were provided."[14]

Spurgeon's aim was to establish a ministerial college that was in its very constitution a benevolent institution. He was eager to recruit men from the lower classes who would minister to the common people of England. Spurgeon often reflected a certain prejudice against the social and intellectual elite of his day.[15] He was a man

---

13. C. H. Spurgeon's Autobiography, 2:148–49.
14. Dallimore, Spurgeon, 105.
15. David W. Bebbington, "Spurgeon and the Common Man," Baptist Review of Theology 5, no. 1 (Spring 1995): 63–75; Bebbington, "British Evangelical Theological Education," 219. In many ways, Spurgeon's background and upbringing conditioned him to maintain certain biases in favor of the common man over the social and intellectual elite. He was, after all, a Liberal, Nonconformist, and Baptist. He had humble origins, having been reared as a coal merchant's son in the heart of rural East Anglia. He was a child of Nonconformity who was educated in Anglican schools. He felt his social inferiority keenly in such environments. He never went to college. He eventually found himself a country boy living in the largest city in the world. He was regularly criticized in some of the leading papers of his day in the first several years of his ministry in London by men of higher education and social standing. Many of these criticisms centered around Spurgeon's supposed crudeness, simplicity, and lack of refinement. Spurgeon's experiences, coupled with his view of the inherent simplicity of plain gospel preaching, engendered within him a certain type of prejudice

of the people, an advocate for the proverbial common man. Spurgeon's championing of the common man bled into his vision for the college. The Pastors' College was a benevolent institution designed to train men of the people who would give themselves tirelessly to ministry among the masses.

In 1857, Spurgeon employed George Rogers, a Congregationalist minister, to serve as acting principal of the college. Under Rogers's leadership, the work of the Pastors' College began to grow as more students enrolled for study.[16] For the first few years, the college's financial support came almost entirely from Spurgeon himself.[17] He committed all of the income he made from his sermon sales in America and supplemented this sum with funds from his savings, which together amounted to about £600 to £800 annually.[18] However, though the college enjoyed a solid start, controversy would soon threaten to kill the operation entirely.

In the late 1850s, Spurgeon became quite vocal in his opposition to slavery, particularly as it was carried on in the American South. As a result of his strong stand against slavery, Spurgeon's publishers in the South refused to continue the publication of his sermons, forcing him to find funding for the college elsewhere.[19] Spurgeon's comments on slavery sparked outrage among many of his American readers, leading to community book burnings of his sermons, widespread criticism in American newspapers, and even death threats should he ever visit America.[20] Chapter 11 will tell the fuller story of Spurgeon's

---

against the elite. In one of his lectures, he quipped, "Go up to his level if he is a poor man; go down to his understanding if he is an educated person. You smile at my contorting the terms in that manner, but I think there is more going up in being plain to the illiterate, than there is in being refined for the polite." C. H. Spurgeon, *Lectures to My Students* (London: Passmore and Alabaster, 1881), 1:141.

16. *C. H. Spurgeon's Autobiography*, 2:148.
17. Mike Nicholls, *Lights to the World*, 33.
18. *C. H. Spurgeon's Autobiography*, 3:138.
19. *C. H. Spurgeon's Autobiography*, 3:138.
20. Christian T. George, preface to *The Lost Sermons of C. H. Spurgeon: His Earliest Outlines and Sermons Between 1851 and 1854*, ed. Christian T. George (Nashville: B&H Academic, 2016), 1:xvii–xix.

assault on the institution of slavery. For now, it should simply be noted that Spurgeon's regard for the poor and the oppressed—in this case, American slaves—was such that he was willing to suffer personal loss, even allowing his convictions in this area to intrude upon the progress of his dearly beloved Pastors' College. In the immediate aftermath of this unanticipated loss of revenue, Spurgeon sought to make up for the lack of funds entirely from his savings. At one point, he even proposed selling his horse and carriage, but Susannah dissuaded him from doing so as he frequently had to travel long distances to preach.[21]

At this stage, Spurgeon began aggressively raising funds for the college, which he did intermittently for the rest of his life.[22] The Metropolitan Tabernacle adopted the Pastors' College as an official church ministry in 1861, and the church consistently supported the college for several decades thereafter.[23] In the mid-1870s, when plans were laid to erect new facilities for the college, much of the £15,000 required for the project Spurgeon either gave directly or raised through his many speaking engagements in other churches and venues.[24] He said of the college in 1875, "Our assured conviction is that there is no better, holier, more useful or more necessary Christian service than assisting to educate young ministers."[25] To him, there was no work worthier of Christian support than the Pastors' College. Spurgeon's friend William Williams wrote, "The Pastors' College was the first philanthropic institution Mr. Spurgeon founded, and to the last it was dearer to his heart than any other."[26]

---

21. *C. H. Spurgeon's Autobiography*, 3:138.
22. *C. H. Spurgeon's Autobiography*, 3:138–39.
23. *C. H. Spurgeon's Autobiography*, 3:139.
24. Dallimore, *Spurgeon*, 142.
25. Spurgeon, "A Plea for the Pastors' College," *Sword and the Trowel*, June 1875, 252.
26. William Williams, *Personal Reminiscences of Charles Haddon Spurgeon* (London: Religious Tract Society, 1895), 131.

Requirements for Admission

The college's requirements for admission can be described simultaneously as both high and low. Spurgeon had high expectations for prospective students in certain areas. He believed they must exhibit high moral character, and he expected them to be known for their godliness and personal holiness.[27] He would not accept students who reflected "a low state of piety, a want of enthusiasm, a failure in private devotion, a lack of consecration."[28] Spurgeon also required incoming students to demonstrate a proven track record in preaching and soul winning.[29] He expected each student to have two years of preaching experience prior to enrollment as well as some evidence of conversions under his preaching.[30] It was his policy to accept into the college only those who were already serving as ministers in some form or fashion.[31] Finally, all incoming students were expected to have demonstrated a commitment to significant church work. Spurgeon wanted students who had proven themselves to be eager and active in various forms of church ministry well before applying to the college. He said, "We want soldiers, not fops, earnest labourers, not genteel loiterers. Men who have done nothing up to their time of application to the college, are told to earn their spurs before they are publicly dubbed as knights."[32]

Spurgeon succinctly summarized these basic requirements in an 1866 article in the *Sword and the Trowel*, writing, "The selection of candidates for admission is principally determined by evidences

---

27. Spurgeon, "Ministry Needed," 225; see also Spurgeon's lecture "The Minister's Self-Watch," in *Lectures to My Students*, 1:1–17. For more on the spirituality of the students of the Pastors' College, see Randall, *School of the Prophets*, 44–57.

28. Spurgeon, "Annual Paper Concerning the Lord's Work in Connection with the Pastors' College, Newington, London, 1888–89," *Sword and the Trowel*, June 1889, 311.

29. Nicholls, *Lights to the World*, 62–64.

30. C. H. *Spurgeon's Autobiography*, 2:148; Spurgeon, *Lectures to My Students*, 1:23–30; Bebbington, "British Evangelical Theological Education," 223–24.

31. Spurgeon, *Lectures to My Students*, 1:33.

32. Spurgeon, *Lectures to My Students*, 1:34.

of eminent piety, of adaptation for public teaching, of great zeal for the salvation of souls, and of instances of actual usefulness."[33] To ensure these standards were met, Spurgeon himself conducted rigorous personal interviews with each applicant.[34] This particular step in the process often led to the rejection of a prospective student. Spurgeon said,

> I have to form an opinion as to the advisability of aiding certain men in their attempts to become pastors. This is a most responsible duty, and one which requires no ordinary care. Of course, I do not set myself up to judge whether a man shall enter the ministry or not, but my examination merely aims at answering the question whether this institution shall help him, or leave him to his own resources. Certain of our charitable neighbors accuse us of having "a parson manufactory" here, but the charge is not true at all. We never tried to make a minister, and should fail if we did; we receive none into the College but those who profess to be ministers already. It would be nearer the truth if they called me a parson killer, for a goodly number of beginners have received their quietus from me; and I have the fullest ease of conscience in reflecting upon what I have so done. It has always been a hard task for me to discourage a hopeful young brother who has applied for admission to the College. My heart has always leaned to the kindest side, but duty to the churches has compelled me to judge with severe discrimination. After hearing what the candidate has had to say, having read his testimonials and seen his replies to questions, when I have felt convinced that the Lord had not called him, I have been obliged to tell him so.[35]

While Spurgeon had high expectations in the aforementioned areas, from another angle, requirements for admission to the college were set rather low. As noted above, Spurgeon determined that

---

33. Spurgeon, "Work of the Metropolitan Tabernacle," *Sword and the Trowel*, March 1866, 135.

34. Nicholls, *Lights to the World*, 64–65.

35. Spurgeon, *Lectures to My Students*, 1:33.

financial and educational disadvantages would never be allowed to present an obstacle to one's entry into the college.[36] Spurgeon wished to draw students from across the socioeconomic spectrum and was especially eager to welcome students from the poorer classes, so long as they met the other requirements for admission. He said, "Let the church, when the Lord sends her a man of rough but great natural ability, and of much grace, meet him all the way, take him up where he is, and help him even to the end."[37]

Some who applied to the college lacked a basic education, and more than a few were effectively illiterate. For incoming students in need of remedial education, the Tabernacle provided free evening classes, beginning in 1862.[38] These classes were open to the entire community and welcomed any who wanted to be educated in basic subjects such as mathematics, science, and grammar. At any given time, these classes had roughly two hundred to three hundred students enrolled, though only approximately half of those enrolled regularly attended.[39] The evening classes also served as both a feeder into the college and a means of providing supplemental education for those who were at a significant educational disadvantage upon entering the college.[40] Through these classes, Spurgeon sought to extend a helping hand to those whose prospects for ministry would otherwise appear dim due to lack of formal education.

The effect of the lowered standards for entry to the Pastors' College was to significantly reshape the makeup of the Baptist ministry in England. Historian Kenneth Brown has highlighted how the Pastors' College contributed more to the increase among Baptist ministers in England than any other training college of the era by far.[41] Brown

---

36. Bebbington, "British Evangelical Theological Education," 224–28.
37. Spurgeon, "Ministry Needed," 224.
38. Nicholls, *Lights to the World*, 78–81; Randall, *School of the Prophets*, 76–78.
39. Randall, *School of the Prophets*, 77; Spurgeon, "The College Report for 1876-7," *Sword and the Trowel*, May 1877, 214.
40. Bebbington, "British Evangelical Theological Education," 227–28.
41. Kenneth D. Brown, *A Social History of the Nonconformist Ministry in England and Wales 1800–1930* (Oxford: Clarendon, 1988), 33, 98. See also J. H. Y. Briggs,

states that by 1871, graduates of the Pastors' College accounted for 10 percent of all Baptist ministers in England and Wales. By 1891, that number had risen to over 20 percent, and by 1911, it was 24 percent. Furthermore, Brown estimates that in 1871, only 58 percent of all Baptist ministers in England had received any formal ministerial training. By 1911, that number had ballooned to nearly 85 percent. A rough calculation based on these numbers would suggest that the Pastors' College accounted for more than half of the growth of education among the Baptist ministry in England from 1871 to 1911. Brown further suggests that the majority of the men trained at the college were from the lower classes, leading Brown to conclude that the low standards for entry into the college with respect to educational and financial ability directly contributed to the overall numerical growth of the Baptist ministry in England as a whole.[42] The Pastors' College provided a unique avenue for men of low social standing to pursue ministerial training. All of this took place during a time when Baptists had begun increasingly to draw ministers from white-collar backgrounds and when educational requirements for entry into Baptist colleges were generally rising.[43]

Preachers for the Masses

Undergirding the Pastors' College was a particular vision of the ideal preacher, a vision that Spurgeon carefully crafted and zealously promulgated. Spurgeon was not interested in producing detached scholars or ivory tower theologians but popular preachers who emerged from among the masses of ordinary people and who possessed the requisite gifts and experience to reach the common man. Spurgeon wanted preachers of the people. He once wrote,

---

The English Baptists of the Nineteenth Century (Didcot, U.K.: Baptist Historical Society, 1994), 3:88–90.

42. Brown, *Social History*, 33–34; Bebbington, "British Evangelical Theological Education," 225.

43. Briggs, *English Baptists*, 88–90; Bebbington, "British Evangelical Theological Education," 218–19.

> It seems to me that many of our churches need a class of ministers who will not aim at lofty scholarship, but at the winning of souls;—men of the people, feeling, sympathizing, fraternizing with the masses of working men;—men who can speak the common language, the plain blunt Saxon of the crowd;—men ready to visit the sick and the poor, and able to make them understand the reality of the comforts of religion. There are many such men among the humbler ranks of society, who might become master-workmen in the Lord's Church if they could get an education to pare away their roughness, and give them more extended information.... Why should not such men have help? Why should they be compelled to enter our ministry without a competent knowledge of Scripture and Biblical literature? Superior in some respects already, let them be educated, and they will be inferior to none. It was the primary aim of this Institution to help such men, and this is still its chief end and design.... Whether the student be rich or poor, the object is the same,—not scholarship, but preaching the gospel,—not the production of fine gentlemen, but of hard-working men.[44]

Spurgeon's ambition was to produce hundreds of popular preachers who would embrace the masses and speak directly to the lives and concerns of the people. "Our men...seek to preach efficiently," he wrote, "to get to the heart of the masses, to evangelize the poor,—this is the College ambition, this and nothing else."[45]

In his efforts to train preachers who could reach the masses, Spurgeon encouraged his students to give significant attention to their speech and manner in the pulpit. Spurgeon criticized the preachers of his day, especially those within the Church of England, for being too contrived, high-sounding, and grandiloquent in the pulpit.[46] He cautioned his students to "Avoid everything which is stilted, official, fussy, and pretentious."[47] Instead he urged them to

---

44. *C. H. Spurgeon's Autobiography*, 3:129.
45. *C. H. Spurgeon's Autobiography*, 2:149.
46. Bebbington, "Common Man," 70–71.
47. Spurgeon, *Lectures to My Students*, 1:180.

"speak plainly."[48] This, he believed, would enable his students to connect broadly with ordinary people.[49] Spurgeon taught this style of preaching both by example and precept. He said,

> The next thing we need in the ministry, now and in all time, is men of plain speech. The preacher's language must not be that of the classroom, but of all classes; not of the university, but of the universe. Men who have learned to speak from books are of small worth compared with those who learned from their mothers their mother tongue—the language spoken by men around the fireside, in the workshop, and in the parlor.... We must have plain preachers. Yet plain speech is not common in the pulpit. Judging from many printed sermons, we might conclude that many preachers have forgotten their mother tongue. The language of half our pulpits ought to be bound hand and foot, and with a millstone about its neck, cast into the sea: it is poisoning the 'wells of English undefiled,' and worse still, it is alienating the working classes from public worship.[50]

The importance of plain speech was not a matter of mere preference for Spurgeon but a matter of evangelistic witness. He believed England's greatest need was preaching that was direct, simple, and unadorned.

Additionally, Spurgeon sought to cultivate preachers for the masses through the type of education offered at the college. Nicholls writes, "This curriculum was designed to give men the education of which many were deprived in childhood and to enable them to proclaim the gospel with interest and relevance."[51] Because Spurgeon

---

48. Spurgeon, *Lectures to My Students*, 1:141; Spurgeon, "Report of the Pastors' College," *Sword and the Trowel*, May 1882, 260; Spurgeon, "Fields White for Harvest," in *Metropolitan Tabernacle Pulpit*, 12:460.

49. Spurgeon's contemporary J. C. Ryle, bishop of Liverpool, wrote a short treatise titled *Simplicity in Preaching*. In it, Ryle mentions Spurgeon, in particular, as a notable exemplar of simple and accessible preaching that appealed to the common man. See John Charles Ryle, *Simplicity in Preaching: A Few Short Hints on a Great Subject* (London: William Hunt, 1882), 20–21.

50. Spurgeon, "Ministry Needed," 217–18.

51. Nicholls, *Lights to the World*, 69.

was not interested in training scholars primarily, he lowered educational standards and the curriculum of the college took on a largely practical focus.[52] "Its training was to be practical rather than literary," Bebbington writes, "a down-to-earth affair rather than an imitation of Oxford or Cambridge. There would be no attempt to compete for scholarly distinctions or to turn theology from a vocational into an academic subject."[53] This was in keeping with the college's mission. "We are not called to proclaim philosophy and metaphysics," Spurgeon told his students, "but the simple gospel."[54]

As Spurgeon sought to produce preachers for the masses, his primary aim was to develop men who possessed true sympathy for the people. Spurgeon believed it was essential for preachers to be authentically connected to their congregations. The congregation had to be convinced that the preacher truly understood their unique trials and burdens and could relate to their experiences. If this could not be achieved, all was lost. The surest way of reaching the masses was to put before them men who understood them. Spurgeon said, "The more our hearts beat in unison with the masses, the more likely will they be to receive the gospel kindly from our lips."[55] This is one of the reasons why Spurgeon intentionally drew men to the college from among the working classes of London. Such men, he believed, could truly sympathize with the people. He said,

> We require men of popular sympathies; men of the people, who feel with them.... Unless a man is a lover of the people in his inmost soul he will never be greatly useful to them. The people do not require more of those gentlemen who condescend to instruct the lower orders.... London's millions spurn the foppery of caste, they yearn for great hearts to sympathize with their sorrows; such may rebuke their sins and lead their minds, but no others may lecture them. The working classes of

---

52. Nicholls, *Lights to the World*, 67–78.
53. Bebbington, "British Evangelical Theological Education," 219–20.
54. Spurgeon, *Lectures to My Students*, 1:83.
55. Spurgeon, "Ministry Needed," 220.

England are made of redeemable material after all; those who believe in them can lead them.[56]

This became the reputation of Spurgeon's men. Commenting on the graduates of the Pastors' College, Spurgeon's close friend Lord Shaftesbury, the great social activist, said, "They had a singular faculty for addressing the population, and going to the very heart of the people."[57]

As Spurgeon himself was a man of the people, determined to reach the common man, the college under Spurgeon's leadership purposed to produce preachers for the masses. "That was the hallmark of Spurgeon's training project," Bebbington writes, "to ensure that all the pastors remained men of the people."[58] What he achieved in this respect was simply extraordinary. Spurgeon successfully marshaled a generation of preachers who brought the gospel to the people with unparalleled zeal and effectiveness.

The Success of the College

By almost any metric, save that of high scholastic achievement, the Pastors' College was profoundly successful during Spurgeon's lifetime. The college trained 863 ministers between 1856 and 1892.[59] At the time of Spurgeon's death, over one-fifth of all the Baptist ministers in England and Wales had been trained at the Pastors' College.[60] Though many of those trained took obscure posts, a number of graduates found themselves in prominent Baptist pulpits all over Britain. Students from the college occupied "some of the pulpits of the denomination most valuable and illustrious in past generations," including T. G. Tarn of St. Andrew's Street Baptist Church, Cambridge, and E. G. Gange of Broadmead Chapel, Bristol.[61] The college

---

56. Spurgeon, "Ministry Needed," 219–20.
57. As quoted in C. H. Spurgeon, *The Metropolitan Tabernacle: Its History and Work, Mr. Spurgeon's Jubilee Sermons, A Memorial Volume* (London: Passmore and Alabaster, 1876), 101.
58. Bebbington, "Common Man," 74.
59. Bebbington, "British Evangelical Theological Education," 221.
60. Brown, *Social History*, 33.
61. Spurgeon, "Concerning College Work as We See It," *Sword and the Trowel*,

also started new churches with men who went on to experience spectacular success in reaching the masses, such as Archibald G. Brown of the East London Tabernacle and William Cuff of the Shoreditch Tabernacle, two churches that were eventually among the largest dissenting churches in London.[62]

The Pastors' College made a concentrated effort to trace basic statistics related to baptisms and membership in the churches where its graduates pastored. Though several of the graduates failed to submit returns regularly, most of them were faithful to report their statistics to the college. In the year that Spurgeon died, the college reported that nearly one hundred thousand people had been baptized in churches pastored by Spurgeon's men.[63] The compilers of Spurgeon's autobiography note, "Truly, if Mr. Spurgeon had done nothing beyond founding and carrying on the Pastors' College, it would have been a noble life-work; yet that was only one of his many forms of labour for the Lord."[64]

The Pastors' College and Social Concern

Readers of this book might be thinking, What does all of this information related to the Pastors' College have to do with the subject of this book? The answer is twofold. In the first place, it should simply be appreciated that the Pastors' College was a significant benevolent enterprise in and of itself. Spurgeon donated thousands of pounds and massive amounts of his time to make the education of these men possible. It was an expression of philanthropy and charity on his part, even as he pursued the strategic end of seeing more pastors trained and churches planted for the evangelization of Britain. The college contributed immensely to the betterment of otherwise poor

---

May 1883, 276. Robert Robinson and Robert Hall both served as pastors of the St. Andrews Street Baptist Church in Cambridge. Spurgeon himself taught Sunday school at the church and participated in the church's lay preacher's association in the late 1840s.

62. Spurgeon, "Concerning College Work as We See It," 276.
63. *C. H. Spurgeon's Autobiography*, 4:330.
64. *C. H. Spurgeon's Autobiography*, 4:330.

and uneducated men and their families and prepared them to plant churches and start ministries among needy people in London and, indeed, throughout the whole country.

Pastors, churches, and seminaries in our own day would do well to consider how men operating at an educational or financial disadvantage will receive the necessary ministerial training and preparation to serve churches today. There are men among needy communities whom God has gifted with real ability to shepherd the Lord's people but who lack access or means to pursue solid ministerial training. Such men are often uniquely able to sympathize with the communities from which they come and are often best positioned to reach them with the gospel. How will they receive training in today's climate in which academic prerequisites are often overvalued, and education is increasingly expensive? It is not my purpose here to provide specific prescriptions for those engaged in theological education but simply to suggest that a fuller consideration of the Pastors' College could provide an important reference point to those interested in pursuing this question further.

Second, the Pastors' College is relevant to the present study because of its particular focus on reaching the common man. From the college's admissions policies to its method of education, it sought to produce men who sympathized with and were determined to reach poor and working-class people. Just as Spurgeon's heart beat with the masses of ordinary people in England, so he endeavored to train men with the same impulse. Spurgeon was not concerned primarily with who would preach to, pastor, and care for society's elite. He had a special burden for humble and needy people. Graduates from the Pastors' College were uniquely fruitful among the working classes, and thus, the college became a vital means of advancing Spurgeon's social concern. Of course, though Spurgeon was eager and earnest about meeting practical and material needs, above all, he wanted to see the poor come to saving faith in Jesus Christ. The following passage, quoted at length from one of Spurgeon's lectures to his students, illustrates well Spurgeon's burden for his students as he called them to reach needy people for Jesus:

If you have to labour in a large town I should recommend you to familiarize yourself, wherever your place of worship may be, with the poverty, ignorance, and drunkenness of the place. Go if you can with a City missionary into the poorest quarter, and you will see that which will astonish you, and the actual sight of the disease will make you eager to reveal the remedy. There is enough of evil to be seen even in the best streets of our great cities, but there is an unutterable depth of horror in the condition of the slums. As a doctor walks the hospitals, so ought you to traverse the lanes and courts to behold the mischief which sin has wrought. It is enough to make a man weep tears of blood to gaze upon the desolation which sin has made in the earth. One day with a devoted missionary would be a fine termination to your College course, and a fit preparation for work in your own sphere.... The world is full of grinding poverty, and crushing sorrow; shame and death are the portion of thousands, and it needs a great gospel to meet the dire necessities of men's souls. Verily it is so. Do you doubt it? Go and see for yourselves. Thus will you learn to preach a great salvation, and magnify the great Saviour, not with your mouth only, but with your heart; and thus will you be married to your work beyond all possibility of deserting it.[65]

---

65. Spurgeon, *Lectures to My Students*, 2:160–61.

9

A Benevolent Ministry

When John B. Gough referred to Spurgeon as "a greater and grander man," he was describing the scene in the infirmary of the Stockwell Orphanage as he observed the tender manner with which Spurgeon comforted a dying boy. Gough, who had witnessed Spurgeon's preaching on many occasions, had his view of Spurgeon enlarged by witnessing this humble scene. It is vital to appreciate that the Spurgeon who cared for London's widows and orphans, fed the hungry, clothed the naked, advocated for the needy, and pleaded the cause of the poor was not a different man from the one who preached to thousands week by week. For Spurgeon, word gave birth to deed, and deed had no life apart from word. Spurgeon the preacher and Spurgeon the philanthropist were the same man. This book has been written out of a concern not only that the former has eclipsed the latter but that a failure to appreciate Spurgeon the philanthropist will impoverish our view of Spurgeon the preacher.

This chapter provides a survey of some of Spurgeon's most prominent benevolent ministries, with a special focus on the Stockwell Orphanage. No single volume could contain the whole story of Spurgeon's many benevolences. This sketch, however, will help readers appreciate how Spurgeon applied the principles he advocated in his teaching on the subject of mercy ministry and social concern.

The Stockwell Orphanage
If the Pastors' College was, as William Williams said, dearest to Spurgeon's heart, then the Stockwell Orphanage followed closely behind.

Established in 1867, the Stockwell Orphanage was another benevolent institution that Spurgeon founded, supported, and led. The beginnings of the orphanage, according to Spurgeon, can be traced to three key occurrences. First, there was an article that appeared in an 1866 issue of the *Sword and the Trowel* in which Spurgeon communicated his burden that "distinctly religious" schools and centers be established for children, where the gospel would be taught so that children might be brought to faith in Christ at an early age.[1] The second major event occurred at a prayer meeting at the Metropolitan Tabernacle that likely took place toward the end of 1866, in which Spurgeon said to his congregation, "Dear friends, we are a huge church, and should be doing more for the Lord in this great city. I want us, tonight, to ask Him to send us some new work; and if we need money to carry it on, let us pray that the means may also be sent."[2]

The third and most remarkable occurrence came in the form of a letter sent to Spurgeon from Anne Hillyard, the wealthy widow of an Anglican priest, just a few days after the prayer meeting mentioned above. In the letter, she offered to commit £20,000 for the purpose of founding an orphanage for needy boys. Mrs. Hillyard had been looking for a way to use these funds in some benevolent cause and had read Spurgeon's article in the *Sword and the Trowel* about religious education for children. In Spurgeon, she was sure she would find a willing and compassionate colaborer. For Spurgeon's part, there was no doubt in his mind that God Himself had sovereignly directed Mrs. Hillyard to him. He wrote, "Here was the new work and the money with which to begin it."[3] Together, Spurgeon

---

1. C. H. Spurgeon, "The Holy War of the Present Hour," *Sword and the Trowel*, August 1866, 339–45; *C. H. Spurgeon's Autobiography, Compiled from His Diary, Letters, and Records by His Wife and His Private Secretary* (London: Passmore and Alabaster, 1899), 3:167. At that time, there was no system of public education in Britain. The British system of public education began with the Public Schools Act of 1868.

2. *C. H. Spurgeon's Autobiography*, 3:168.

3. *C. H. Spurgeon's Autobiography*, 3:168–69.

and Hillyard embarked upon this new labor and would go on, over the coming years, to rescue hundreds upon hundreds of orphans. In the final orphanage report during Spurgeon's lifetime, composed in 1891, Spurgeon recorded the number of orphans who had been supported as being over fifteen hundred. They decided early on that they would not discriminate against children based on denominational backgrounds. Thus, roughly six hundred of these children came from Anglican backgrounds, and other children came from Baptist, Congregationalist, Wesleyan, Presbyterian, and even Roman Catholic backgrounds.[4]

In most cases, the orphans were children who had no fathers and whose mothers, though living, could not provide adequately for them. In this way, Spurgeon deliberately designed the orphanage to help both the fatherless and the widow. Spurgeon frequently drew attention to the destitute cases of many of the widows. He wrote, "Often sickly themselves, altogether without business capacity, grieving for the loss of their husbands, and having half-a-dozen or more children tugging at their skirts, they are true objects of Christian sympathy."[5] For Spurgeon, the Stockwell Orphanage was as much about ministering to these women as it was about ministering to the orphans themselves. He wrote, "The relief afforded by our taking one child has often inspired a poor woman with hope, given her a little breathing-space, and enabled her to accomplish the difficult task which still remained."[6]

Though the orphanage undoubtedly addressed many cases of extreme need, it did not meet the needs of those who might be considered the most desperate, as it did not usually permit children born out of wedlock.[7] The orphanage report of 1876–77 stated

---

4. Lewis A. Drummond, *Spurgeon: Prince of Preachers*, 3rd ed. (Grand Rapids: Kregel Publications, 1992) 427.
5. Spurgeon, "Annual Report of the Stockwell Orphanage, 1882–83," *Sword and the Trowel*, July 1883, 403.
6. Spurgeon, "Annual Report of the Stockwell Orphanage, 1882–83," 404.
7. Peter Shepherd, "Spurgeon's Children," *Baptist Quarterly* 42, no. 2, part 1 (April 2007): 93.

plainly, "The cases of illegitimate children are not within the scope of this Institution."[8] Admission to the orphanage of any child universally required that the parent(s) provide a certificate of marriage.[9] There is no record from Spurgeon himself or the administration of the orphanage as to why this was the policy. One might speculate that providing for children born out of wedlock could be viewed as making accommodations for extramarital sex or the widespread practice of prostitution.[10] The highly controversial "Bastardy Clause" of the 1834 Poor Law was essentially the product of precisely this line of reasoning. The clause effectively made mothers of illegitimate children solely responsible for the support of their children until the age of sixteen as a deterrent to fornication and sexual promiscuity. Additionally, the new law made it almost impossible for mothers to pursue remuneration from the putative fathers.

The policy of Spurgeon's orphanage with respect to illegitimate children, though perhaps disappointing by today's standards, was not at all unique in the nineteenth century, a point that one must keep in mind. Many such institutions refused aid to children on the basis of illegitimacy.[11] A prominent example was one of Spurgeon's models, George Müller, who only admitted children into his orphan-

---

8. Spurgeon, "Report of the Stockwell Orphanage," 347. Spurgeon considered rising illegitimacy in England to be among the clearest signs of the "awful wickedness of this land." Spurgeon, "A Prophetic Warning," *Sword and the Trowel*, October 1883, 522.

9. Spurgeon, "Report of the Stockwell Orphanage," 347.

10. R. J. Helmstadter makes this suggestion in "Spurgeon in Outcast London," in *The View from the Pulpit: Victorian Ministers and Society*, ed. P. T. Phillips (Toronto, Ont.: Macmillan of Canada, 1978), 184.

11. Policies barring illegitimate children from admission to orphanages were fairly common in the eighteenth and most of the nineteenth century; see Ivy Pinchbeck and Margaret Hewitt, *Children in English Society*, vol. 2, *From the Eighteenth Century to the Children Act of 1948* (London: Routledge & K. Paul, 1973), 583–84. For example, in Spurgeon's day, of the roughly fifty-five London creches (essentially day care centers for working mothers), twenty-five of them expressly prohibited admission of illegitimate children; see Anna Davin, *Growing Up Poor: Home, School and Street in London, 1870–1914* (London: Rivers Oram, 1996), 93.

age who were "lawfully begotten."¹² However, in the latter half of the nineteenth century, more institutions began to open their doors to illegitimate children. One famous example was Thomas Barnardo's homes for poor children.¹³ Barnardo wrote in 1879, "Indeed, common humanity urges us to do something on behalf of so helpless a class."¹⁴ Whatever the reason, Spurgeon did not admit such children into the Stockwell Orphanage. The typical boy or girl at Spurgeon's orphanage was one who came from a family in which the father had died, and the mother was poor.

It was important to Spurgeon that the overall design and organization of the orphanage allow for as normal a family atmosphere for the orphans as possible. Spurgeon did not want all the orphans to be placed together in very large rooms. Instead, he arranged for small "families" of orphans to be gathered into individual family homes, with one "house mother" assigned to each family home.¹⁵ This method of organization was common among the orphanages of the Victorian era.¹⁶ Spurgeon did all he could to make sure that the orphans did not feel like they were abnormal or somehow

---

12. George Müller, *A Narrative of Some of the Lord's Dealings with George Müller* (London: J. Nisbet, 1874), 3:559. Spurgeon greatly admired George Müller and developed a close friendship with him over the years. Spurgeon visited Müller's orphanage in 1855, spent many days with him in Mentone, France, and even had Müller preach at the Tabernacle in 1875; see Christian T. George's footnote in *The Lost Sermons of C. H. Spurgeon: His Earliest Outlines and Sermons Between 1851 and 1854*, ed. Christian T. George (Nashville: B&H Academic, 2016), 1:414n7; and Peter J. Morden, *Communion with Christ and His People: The Spirituality of C. H. Spurgeon* (Eugene, Ore.: Pickwick Publications, 2013), 159–60, 208–11. When Spurgeon was first offered money from Anne Hillyard to start his own orphanage, he suggested that the funds might be put to better use if given to George Müller for his orphan homes; see *C. H. Spurgeon's Autobiography*, 3:170.

13. Shepherd, "Spurgeon's Children," 93.

14. Thomas Barnardo, "Personal Notes," *Night and Day: A Monthly Record of Christian Missions and Practical Philanthropy Edited by Dr. Barnardo*, December 1879, 145.

15. Richard E. Day, *The Shadow of the Broad Brim: The Life Story of Charles Haddon Spurgeon, Heir of the Puritans* (Philadelphia: Judson, 1934), 124.

16. Kathleen Heasman, *Evangelicals in Action: An Appraisal of Their Social Work in the Victorian Era* (London: Geoffrey Bles, 1962), 98–99.

disadvantaged. In the 1885 annual report for the orphanage, Spurgeon highlighted the fact that the children were not required to wear special uniforms for this very reason. He wrote, "Orphanhood is a child's misfortune, and he should not be treated as though it were his fault. In a garb which is a symbol of dependence, it is difficult, if not impossible for an orphan to preserve a feeling of self-respect."[17]

In 1879, Spurgeon established a girls' orphanage alongside the one for boys.[18] Together, between the girls' and boys' wings, the Stockwell Orphanage housed approximately five hundred children at any given time. Spurgeon frequently visited the orphanage, and the children there universally regarded him with affection and delight. He made it his habit to spend every Christmas with the orphans. Reflecting on his visits, Spurgeon said of the orphans that "they compassed me about like bees."[19] An 1880 article in the *Daily Telegraph* captured the scene: "As to the happiness of the orphans, there is no doubt about it. When Mr. Spurgeon opened the door there was a shout of delight at the appearance of their friend. It was like a welcome to an old school fellow, and was repeated in every house we entered. Not the kind of cheer that requires a lead, but one that sprang up on the instant when it was known that Mr. Spurgeon was at the orphanage."[20] Spurgeon also made it a point to be present in times of sorrow in order to cheer the children. As Dallimore notes, "He made it a particular point to call on any children who might be in the infirmary, to pray for them and show whatever special kindness he could."[21] Throughout his life and ministry, the orphanage remained a source of special joy and delight to Spurgeon.

---

17. Spurgeon, "Report of the Stockwell Orphanage," 460.
18. Shepherd, "Spurgeon's Children," 96; Spurgeon, "The Girls' Orphanage, Stockwell," *Sword and the Trowel*, June 1880, 281.
19. *C. H. Spurgeon's Autobiography*, 3:179.
20. W. Y. Fullerton, *C. H. Spurgeon: A Biography* (London: Williams and Norgate, 1920), 245.
21. Arnold Dallimore, *Spurgeon: A New Biography* (Edinburgh: Banner of Truth, 1985), 129.

As with the Pastors' College, Spurgeon frequently promoted the work of the Stockwell Orphanage and was not the least bit shy about soliciting funds from his readers for its support. Spurgeon believed orphan care should be a cause of universal concern to Christians, and thus he expected to find hearty support among his fellow believers. In an 1881 issue of the *Sword and the Trowel*, Spurgeon wrote, "The duty of each Christian to the mass of destitute orphanhood is clear enough, and if pure minds are stirred up by way of remembrance there will be no lack in the larder, no want in the wardrobe, no failing in the funds of our Orphan House."[22] As James 1:27 says, "Pure religion and undefiled before God and the Father is this, to visit the fatherless and widows in their affliction." With this verse in mind, Spurgeon wrote in an 1881 article, "The work of caring for the widow and the fatherless is specially mentioned by the Holy Spirit as one of the most acceptable modes of giving outward expression to pure religion and undefiled before God and the Father, and therefore the Lord's people will not question that they should help in carrying it out."[23] Again, Spurgeon wrote, "The objects of our care are not far to seek; there they are at our gates—widows worn down with labour, often pale, emaciated, delicate, and even consumptive—boys half-famished, growing up neglected, surrounded with temptation! Can you look at them without pity? We cannot. We will work for them, through our Orphanage, as long as our brain can think, and our pen can write, and our heart can love; neither sickness nor weariness shall tempt us to flag in this sacred enterprise."[24]

The Stockwell Orphanage is today known as Spurgeon's Children's Charity and is one of the most successful children's organizations in the United Kingdom, helping over thirty-seven thousand children and young people. On the charity's website, they include a statement about their founder that captures the spirit of his

---

22. Spurgeon, "Report of the Stockwell Orphanage, 1880–81," 432.
23. Spurgeon, "Report of the Stockwell Orphanage, 1880–81," 440.
24. Spurgeon, "Report of the Stockwell Orphanage, 1880–81," 13.

social concern: "As a prominent Christian of his day, Spurgeon's practical response to the Bible's teaching was to provide orphaned and vulnerable children in London with shelter, education and the hope of a better future.... Spurgeons was founded in 1867 as a compassionate and distinctively Christian response to the plight of orphaned and vulnerable children in London." The charity states on their website that Spurgeon and his associates were "motivated by their faith." They go on to add, "We are very proud of our heritage and we still bear our founder's name. By keeping Charles Spurgeon at the heart of our identity and mission, it reaffirms our commitment to continue the work he started."[25]

Few ministries were a greater source of joy to Spurgeon than the orphanage. A particular passing reference in his autobiography testifies to just how important the orphanage was to him. In a chapter written by his wife Susannah, she recorded that it was Spurgeon's desire to be buried in the middle of the Stockwell Orphanage grounds. Knowing that thousands upon thousands of people would come to visit his grave, he hoped that those who came would see the orphans and would be moved to support their cause.[26] Thus, even in his death, Spurgeon considered how he could advocate for the poor and the needy.

Other Benevolences

The Pastors' College and the Stockwell Orphanage were undoubtedly the foremost among Spurgeon's benevolences. Nonetheless, Spurgeon's zeal for good works led him to multiply his various charitable efforts at such an astounding rate that by 1884, no less than sixty-six separate benevolent ministries operated under the auspices of the Metropolitan Tabernacle. The full list of these ministries is worth including at length,

---

25. "Our Heritage," Spurgeons, accessed on January 6, 2020, https://www.spurgeons.org/about-us/our-heritage/.

26. C. H. Spurgeon's Autobiography 4:372–73.

A Benevolent Ministry

The Almshouses; the Pastors' College; the Pastors' College Society of Evangelists; the Stockwell Orphanage; the Colportage Association; Mrs. Spurgeon's Book Fund, and Pastors' Aid Fund; the Pastors' College Evening Classes; the Evangelists' Association; the Country Mission; the Ladies' Benevolent Society; the Ladies' Maternal Society; the Poor Ministers' Clothing Society; the Loan Tract Society; Spurgeon's Sermons' Tract Society; the Evangelists' Training Class; the Orphanage Working Meeting; the Colportage Working Meeting; the Flower Mission; the Gospel Temperance Society; the Band of Hope; the United Christian Brothers' Benefit Society; the Christian Sisters' Benefit Society; the Young Christians' Association; the Mission to Foreign Seamen; the Mission to Policemen; the Coffee-House Mission; The Metropolitan Tabernacle Sunday School; Mr. Wigney's Bible Class; Mr. Hoyland's Bible Class; Miss Swain's Bible Class; Miss Hobbs's Bible Class; Miss Hooper's Bible Class; Mr. Bowker's Bible Class for Adults of both Sexes; Mr. Dunn's Bible Class for Men; Mrs. Allison's Bible Class for Young Women; Mr. Bartlett's Bible Class for Young Women; Golden Lane and Hoxton Mission (Mr. Orsman's); Ebury Mission and Schools, Pimlico; Green Walk Mission and Schools, Haddon Hall; Richmond Street Mission and Schools; Flint Street Mission and Schools; North Street, Kennington, Mission and Schools; Little George Street Mission, Bermondsey; Snow's Fields Mission, Bermondsey; the Almshouses Missions; the Almshouses Sunday Schools; the Almshouses Day Schools; the Townsend Street Mission; the Townley Street Mission; the Deacon Street Mission; the Blenheim Grove Mission, Peckham; the Surrey Gardens Mission; the Vinegar Yard Mission, Old Street; the Horse Shoe Wharf Mission and Schools; the Upper Ground Street Mission; Thomas Street Mission, Horselydown; the Boundary Row Sunday School, Camberwell; the Great Hunter Street Sunday School, Dover Road; the Carter Street Sunday School, Walworth; the Pleasant Row Sunday Schools, Kennington; the Westmoreland Road Sunday Schools, Walworth; Lansdowne Place Sunday School; Miss Emery's Banner Class,

Brandon Street; Miss Miller's Mothers' Meeting; Miss Ivimey's Mothers' Meeting; Miss Francies' Mothers' Meeting.[27]

This list was read out before a large assembly at Spurgeon's fiftieth-birthday celebration at the Metropolitan Tabernacle. Spurgeon's close friend Anthony Ashley-Cooper, often referred to simply as Lord Shaftesbury, chaired the festivities. Shaftesbury, an Anglican churchman himself, was the leading social reformer in Britain in the nineteenth century. After the list was read, he commented, "What a tale of his agencies [was] read to you just now! How it showed what a powerful administrative mind our friend has. That list of associations, instituted by his genius, and superintended by his care, were more than enough to occupy the minds and hearts of fifty ordinary men."[28]

With the rest of this chapter, I highlight just a few of Spurgeon's foremost benevolences outside the Pastors' College and the Stockwell Orphanage. Spurgeon was engaged on some level in all the Tabernacle's ministries, but he was involved in some more than others. Below, I survey just a few of Spurgeon's benevolences that received a special degree of his attention and care.

Missions Stations and Schools

Prominent among the long list of ministries above are the numerous mission stations and schools. Spurgeon's many mission stations varied in terms of how they operated, but they generally had as their object the evangelization of a particular area, as well as the meeting of practical and material needs in the target community. The Metropolitan Tabernacle supported twenty-two such missions in Spurgeon's day, many of which continued to operate long after his

---

27. *Memorial Volume, Mr. Spurgeon's Jubilee: Report of the Proceedings at the Metropolitan Tabernacle on Wednesday and Thursday Evenings, June 18th and 19th, 1884* (London: Passmore & Alabaster, 1884), 7–8; Spurgeon, "Mr. Spurgeon's Jubilee Meetings," *Sword and the Trowel*, July 1884, 373.

28. G. Holden Pike, *The Life and Works of Charles Haddon Spurgeon* (London: Passmore and Alabaster, 1894), 6:275.

death.[29] These missions regularly drew people to the Tabernacle and sometimes turned into new churches themselves. Spurgeon often provided updates on the various missions in a section in the *Sword and the Trowel* simply titled "Notes." A typical description of one of the mission sites reads as follows: "*Green Walk Mission, Bermondsey.*—President, W. Olney, Junr. A mighty warfare against sin has been carried on here, and very many brought to Jesus and added to the Tabernacle church. Hall thronged to hear the gospel. About 350 children in the schools. Mothers meetings, Band of Hope, Tract Society, Open air mission, Bible and singing classes, and Children's special service. All at work and all alive. *Here a good hall must be built.* If some generous friend would build a place for this mission, the money would be well laid out."[30]

The schools mentioned in the list of Tabernacle ministries were either Sunday schools or what were known as *ragged schools*. In Spurgeon's day, Sunday schools were principally for religious instruction and usually operated on Sunday afternoons.[31] When the Sunday school movement began in the late eighteenth century, many of the Sunday schools also addressed subjects of more general education. However, Spurgeon's utilization of the Sunday schools was similar to that of many in the Victorian era—namely, for the religious instruction of the children of the poor and lower-middle class.[32]

---

29. *C. H. Spurgeon's Autobiography*, 4:336; Eric W. Hayden, *A History of Spurgeon's Tabernacle* (Pasadena, Tex.: Pilgrim Publications, 1971), 28–33.

30. C. H. Spurgeon, *The Metropolitan Tabernacle: Its History and Work, Mr. Spurgeon's Jubilee Sermons, A Memorial Volume* (London: Passmore and Alabaster, 1876), 118.

31. J. H. Y. Briggs, *The English Baptists of the Nineteenth Century* (Didcot, U.K.: Baptist Historical Society, 1994), 3:308–18; Hugh McLeod, *Religion and Society in England, 1850–1914* (New York: St. Martin's, 1996), 78–82; John Wolffe, *God and Greater Britain: Religion and National Life in Britain and Ireland, 1843–1945* (London: Routledge, 1994), 88, 92–93.

32. For general studies of the Sunday school movement in England, see Phillip B. Cliff, *The Rise and Development of the Sunday School Movement in England, 1780–1980* (Redhill, U.K.: National Christian Education Council, 1986); J. H. Y. Briggs and Stephen Orchard, eds., *The Sunday School Movement: Studies in the Growth and*

Hugh McLeod notes that Sunday schools were "an established part of working class life" and that "many middle-class children attended Sunday school too."[33] John Wolffe also observes, "Sunday School was felt to provide a necessary part of the upbringing of children, and the rites of passage required formal religious sanction."[34] Thus, Sunday schools were one of the primary means for churches to establish contact with the working poor. The Metropolitan Tabernacle under Spurgeon's leadership heavily promoted Sunday school ministry. By 1883, over fourteen hundred children participated in the Metropolitan Tabernacle Sunday schools.[35] Spurgeon regularly made appeals for Christians to serve in this vital ministry. The following quote is a typical example:

> Can you see these streets swarming with children and not come forward to help the Sunday-school? Can you watch the multitudes of boys and girls streaming out of the Board School and not say to yourself, "What is done with these on the Lord's day? Others must be hard at work with them, why am I not doing something?" Everywhere, on all hands, work is suggested, and especially by the activity of our adversaries. See how they compass sea and land to make one proselyte! See how the devil incessantly goes about seeking whom he may devour! He appears to have lost his eyelids. He never sleeps. He is intent continually upon devouring the souls of men; and all the incidents and accidents we meet with say to us, "Are you Christians? Then bestir yourselves. Are you the King's servants? Then be up and doing, for there are ten thousand things that

---

Decline of Sunday Schools (Milton Keynes, U.K.: Paternoster, 2007); T. W. Laqueur, *Religion and Respectability: Sunday Schools and Working-Class Culture, 1780–1850*, (New Haven: Yale University Press, 1976); William H. Groser, *A Hundred Years' Work for the Children: Being a Sketch of the History and Operations of the Sunday School Union, from Its Formation in 1803 to Its Centenary in 1903* (London: Sunday School Union, 1903).

33. McLeod, *Religion and Society*, 78.
34. Wolffe, *God and Greater Britain*, 93.
35. Spurgeon, "Notes," *Sword and the Trowel*, May 1883, 247.

must be done at once, if done at all, without waiting to discuss the best way of doing them."[36]

Alongside the religious education offered through Sunday school ministry, Spurgeon also promoted the work of ragged schools, which provided poor children with free education in basic subjects such as reading and mathematics. The ragged schools emerged in the early to mid-nineteenth century, with Lord Shaftesbury founding the Ragged School Union in 1844.[37] These schools would normally meet in the evenings during the week so as not to interfere with the work day.[38] Historian Owen Chadwick summarizes the utility and scope of the ragged schools, noting, "The ragged schools, established in slum areas by Lord Shaftesbury and others, for the purpose of instructing poor children in the three Rs and in the Bible, were 132 in number during 1870, with a total attendance of 23,132. They really aimed at taking waifs off the streets."[39] In a nation that lacked a system of public education for most of the nineteenth century, ragged schools were vital for the education of the lower classes.[40] Spurgeon was, thus, an enthusiastic proponent of ragged schools. He believed that part of his and every Christian's service to Christ should include ministering to needy children. He frequently encouraged his listeners to make poor children the special object of their benevolent care, and he commended the work of Sunday schools and ragged schools as an appropriate expression of Christian service in this arena. In

---

36. Spurgeon, "With the King for His Work!" in *The Metropolitan Tabernacle Pulpit: Sermons Preached and Revised by C. H. Spurgeon* (Pasadena, Tex.: Pilgrim Publications, 1972), 24:115.

37. David Furse-Roberts, *The Making of a Tory Evangelical: Lord Shaftesbury and the Evolving Character of Victorian Evangelicalism* (Eugene, Ore.: Pickwick Publications, 2019), 119–21, 178–79.

38. Shepherd, "Spurgeon's Children," 92.

39. Owen Chadwick, *The Victorian Church*, vol. 2, *1860–1901* (London: SCM, 1972), 307.

40. Laura M. Mair, *Religion and Relationships in Ragged Schools: An Intimate History of Educating the Poor, 1844–1870* (New York: Routledge, 2019); Heasman, *Evangelicals in Action*, 69–87.

an 1881 article in the *Sword and the Trowel*, Spurgeon commended Shaftesbury and the work of the ragged schools, writing,

> Let us attempt great things, for those who believe in the name of the Lord succeed beyond all expectation. By faith the worker lives. The right noble Earl of Shaftesbury said the other afternoon of Ragged-school teachers and their work,—"It was evident to all thinking persons that we had a great danger in the ignorance of the children of the lower classes, and so the senators began to think of it, and the philosophers began to think of it, and good men of all sorts began to think of it; but while they were all engaged in thinking, a few plain, humble people opened Ragged-schools, *and did it*." This is the kind of faith of which we need more and more: we need so to trust in God as to put our hand to the plough in his name. It is idle to spend time in making and altering plans, and doing nothing else; the best plan for doing God's work is to do it.[41]

By the end of Spurgeon's life, the Metropolitan Tabernacle supported 27 Sunday and ragged schools, with 612 teachers and over 8,000 scholars enrolled.[42]

The Colportage Association

A lesser-known ministry, yet one that, nonetheless, factored largely into the benevolent program of the Tabernacle, was what became known as the Colportage Association.[43] This ministry was always something of a third child to Spurgeon, after the Pastors' College and the Stockwell Orphanage. The Colportage Association was a confed-

---

41. Spurgeon, "Inaugural Address," *Sword and the Trowel*, August 1881, 378.
42. *C. H. Spurgeon's Autobiography*, 4:336; Helmstadter, "Spurgeon in Outcast London," in Phillips, *View from the Pulpit*, 181.
43. Spurgeon scholars have generally overlooked the significance of the Colportage Association to Spurgeon's ministry. However, two of the most significant treatments of the Colportage Association are found in Albert R. Meredith, "The Social and Political Views of Charles Haddon Spurgeon, 1834–1892" (PhD diss., Michigan State University, 1973), 132–42; and Tom Nettles, *Living by Revealed Truth: The Life and Pastoral Theology of Charles Haddon Spurgeon* (Scotland: Christian Focus Publications, 2013), 387–91.

eration of traveling salesmen, called *colporteurs*, who sold Christian literature at highly discounted prices in various districts, towns, and villages across the United Kingdom. The Colportage Association had its origins in an August 1866 article in the *Sword and the Trowel* titled "The Holy War of the Present Hour."[44] In that article, Spurgeon wrote against the incursions of what he referred to as Tractarianism, or Puseyism, into the religious life of Britain. He viewed this as a latent form of Roman Catholicism present within the Church of England.[45] To combat the errors of Tractarianism, Spurgeon proposed a number of initiatives, one of which was to promote the mass distribution of religious literature that could engage the public on crucial religious questions. Spurgeon wrote, "We should like to see the country flooded, and even the walls placarded with bold exposures of error and plain expositions of truth. We will take our own share in the effort if any friends should be moved to work *with us*."[46] Thus, the Colportage Association was born. Spurgeon believed that putting inexpensive literature in the hands of the working classes would give them access to rich truth that could help them better understand the truth and grow in the grace of God.

As the Colportage Association expanded its operations over the years, Spurgeon frequently shared reports on its productivity and regularly included appeals for its financial support. By 1878, there were ninety-four colporteurs in the association who were engaged

---

44. Spurgeon, "The Holy War of the Present Hour," *Sword and the Trowel*, August 1866, 339–45. This was the same article that led to the founding of the Stockwell Orphanage; see *C. H. Spurgeon's Autobiography*, 3:161.

45. Tractarianism and Puseyism were two names given to the Oxford Movement—a movement among High Church Anglicans in the early to mid-nineteenth century to reintroduce older church practices associated with Roman Catholicism in the theology and liturgy of the Church of England. John Henry Newman, E. B. Pusey, and John Keble were prominent leaders in the movement. For more on the Oxford Movement, see Chadwick, *Victorian Church*, 1:167–231; Stewart J. Brown, Peter B. Nockles, and James Pereiro, eds. *The Oxford Handbook of the Oxford Movement* (Oxford: Oxford University Press, 2017); George Herring, *What Was the Oxford Movement?* (New York: Continuum, 2002).

46. Spurgeon, "Holy War," 343.

full-time in distributing literature and ministering to men and women around the country.[47] By the end of Spurgeon's life, the colporteurs had paid nearly twelve million home visits and sold £153,784 worth of literature.[48]

The Almshouses

One of Spurgeon's most significant benevolent projects was the Tabernacle Almshouses, which John Rippon, one of Spurgeon's predecessors, pioneered some years earlier.[49] Under Spurgeon, this ministry expanded substantially.[50] Throughout the course of his ministry, Spurgeon built seventeen almshouses, which housed numerous poor widows. These almshouses were dear to Spurgeon and were the object of his special care. Peter Morden writes, "For some years he met the women's basic expenses, for example the costs of heating and lighting, from his own pocket. Spurgeon was not just the people's preacher—he was a man who helped ordinary people in practical ways."[51] In 1879, on the occasion of Spurgeon's silver wedding celebration, the Tabernacle congregation presented Spurgeon with a gift of £6,233. Spurgeon immediately gave £5,000 of it as an endowment for the almshouses, with the balance going to some of Spurgeon's other benevolent ministries.[52]

In Spurgeon's day, widows were unusually vulnerable, especially in London. Out of his selfless devotion to helping the weak and ministering to the afflicted, he made these widows the special object of his care and attention. Throughout his career in London, even as his celebrity grew, he was always available to the widows of the almshouses to provide support, aid, and counsel.

---

47. Morden, *C. H. Spurgeon*, 152.
48. Fullerton, *C. H. Spurgeon*, 288.
49. *C. H. Spurgeon's Autobiography*, 2:313–14.
50. Spurgeon, *Metropolitan Tabernacle*, 52–53, 93–95; Hayden, *History of Spurgeon's Tabernacle*, 20–21; Mike Nicholls, *C. H. Spurgeon: The Pastor Evangelist* (Didcot, U.K.: Baptist Historical Society, 1992), 56–57.
51. Morden, *C. H. Spurgeon*, 153.
52. Spurgeon, "Notes," March 1884, 145.

Important Principles for Christians Today

As we draw this chapter to a close, it's worth highlighting a few principles that gave shape to Spurgeon's efforts in benevolence and social ministry. There are five worth noting, in particular, that may be especially helpful for pastors and churches today.

First, it must be observed that *in all of Spurgeon's social ministries, good works served witness*. Practically every one of Spurgeon's benevolences incorporated gospel proclamation in some way. This was certainly the case with the many missions, classes, and children's ministries he founded or ran. It was also the case with other benevolent institutions like the Colportage Association. In all his efforts in mercy ministry, Spurgeon aimed to connect his good works to the proclamation of truth and to make the link between word and deed as explicit as possible.

Second, *many of Spurgeon's benevolent ministries rose from the ground up*. By this, I mean that many of the Tabernacle ministries did not originate with Spurgeon at all. Rather, he sought to be responsive to the burdens of his people and endeavored to resource and encourage them as they brought ideas to the table. Many of the classes and mission stations began through a suggestion brought to him by one of his members or, perhaps, an elder or deacon. Even the Stockwell Orphanage was primarily the product of Anne Hillyard's vision. Though many of the Tabernacle's ministries and institutions originated with Spurgeon, the benevolent program of the church was not strictly top down. Spurgeon was keen to collaborate, and he welcomed the ideas and contributions of his members. He was always eager to get behind the zeal of his own members in their efforts to do good.

A third principle that shaped Spurgeon's approach to benevolence was *his responsiveness to the providence of God*. Spurgeon was a steward of the opportunities God presented him, and he looked to the Lord to guide him in choosing his benevolent work. A signal example is the founding of the orphanage. Spurgeon called his church to pray that God would guide them by sending them some "new work" and that the Lord would provide all the necessary means to support it. Only a few days later, he received the letter from Anne Hillyard pledging £20,000 to start the orphanage. Spurgeon always sought to be responsive to God's providential direction in his benevolent work. Several more cases could be marshaled to illustrate this point, from the Pastors' College to Mrs. Spurgeon's book fund. Spurgeon was at home waiting on God, and he was ready when God's direction came.

Fourth, *children and other uniquely vulnerable groups should be the special objects of the church's care and concern.* Though practically no one fell outside the umbrella of Spurgeon's compassionate care, he, along with the members of his church, evinced a special commitment to those who were most defenseless in Victorian society, especially children and widows but also the poor, the disabled, and the oppressed. From London's forgotten blind to America's slaves, Spurgeon directed his compassion toward especially vulnerable people.

A fifth and final principle worth noting is that *Spurgeon studied the needs of his community.* He wanted to bring specific aid to meet specific needs. He studied the aches and pains of London and sought to educate himself on the areas of greatest deprivation and want in the city. This approach often gave life to new ministries, such as the Tabernacle's ragged schools or the ministry to poor pastors. Spurgeon's attention to the particular needs of his community played a part in directing and shaping his social ministries.

These and many other lessons can inform churches today as they endeavor to promote benevolence and mercy ministry among their own people. Though it is easy to imagine that the administration of the Tabernacle's many benevolent institutions became somewhat complex over time, the convictions that gave rise to them were simple. The surge of ministries that erupted forth from the Tabernacle and overflowed into the needy streets of London proceeded from the foundational belief that God calls his people to good works of charity and love on behalf of the needy. This belief was operative in the infirmary of the Stockwell Orphanage, as Gough beheld the mighty preacher as an even greater and grander man.

10

The Metropolitan Tabernacle

In 1867, General James A. Garfield, the future twentieth president of the United States, visited the Metropolitan Tabernacle. The experience left a singular impression on him that he would remember for the rest of his life. In his journal, he wrote of the immense crowds and of the singing that "made itself as a living, throbbing presence… and swept you away in its resistless current." He wrote of Spurgeon's preaching, commenting on his unusual authority, clarity, and earnestness in the pulpit. As he concluded his commentary on Spurgeon and the work of the Metropolitan Tabernacle, he wrote, "Every good man ought to be thankful for the work Spurgeon is doing.… I felt that Spurgeon had opened an asylum where the great untitled, the poor and destitute of this great city, could come and find their sorrows met with sympathy; their lowliness and longings for a better life touched by a large heart and an undoubted faith. God bless Spurgeon!"[1]

Spurgeon understood the local church to occupy a place of primacy in God's plans and purposes for the world. Thus, his own local church was at the center of his ministry. The Metropolitan Tabernacle was command central for the broad network of interlocking ministries that formed the bedrock of Spurgeon's far-reaching program of philanthropy and benevolence. The Metropolitan Tabernacle sponsored sixty-six benevolent ministries by 1884, many of which Spurgeon oversaw himself. The Tabernacle under his leadership

---

1. H. L. Wayland, *Charles H. Spurgeon: His Faith and Works* (Philadelphia: American Baptist Publication Society, 1892), 234.

enjoyed the resources of a small denomination, and it essentially functioned like one by administering a central budget, overseeing a ministerial college, planting new churches, sending out missionaries, fueling extensive publishing efforts, maintaining meticulous records of cooperating agencies and churches that had their origins in the Tabernacle, and issuing a monthly magazine, which documented the activities of the church and other churches within its broad network. Of course, Spurgeon himself rejected the idea of forming his own denomination, though the opportunity was open to him.[2] Nonetheless, Spurgeon and the Tabernacle possessed unusual organizational power, missional cohesion, and administrative efficiency that mirrored many denominations of the day and even exceeded some in terms of scope and influence.

The Metropolitan Tabernacle teemed with activity, like a hive of bees in spring. This was, in part, due to Spurgeon promoting the concept of the "working church," one in which every member was active in service, and the church's facilities and resources were utilized to their maximum capacity. The church building was open seven days a week, from seven in the morning until eleven at night.[3] The Tabernacle was the center for meetings, classes, and gatherings of all sorts. The church hosted teas, lunches, food pantries, bazaars, society meetings, and a variety of missions. On Sundays, no room was left unused. The Tabernacle was a thriving center of metropolitan ministry in the heart of South London. Spurgeon's administrative genius fueled this hive of activity. It is fascinating to read the minutes of many of even the smallest of the Tabernacle's ministries and to learn just how involved Spurgeon was in chairing meetings, organ-

---

2. C. H. Spurgeon, "Spurgeonism," *Sword and the Trowel*, March 1866, 138; W. Y. Fullerton, *C. H. Spurgeon: A Biography* (London: Williams and Norgate, 1920), 317–20; David W. Bebbington, "Spurgeon and British Evangelical Theological Education," in *Theological Education in the Evangelical Tradition*, ed. D. G. Hart and R. A. Mohler Jr. (Grand Rapids: Baker Books, 1996), 231–32.

3. Arnold Dallimore, *Spurgeon: A New Biography* (Edinburgh: Banner of Truth, 1985), 155.

izing affairs, and recruiting support. Dallimore writes, "The entire enterprise depended on Spurgeon for leadership.... With the exception of the Almshouses each institution had originated under his influence, he had planned its form of organization and had overseen its growth, and his word was supreme in all its affairs."[4] This is not to say that Spurgeon micromanaged or failed to invite collaboration in the Tabernacle's benevolences. However, he did exert tremendous influence and felt at home when exercising administrative oversight. He depended on the contributions of thousands of volunteers, which was precisely in keeping with Spurgeon's vision for how the church should operate.

An Active Church

Spurgeon embraced and promoted a vision for an active church. "The Christian church," he wrote, "was designed from the first to be aggressive."[5] He urged his members, "We must go from strength to strength, and be a missionary church."[6] Spurgeon described the Tabernacle itself as "a truly living, intensely earnest, working organization."[7] He believed the church should be an energetic and dynamic force for good in the world. He did not view the church as primarily a maintenance project. The church, he believed, should never be satisfied with merely preserving the status quo. Stagnation in mission and ministry was intolerable for Spurgeon. The church was designed by Christ to be proactive and to be aggressively engaged in the proclamation of truth and deeds of mercy.

Under Spurgeon's leadership, the Tabernacle feverishly multiplied ministries that extended into the local community and even the country at large. These ministries addressed almost every major area

---

4. Dallimore, *Spurgeon*, 154.
5. Spurgeon, "Metropolitan Tabernacle Statistics," *Sword and the Trowel*, April 1865, 174.
6. C. H. *Spurgeon's Autobiography, Compiled from His Diary, Letters, and Records by His Wife and His Private Secretary* (London: Passmore and Alabaster, 1898), 2:329.
7. Spurgeon, "The Ministry Needed by the Churches, and Measures for Providing It," *Sword and the Trowel*, May 1871, 226.

of human need, especially spiritual needs. Geoff Chang observes, "Spurgeon longed to see active churches. Too often, churches were marked by endless meetings, fruitless resolutions, and territorialism, but very little real action. Thus in his church, Spurgeon urged all his members to do something in the war for truth. This was the point of all church order, not to hinder the work of the church, but to facilitate the members' ability to engage in the work."[8] The activist spirit that permeated the Tabernacle was the product of the activist vision of its pastor.

As Spurgeon believed gospel proclamation should be central to the church's mission, so it was central to the ministry of the Metropolitan Tabernacle. Spurgeon's church was profoundly fruitful in the arenas of evangelism, church planting, and ministerial training. The work of evangelism was prominent in many of the Tabernacle's foremost ministries, including the church's many street missions, the Evangelists' Association, the Colportage Association, the Country Mission, the Tabernacle Sunday School, and the large number of Bible classes. Spurgeon saw his Sunday sermons as only a part of the church's overall evangelistic program. The gospel was proclaimed not only from the pulpit on Sundays but in scores of ministries and meetings across the city throughout the week by hundreds of the Tabernacle's members.

To promote the spread of the gospel throughout Britain—and, indeed, the world—Spurgeon founded the Pastors' College. Over the years, the bond between the college and the Tabernacle only grew stronger. What started as Spurgeon's private endeavor to train men eventually became one of the church's official ministries. The Tabernacle began to provide a large portion of the required support for the Pastors' College after Spurgeon lost funding from his American publishers due to his stand against slavery in the American South.[9] Many

---

8. Geoffrey Chang, "The Militant Ecclesiology and Church Polity of Charles Haddon Spurgeon" (PhD diss., Midwestern Baptist Theological Seminary, 2020), 236–37.

9. Mike Nicholls, *Lights to the World: A History of Spurgeon's College, 1856–1992*

of the church's members lodged students in their homes in order to support the work of the college.[10] For a number of years, the Tabernacle facilities hosted the various classes of the Pastors' College, and many of the school's students were drawn from the Tabernacle membership.[11] Spurgeon delighted in the strong connection between the Tabernacle and the college and saw such a relationship as providing an optimal context for the ongoing growth and maturation of the students. In 1871, he said,

> In order to achieve all these things, it is a very grand assistance to our College that it is connected with an earnest Christian Church. If union to such a church does not quicken his spiritual pulse it is the student's own fault. It is a serious strain upon a man's spirituality to be dissociated during his student-life from actual Christian work, and from fellowship with more experienced believers. At the Pastors' College our brethren can not only meet, as they do every day, for prayer by themselves, but they can unite daily in the prayer-meetings of the church, and can assist in earnest efforts of all sorts. Through living in the midst of a church which, despite its faults, is a truly living, intensely earnest, working organization; they gain enlarged ideas, and form practical habits. Even to see church management and church work upon a large scale, and to share in the prayers and sympathies of a large community of Christian people, must be a stimulus to right-minded men. Our circumstances are peculiarly helpful, and we are grateful to have our institution so happily surrounded by them. The College is recognized by the Tabernacle church as an integral part of its operations, and supported and loved as such. We have the incalculable benefit of its prayers, and the consolation of its sympathies.[12]

(Harpenden, U.K.: Nuprint, 1994), 33; Ian Randall, *A School of the Prophets: 150 Years of Spurgeon's College* (London: Spurgeon's College, 2005), 3.

    10. Randall, *School of the Prophets*, 20.

    11. Nicholls, *Lights to the World*, 62; Dallimore, *Spurgeon*, 155; Randall, *School of the Prophets*, 3.

    12. Spurgeon, "Ministry Needed," 226. See also Spurgeon, "Work of the Metropolitan Tabernacle," *Sword and the Trowel*, March 1866, 137.

Amid all the efforts at gospel proclamation, the church also pioneered dozens of benevolence ministries. The members of the Tabernacle sent parcels of clothes to poor people across the country, provided meals for the hungry, sent flowers to the sick, prepared cards for the bereaved, hosted special tea meetings for the blind, prepared gifts for expectant mothers, taught practical courses to London's lower classes, and raised funds to support widows and orphans. Virtually no needy group fell outside the pale of the Tabernacle's benevolence.

The Metropolitan Tabernacle swelled with activity throughout the week. Dallimore writes, "The Metropolitan Tabernacle was not, as some have assumed, merely a highly popular preaching center.... The Tabernacle was a great, working church.... There were activity and work that brought great numbers to the Tabernacle on many occasions during the week."[13] In the *Sword and the Trowel*, Spurgeon regularly recorded some of the various activities taking place at the Tabernacle from week to week. He did so in a journal-entry style under the "Notes" section. Almost every issue of the magazine, from 1873 onward, contained these notes on various church activities, though they did not include everything taking place in the building on a regular basis. Below is a typical example from a section of the magazine's notes in 1880:

> On *Friday evening, May* 14, the eleventh annual meeting of the Metropolitan Tabernacle Country Mission was held in the Lecture-hall under the presidency of C. H. Spurgeon. The Orphanage choir sang at intervals selections from Mr. Charlesworth's Service of Song, "*Valour and Victory*." Friends would find these "services" very useful for their choirs: they are cheap and excellent. The report referred to the fact that, through the agency of the mission, churches have been formed at Putney, Carshalton, Waltham-stow, and St. Mary Cray; and then described the present position of the work at Tooting, Southgate, Teddington, Bell Green, North Cheam, Pope Street, King's

---

13. Dallimore, *Spurgeon*, 153.

Langley, Tiptree, Great Warley, Brentwood, Stratford, and Isleworth. The treasurer, Mr. R. Hayward, read the balance-sheet for the year, which showed receipts £183 11s. 9 1/2d., and expenditure £167 3s. 0 1/2d....

The same work as that which is done by the Country Mission for the suburbs is done for London itself by our Tabernacle Evangelists' Association, which held its meeting on *Monday, May* 24, in connection with the prayer-meeting. Mr. Elvin, the secretary, stated that in the five months since the beginning of the year 1,004 services had been conducted by members of the Association. The pastor cordially commended the work as one of the cheapest and most direct forms of carrying the gospel to the people. Messrs. Cox and Hunt gave interesting reports of their evangelistic labors. We have to find a large proportion of the money which is needed for the carrying on of this admirable effort, and we shall be very glad if more friends will share with us the privilege of supporting its operations....

On *Friday evening, June* 4, the Royal Hand-Bell Ringers, Poland-street, London, gave an entertainment to the Tabernacle Sunday-school, as the commencement of a series of similar gatherings of Sunday-scholars. The pastor presided, and at the close of the entertainment, expressed his hearty approval of the manner in which Mr. Duncan S. Miller and his merry men had combined useful moral lessons with the sweetest of music and the happiest of talk....

On *Monday evening, June* 7, the annual meeting of the Metropolitan Tabernacle Missionary Working Society was held in the lecture-hall. The pastor presided, and spoke in praise of the object of the society, which is to supply clothes to the families of poor pastors, missionaries, and colporteurs....

On *Wednesday evening, June* 9, the annual meeting of the Spurgeon's Sermons Tract Society was held in the Lecture-hall. The chair was taken by C. F. Allison, Esq., our last elected deacon; addresses were delivered by Messrs. Murrell, Carr, Charlesworth, Goldston, Perkins, and Dunn; Mr. Cornell's report stated that upwards of 17,000 of the Pastor's sermons had been circulated by the Society during the past year, many of them going to places where no gospel preacher is laboring.

By supplying these sermons to those who lend them out from door to door their usefulness is greatly promoted. This is a capital idea, and it is vigorously carried out....

Metropolitan Tabernacle Flower Mission.—Miss Higgs asks us to mention that flowers and texts are much needed for the Flower Mission. She says:—"We have several applications from City Missionaries who find that the flowers give them an easy introduction into houses where otherwise they would not be received, and we are sorry not to be able to let them have as many as they want." Hampers should be sent off, *carriage paid*, addressed to

> The Secretary of the Flower Mission,
> Metropolitan Tabernacle,
> Newington,

in time to arrive on Wednesday morning. Surely those who have an abundance in their gardens will help our poor Londoners to see a flower, and will aid our beloved sisters by this means to spread the sweetness and perfume of the Rose of Sharon. All our societies delight us. Each one seems to be the best: but assuredly the Flower-mission is the pink of them all, or as the lily among all the beauties of the Tabernacle garden.[14]

The sorts of activities summarized in these notes proceeded daily at the Tabernacle. Not only did these ministries have their regular weekly activities, but most of them also held their annual meetings at the Tabernacle. Dallimore stated, "The Tabernacle was the center for the various institutions' annual meetings—so many of them that one was held almost every week."[15]

It was important to Spurgeon that the local church itself superintend almost all of these ministries. Spurgeon did not found ministries and organizations that remained detached from his local church. Rather, the local church was to be the true locus of ministry. Thus, the Tabernacle hosted these ministries with their facilities, staffed them

---

14. Spurgeon, "Notes," *Sword and the Trowel*, July 1880, 357–58.
15. Dallimore, *Spurgeon*, 155.

with their volunteers, and supported them from the church's central budget and regular subscriptions. The church as a corporate entity was at the center of Spurgeon's strategic approach to mercy ministry.

An Active Membership

Earlier in this book, it was argued that Spurgeon believed every church member is called to good works and to be active in service to Christ and His church. One of the reasons the Metropolitan Tabernacle was so productive was because Spurgeon's teaching routinely enlisted every member in the work of the church. Spurgeon believed the humblest layperson has a part to play in the spread of the gospel and ministry to the needy. It is not that God calls each member to be a pastor or a missionary. Nonetheless, each member has a part to play in the church's overall mission.

With this imagery, Spurgeon was able to emphasize the duty and service each man and woman owe to Christ. He said, "As in the ranks each man has his place, and each rank has its particular phase in the battalion, so in every rightly constituted church each man, each woman, will have, for himself or herself, his or her own particular form of service, and each form of service will link in with every other, and the whole combined will constitute a force which cannot be broken."[16] This view required all the members of the church to feel a sense of duty to give themselves to Christian work for Christ. The particular type of work might look different from individual to individual, but the idea was that every member had his or her own sphere of labor. Early in his London ministry, he said,

> We have each an allotted work to do, if we are the Lord's elect; let us take care that we do it. You are a tract distributor; go on with your work, do it earnestly. You are a Sunday-school teacher; go on, do not stay in that blessed work, do it as unto God, and

---

16. C. H. Spurgeon, "The Church as She Should Be," in *The Metropolitan Tabernacle Pulpit: Sermons Preached and Revised by C. H. Spurgeon* (Pasadena, Tex.: Pilgrim Publications, 1971), 17:195.

not as unto man. You are a preacher; preach as God giveth you ability.... Are you like Zebulon, one that can handle the pen? Handle it wisely; and you shall smite through the loins of kings therewith. And if you can do but little, at least furnish the shot for others, that so you may help them in their works of faith and their labors of love. But let us all do something for Christ. I will never believe there is a Christian in the world who cannot do something.[17]

Spurgeon wanted his members to feel empowered to work for the Lord and to feel they each had a part to play in service to Christ. To work for Jesus is a privilege and responsibility belonging to every Christian.

Further, Spurgeon wanted all of his hearers to feel as though a great deal rested on their shoulders. The mission was urgent, and the efforts of each member were of the utmost importance. Each member was to man his post and every Christian was to have his own job. With so many outlets for service in the church, no member needed to go without regular and manifold opportunities to serve. Chang writes,

> Under the leadership of the Tabernacle, the church organized numerous ministries. For many members, this meant serving as a Sunday School teacher and bringing the gospel to poor children. For others, it was participating in the various mission stations and supporting the work of the college students. With all the publishing happening out of the Tabernacle, many members looked for ways to distribute gospel literature. Some members even joined in cross-cultural mission work, taking the gospel to lands that had no witness.[18]

---

17. C. H. Spurgeon, "The War of Truth," in *The New Park Street Pulpit: Containing Sermons Preached and Revised by the Rev. C. H. Spurgeon, Minister of the Chapel* (Grand Rapids: Baker Book House, 2007), 3:45–46.

18. Chang, "Militant Ecclesiology," 237.

Chang argues that active service in the life of the church was an expectation of every member at the Tabernacle.[19] An active church required an active and engaged membership. The mission of the church was not a mission given to one individual leader—or even a group of leaders. Every member had a contribution to make to the overall mission, and every member had a part to play in the "working church."

An Active Diaconate

When Spurgeon came to New Park Street Chapel in 1854, the church had a well-established diaconate but no elders. In 1859, Spurgeon led the church to install elders to aid in the spiritual care of the congregation.[20] The deacons, however, were in some ways more pivotal to the day-to-day operations of the church. The Tabernacle deacons were some of Spurgeon's closest friends and most intimate partners in ministry, and he relied heavily on them in the execution of his many plans and initiatives. Ernest LeVos writes, "Spurgeon viewed and treated his deacons as more than good advisors; they were co-workers in the propagation of the Gospel."[21]

Spurgeon greatly appreciated and admired the deacons who served alongside him in his first pastorate at Waterbeach. He would reflect on them with fondness many times throughout his later ministry in London. He once wrote of them, "The deacons of our first village ministry were in our esteem the excellent of the earth, in whom, we took great delight. Hard-working men on the weekday, they spared no toil for their Lord on the Sabbath; we loved them sincerely, and do love them still.... In our idea they were as nearly the perfection of deacons of country church as the kingdom could

---

19. Chang, "Militant Ecclesiology," 141–42.
20. Eric W. Hayden, *A History of Spurgeon's Tabernacle* (Pasadena, Tex.: Pilgrim Publications, 1971), 59.
21. Ernest LeVos, *C. H. Spurgeon and the Metropolitan Tabernacle: Addresses and Testimonials, 1854–1879* (Bloomington, Ind.: iUniverse, 2014), xi.

afford."[22] Spurgeon's appreciation for the office of deacon did not diminish when he moved to London to pastor the New Park Street Chapel. His personal admiration for his new deacons was immense, as was his sense of their usefulness in the church's ministry. By 1861, the Metropolitan Tabernacle had twelve deacons, all of whom were elected by the church and were appointed for life.[23] Spurgeon referred to them as "peculiarly lovable, active, energetic, warm-hearted, generous men, every one of whom seems specially adapted for his own particular department of service."[24] Eric Hayden wrote,

> He himself, however, felt he was surrounded by a band of loving and loyal deacons. He frequently insisted that his was not a "one-man-ministry," and he had his office-bearers sitting behind him on the pulpit rostrum in the Tabernacle as a sign that they fully supported his ministry of the Word of God.... He felt the Church of God everywhere owed an "immeasurable debt of gratitude" to men who gave up so much time, home comforts, money, and so forth in order to prosper the work of the Church and its members.[25]

The church developed an active diaconate and maintained high expectations for those who served in the office. Their responsibilities included care for the poor, visitation of the sick, various other forms of mercy ministry, supervision of the church's financial affairs, oversight of the church's facilities, participation in many of the church's vital ministries (especially the Sunday school classes and the church's many local missions stations), and regular meetings with Spurgeon to discuss church matters.[26] Every deacon was involved in a significant way in the leadership of some form of ministry at the Tabernacle.

---

22. Spurgeon, "The Good Deacon," *Sword and the Trowel*, June 1868, 244.
23. Hayden, *History of Spurgeon's Tabernacle*, 60; C. H. Spurgeon's *Autobiography*, 3:23.
24. C. H. Spurgeon's *Autobiography*, 3:18.
25. Hayden, *History of Spurgeon's Tabernacle*, 59.
26. Hayden, *History of Spurgeon's Tabernacle*, 59–65.

It was not uncommon for new classes, missions, and ministries to begin by default under the oversight of one of the church's deacons.

Spurgeon made every effort to champion the office of deacon. He viewed it as a high calling that should attract only the best of men. He regularly praised the deacons of the Tabernacle in public and in print. Foremost among the church's deacons was Thomas Olney—or Father Olney, as Spurgeon was fond of calling him. Hayden wrote, "Of all C. H. Spurgeon's office-bearers he seemed to hold Thomas Olney in highest regard."[27] Olney was a member of the church for sixty years. Spurgeon described him as a man of "ceaseless earnest activity."[28] He served the church variously as a deacon, an elder, and the church's treasurer. In the June 1868 issue of the *Sword and the Trowel*, Spurgeon included a glowing tribute to Thomas Olney while the senior deacon was still living. In the article, he wrote, "The church owes an immeasurable debt of gratitude to those thousands of godly men who study her interests day and night, contribute largely of their substance, care for her poor, cheer her ministers, and in times of trouble as well as prosperity remain faithfully at their posts.... Deprive the church of her deacons and she would be bereaved of her most valiant sons; their loss would be the shaking of the pillars of our spiritual house and would cause desolation on every side."[29] After Thomas Olney died a year later in 1869, Spurgeon included another tribute to him in the January 1870 issue of the *Sword and the Trowel*. He wrote,

> Of his love and devotion to both the pastor and the church we all are witnesses. His greatest pride, we might almost use that word, was the work of God at the Tabernacle. He gloried and rejoiced in all that concerned the church. Every institution received his cordial co-operation; he loved college, orphanage, and almshouses, and helped them all to the extent of his ability.... In our departed "Father" the poor have lost a friend.

---

27. Hayden, *History of Spurgeon's Tabernacle*, 60.
28. LeVos, *Spurgeon and the Metropolitan Tabernacle*, 118.
29. Spurgeon, "The Good Deacon," 243.

The poor, especially the poor of the church, always found in him sincere sympathy and help.... Never minister had a better deacon; never church a better servant.[30]

Among the other prominent deacons of the Tabernacle was Thomas Olney's son William, who also became a senior deacon. William served among many of the church's mission stations and also regularly visited the sick.[31] Another of Spurgeon's deacons was Joseph Passmore, who grew up attending New Park Street Chapel and went on to supervise all of Spurgeon's publishing efforts.[32] William Higgs was a builder by trade and constructed the Metropolitan Tabernacle. He also supervised construction on a number of other building projects related to the church's ministry.[33] William Payne first served as an elder and then as a deacon. He also served for a number of years as a ragged school worker and a Sunday school teacher.[34]

These men, along with the rest of the Tabernacle deacons, embodied Spurgeon's ideal for an active diaconate. They were responsible in a special way for advancing the benevolent work of the Metropolitan Tabernacle. They led the way in the church's far-reaching mercy ministries and put hands and feet to many of Spurgeon's plans and initiatives. Spurgeon strongly believed that without its deacons, the Tabernacle could never have been what it was.

The Vital Role of the Whole Church in Mercy Ministry

Though Spurgeon was a spectacular individual philanthropist in his own right (see chapter 11), and though he certainly led the church by casting vision and setting general policy, he nonetheless depended heavily on the help of the Metropolitan Tabernacle's many members

---

30. LeVos, *Spurgeon and the Metropolitan Tabernacle*, 120–21.
31. Hayden, *History of Spurgeon's Tabernacle*, 60.
32. Hayden, *History of Spurgeon's Tabernacle*, 61.
33. Hayden, *History of Spurgeon's Tabernacle*, 61. Higgs built the first Metropolitan Tabernacle building, which was completed in 1861. After his death, his firm went on to rebuild the Tabernacle in 1900, after it was burned down in 1898.
34. Hayden, *History of Spurgeon's Tabernacle*, 61.

to advance the church's program of benevolence. The Tabernacle's broad network of mercy ministries needed more than Spurgeon to be successful. To borrow the kind of military imagery he loved to employ, Spurgeon was like the general, his deacons the lieutenants, and his members the foot soldiers. And just as battles are not won by one general but by troops on the ground, so the Tabernacle's mercy ministry was advanced not only by Spurgeon but by an entire army of Christian workers.

One of the important lessons we learn from Spurgeon's example is that when it comes to mercy ministry, the whole church has a part to play. Spurgeon valued the contribution of every member in the church's benevolent ministries. It is important to remember that for Spurgeon, good works in the Christian life were not merely understood to be optional or preferable but were seen as vital and essential. All Christians should be zealous for good works and active in serving needy people through acts of charity and kindness. Spurgeon was able to excite significant participation from his members in the church's many benevolence ministries because he taught them a high view of the importance of good works and an equally high view of every-member ministry. All the members of the Tabernacle had a part to play when it came to the church's mercy ministry.

Alongside a high view of every-member ministry, Spurgeon also maintained the highest possible view of the office of deacon. At the Tabernacle, the deacons were prominent, especially in the church's benevolence ministry. Spurgeon did not view his deacons simply as finance and facilities gurus. They were men full of the Spirit and of wisdom (Acts 6:3). They were devoted to the work of the Tabernacle and cared deeply for the needy people of the church and of London. They were utterly indispensable to the church's many ministries and operations, and they were a large part of the church's overall success. Though Spurgeon would have never supported the practice of some churches today that more or less view deacons as de facto elders, he would nonetheless urge Christians today to recover something of a biblical understanding of the crucial role of deacons in the ministry of the church. He would also impress upon churches today the crucial need to recover the heart of diaconal work, which is ultimately benevolent ministry—a ministry that addresses real practical needs both in the church and in the community. Much can be gained by churches today from a thorough study of Spurgeon's deacons and how they were deployed in the ministry of the Metropolitan Tabernacle.

A final point worth noting is how the Tabernacle, through its many volunteers, was able to address so wide a range of practical issues, including education, hunger, clothing, orphan care, housing, support for medical institutions, ministries to the disabled, and a host of other challenges facing the community. It is unlikely that most churches will have the capability of attending to such a variety of needs in their mercy ministry. However, there is something to be said for an eagerness to do good to all and not limit one's efforts to addressing one need only. Large churches often have the resources to provide help and support across a broad range of challenges and issues. Yet even small to midsize churches can, perhaps, highlight a half dozen benevolent concerns in the community to begin to address. The point is to know the needs of the community and to consider practical ways in which the church can be organized to meet such needs. The most important issue is not the size or scope of the church's mercy ministry but simple faithfulness in serving needy people in whatever areas providence allows. As a local church focuses on faithfulness in serving practical needs, the church can potentially gain a reputation for being a friend of the community and may thereby enhance the church's witness among outsiders. This is what Spurgeon aimed for in his leading of the Tabernacle's program of benevolence, and in this effort, he was enabled by God to be spectacularly fruitful.

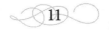

The Good Samaritan in London

Spurgeon accomplished much of his benevolent work through his leadership of a number of key institutions, such as the Metropolitan Tabernacle, the Pastors' College, and the Stockwell Orphanage. Within these organizations, he provided direction, oversight, and vision. However, our view of Spurgeon's mercy ministry would be impoverished if we limited our view of him to his work as a leader of various ministries and organizations. To round out our picture of Spurgeon, we must appreciate something of his many individual acts of ordinary charity and philanthropy. Spurgeon's life was populated with deeds of kindness and works of mercy toward others. As Mike Nicholls writes, "Spurgeon was a big man, with a big heart, and this found expression in many acts of charity."[1] He gave from his own resources to provide material support for a host of needy people, he cared for the sick and the dying, and he regularly advocated for those in need, often using his platform to plead the case of the disenfranchised. As in his public life, so in his private life, he was a man singularly devoted to good works.

Personal Charity
As a popular preacher and author, Spurgeon generated significant income over the course of his life. The Spurgeon Center in Kansas City has estimated that Spurgeon earned the equivalent of over $25

---

1. Mike Nicholls, *C. H. Spurgeon: The Pastor Evangelist* (Didcot, U.K.: Baptist Historical Society, 1992), 56.

million in his lifetime.² He lived in large homes, traveled quite comfortably, and collected one of the largest and most valuable personal libraries of any preacher in Britain. Nonetheless, he lived far below his massive income and died with a relatively small estate. Susannah Spurgeon told a newspaper that her husband only left behind £2,000.³ One of the reasons Spurgeon died with very little money to his name was because of his famous generosity. Spurgeon almost perpetually gave away his money to all kinds of benevolent causes. As his student and friend W. Y. Fullerton said, "His generosity knew scarcely any bounds."⁴

The foremost beneficiaries of his storied largesse were his various organizations and ministries, starting with his church. After Spurgeon came to London to pastor New Park Street Chapel, he began to pay for many of the church's expenses, such as cleaning and lighting, from his own income.⁵ Within a few years, he ceased accepting a salary from the church. When it came time to erect the Metropolitan Tabernacle, Spurgeon personally gave £5,000 pounds and then traveled the country on a preaching tour to raise the majority of the needed balance.⁶

The Pastors' College also benefited from Spurgeon's generosity, and his students were often the special objects of his charity. As noted in chapter 8, Spurgeon provided for all the expenses of the

---

2. Spurgeon Center, "4 Reasons Spurgeon Died Poor," *Spurgeon Center* (blog), October 11, 2016, https://www.spurgeon.org/resource-library/blog-entries/4-reasons-spurgeon-died-poor. This figure was converted from pounds to dollars and has also accounted for inflation.

3. Christian T. George, "A Man of His Time," in *The Lost Sermons of C. H. Spurgeon: His Earliest Outlines and Sermons Between 1851 and 1854*, ed. Christian T. George (Nashville: B&H Academic, 2016), 1:13.

4. W. Y. Fullerton, *C. H. Spurgeon: A Biography* (London: Williams and Norgate, 1920), 202.

5. *C. H. Spurgeon's Autobiography, Compiled from His Diary, Letters, and Records by His Wife and His Private Secretary* (London: Passmore and Alabaster, 1898), 2:123–24.

6. *C. H. Spurgeon's Autobiography*, 2:124; Ernest LeVos, *C. H. Spurgeon and the Metropolitan Tabernacle: Addresses and Testimonials, 1854–1879* (Bloomington, Ind.: iUniverse, 2014), 99.

Pastors' College out of his own pocket for the first few years of the college's existence. As Susannah said, they "planned and pinched" to make ends meet in those early days in order to support the college. Throughout the college's life, Spurgeon often paid to provide his students with books, suitable clothes, and occasionally even pocket money.[7] J. C. Carlile writes, "How many were the men he started financially on their ministerial or missionary careers! Not a few told me that they had gold coins put into their hands when, as students, they had given a good college address at the Tabernacle."[8]

When it came time to erect new facilities for the Pastors' College in 1874, most of the £15,000 required came from Spurgeon himself.[9] He also gave regularly to support the many churches that were planted by students of the Pastors' College.[10] On at least a few occasions, Spurgeon even purchased chapels at auction that he donated as meeting places for various church plants.[11] His generosity was not limited to his students but extended to their families. An illustration of Spurgeon's personal care and concern for the families of his students is found in this moving anecdote from Carlile: "At one time [Spurgeon] addressed a personal letter to each of the children of his former students. These epistles expressed tender solicitude of the child's future, and a deep desire that each should know the Savior Who was so precious to himself. There are men and women who can look back to a great day in the manse when they received a letter all their own, sign C. H. Spurgeon."[12]

---

7. Arnold Dallimore, *Spurgeon: A New Biography* (Edinburgh: Banner of Truth, 1985), 104–5.

8. J. C. Carlile, *C. H. Spurgeon: An Interpretive Biography* (London: Kingsgate, 1933), 8.

9. Dallimore, *Spurgeon*, 142.

10. C. H. Spurgeon, "Annual Paper Concerning the Lord's Work in Connection with the Pastors' College, Newington, London, 1883–84," *Sword and the Trowel*, June 1884, 323; Dallimore, *Spurgeon*, 121.

11. Spurgeon, "Annual Paper," 268–69; Ian Randall, *A School of the Prophets: 150 Years of Spurgeon's College* (London: Spurgeon's College, 2005), 29.

12. Carlile, *C. H. Spurgeon*, 181–82.

Spurgeon's generosity extended to other institutions of his as well. As noted in chapter 9, Spurgeon paid the basic expenses for the women of the almshouses for several years.[13] Spurgeon loved to give various gifts and trinkets to the children of the orphanage. As Dallimore writes, "Whenever Spurgeon visited the orphanage the children thronged around him. He knew virtually all of them by name, and he always had a penny—a coin of some value in those days—for each of them."[14] Spurgeon's congregation presented him with over £10,000 between his silver wedding anniversary (twenty-five years as the Tabernacle's pastor) in 1879 and his jubilee celebration (fiftieth birthday) in 1884, almost all of which he gave to his various benevolent institutions.[15] In 1879, William Olney, one of Spurgeon's deacons, said,

> For many years, the most generous helper of all the institutions connected with this place of worship has been Mr. Spurgeon. He has set us an example of giving. He has not stood to preach to us here for what he has got by preaching, but he has set an example to every one of us, to show that every institution here must be maintained in full vigour and strength. The repairs in connection with this place of worship, the maintenance of it, the management of all its institutions, and of everything connected with the building, and the property, and everything else,—all has been under his fostering care. Not only so, but the proceeds to which he was fully entitled have never been taken by him from the first day until now, and he does not take them at the present moment.... He has expended upon the Lord's work so much of what he has received for preaching in the Tabernacle that he has, during some of the years, returned as much as he received.[16]

---

13. Peter J. Morden, *C. H. Spurgeon: The People's Preacher* (Farnham, U.K.: CWR, 2009), 153; Carlile, *C. H. Spurgeon*, 225.

14. Dallimore, *Spurgeon*, 129.

15. Spurgeon, "Notes," *Sword and the Trowel*, March 1884, 145; Spurgeon, "Mr. Spurgeon's Jubilee," *Sword and the Trowel*, July 1884, 377.

16. *C. H. Spurgeon's Autobiography*, 2:124–25.

Beyond the contributions to his various ministries and institutions, Spurgeon regularly gave to the support of needy individuals, especially those who were close to him. Spurgeon gave a great deal of money to family members who were in need, including his parents, whom he supported for most of his life.[17] When Spurgeon first left his parents' home as a teenager, he went to study at Newmarket Academy in Cambridgeshire. While there, he came under the influence of a humble cook at the school named Mary King. Spurgeon was only fifteen years old when he met Ms. King, and she would come to have a tremendous influence on him over the following two years as the pair carried on a friendship together. It is not an overstatement to say she functioned as something of an early mentor to Spurgeon. Spurgeon said of King, "She was a good old soul [and] liked something very sweet indeed, good strong Calvinistic doctrine.... Many a time we have gone over the covenant of grace together, and talked of the personal election of the saints, their union to Christ, their final perseverance, and what vital godliness meant; and I do believe I learnt more from her than I should have learned from any six doctors of divinity of the sort we have nowadays."[18] Some years later, as Ms. King grew old, she became unwell. After Spurgeon became aware of Ms. King's poor health, he eagerly supported her financially for the rest of her life to honor the contribution she had made to his spiritual growth.[19]

Hundreds of other cases of personal charity could be enumerated. In the Victorian era, photographs of well-known people could be sold for a substantial profit. Though never eager to sit for his own photograph, Spurgeon often did so because he devoted all the sales of his photographs to a needy widow.[20] It was quite common for Spurgeon to send £5 notes to various correspondents who were in

---

17. Spurgeon Center, "4 Reasons Spurgeon Died Poor."
18. *C. H. Spurgeon's Autobiography*, 1:53.
19. *C. H. Spurgeon's Autobiography*, 1:54–55.
20. Fullerton, *C. H. Spurgeon*, 202–3.

need, many of whom he did not know particularly well.[21] Drummond comments, "He was always a 'soft touch' for anyone in real need. Throughout his life, hundreds of thousands of pounds passed through his hands.... His generosity was legendary."[22]

When Spurgeon was on his deathbed, he continued to give away money for benevolent purposes. His last conscious act before he died was to give £100 to the Tabernacle thank offering for the support of the church and its various ministries. His final telegram read, "Self and wife, £100, hearty thankoffering towards Tabernacle General Expenses. Love to all Friends." Spurgeon's secretary, Joseph Harrald, recorded, "That was his last generous act, and his last message."[23]

Hospitality

The Spurgeons lived in three homes throughout their married life. They first settled as newlyweds on New Kent Road in 1856, just a short walk from the then future site of the Metropolitan Tabernacle. After their twins were born, they relocated to Nightingale Lane, where they lived from 1857 to 1880 in a home they called Helensburgh House. Finally, they moved to a fairly spacious house called Westwood in Beulah Hill, situated on a charming thirty acres about six miles south of the Tabernacle.[24] Ray Rhodes Jr. describes the Spurgeon home as "a warm and comfortable refuge."[25] Yet it was more than a cozy nest for the happy couple; it was also a bustling hub for the Spurgeons' bountiful hospitality and generosity. Rhodes went on to write, "Home was the base of their larger ministry and the starting point of all that was good in their service to others."[26]

---

21. Fullerton, *C. H. Spurgeon*, 203.
22. Lewis A. Drummond, *Spurgeon: Prince of Preachers*, 3rd ed. (Grand Rapids: Kregel Publications, 1992), 403.
23. *C. H. Spurgeon's Autobiography*, 4:371.
24. Ray Rhodes Jr., *Susie: The Life and Legacy of Susannah Spurgeon, Wife of Charles H. Spurgeon* (Chicago: Moody, 2018), 113.
25. Ray Rhodes Jr., *Yours, till Heaven: The Untold Love Story of Charles and Susie Spurgeon* (Chicago: Moody, 2021), 142.
26. Rhodes, *Yours, till Heaven*, 156.

Their home was constantly filled with friends and visitors from far and wide. For many years, students of the Pastors' College enjoyed a standing invitation to visit Spurgeon in his garden on Saturday mornings for tea and conversation.[27] Spurgeon was completely at ease in these types of settings. He loved to offer various proverbs and advice to his students, and he allowed his famous sense of humor to shine when he was in their company. The Spurgeons also frequently entertained many famous men of the day, such as John Ruskin, Lord Shaftesbury, and the prime minister, William Gladstone. Carlile writes, "Mr. Spurgeon kept an ever-open door. No doubt his hospitality was not infrequently abused, and friends from other lands told wonderful stories of what they had heard and seen. Missionaries, preachers and public men from all over the world found their way to Westwood. Spurgeon was a great host, with dignity and courtesy and abounding generosity. He delighted to entertain his visitors."[28]

In addition to being a base for hospitality, the Spurgeon home was also a vibrant center for ministry. Susannah Spurgeon's famous book fund carried on operations in their home, with parcels of books for poor pastors being prepared in various corners and rooms. Spurgeon's massive study was often the venue for important meetings with the officers of the Metropolitan Tabernacle. Moreover, pockets of the property were utilized for ministry as well. H. L. Wayland records that the Spurgeons kept ten milk cows, selling the milk locally and using the proceeds to support a nearby ministry.[29] Spurgeon also had a special appreciation for flowers of all varieties, and he loved to take visitors on tours through his gardens. However, the flowers were for more than just beautifying his property. In 1877, a group of young women from the Tabernacle established the Flower Mission, which was founded to deliver flowers with Scripture texts appended to

---

27. Carlile, *C. H. Spurgeon*, 193.
28. Carlile, *C. H. Spurgeon*, 194.
29. H. L. Wayland, *Charles H. Spurgeon: His Faith and Works* (Philadelphia: American Baptist Publication Society, 1892), 234.

them to local hospitals.[30] Spurgeon himself regularly donated flowers to the Flower Mission from his own gardens at Westwood.[31]

The Spurgeons sought to utilize their home to create an inviting and hospitable atmosphere for their visitors. They also tried to employ their home and property to serve various ministries. They always endeavored to be liberal and openhanded with their time and resources. Spurgeon's commitment to philanthropy did not diminish when he retreated from the public arena to the domestic sphere. He was committed to good works in public as well as in private.

Advocacy and Relief

Spurgeon's social concern often came to expression in his advocacy for the poor and disenfranchised. Carlile notes, "Charles Dickens in his crowded pages gave special care to 'the thousand and one next to nothings' that make up the life of the common people. It was so with Spurgeon."[32] On numerous occasions, Spurgeon endeavored to give voice to the oppressed and the afflicted in his sermons and in the pages of the *Sword and the Trowel*. As has already been noted, he founded institutions that provided support for orphans and widows through the Stockwell Orphanage and the Tabernacle Almshouses. Spurgeon believed these two groups were uniquely worthy of Christian advocacy, especially in light of James's statement in James 1:27, "Pure religion and undefiled before God and the Father is this, To visit the fatherless and widows in their affliction." Yet, this impulse to defend the defenseless and advocate for the needy extended to other groups as well. For example, Spurgeon established ministries for the blind, calling such ministries "Christly work."[33] He even personally hosted an annual party for the Tabernacle Blind Society.[34] Another group who came within the sphere of Spurgeon's compassion was the

---

30. Spurgeon, "Notes," June 1877, 286.
31. Rhodes, *Susie*, 163.
32. Carlile, *C. H. Spurgeon: An Interpretive Biography*, 19.
33. Spurgeon, "Notes," August 1876, 384.
34. Spurgeon, "Notes," April 1876, 187.

"neglected souls" of foreign seamen who often docked in ports in and around London and were frequently subjected to mistreatment.[35]

Another cause that drew Spurgeon's advocacy was the plight of poor pastors.[36] In an 1867 article titled "The Pastors' Advocate," Spurgeon wrote,

> An exceedingly great and bitter cry has gone up unto heaven concerning many of us.... It is wrung from hundreds of poor, but faithful ministers of Christ Jesus who labour in our midst in word and doctrine, and are daily oppressed by the niggardliness of churls among us. Many of our churches honourably discharge towards their pastors the duty of ministering to them in temporal things, but by far the larger number dole out to them a pittance upon which they do not live but barely exist.... The wages of workmen have advanced but not the incomes of the workers for God. Bricklayers, carpenters, printers, all draw their extra pay at the week's end, but there is no increase to the scanty quarterage of the poor preacher.... £100 per annum, for a man with a wife and children, is not wealth, but far from it, and yet how many ministers would be happy if their incomes came near to this moderate sum.[37]

Spurgeon eventually helped to start a ministry to provide clothing for poor pastors. This work began as the Tabernacle Home and Foreign Missionary Society, which eventually gave birth to the Poor Ministers' Clothing Society.[38] Describing the mission of the society, Spurgeon said, "Our friends send out clothing for the pastor's wife and children as well as for himself.... We are sorry that any minister

---

35. Spurgeon, "Notes," January 1874, 45.

36. Salaries among Nonconformist pastors were generally quite poor, especially among the Baptists. The Baptist Union estimated in 1873 that the average annual salary among Baptist pastors in England was a mere £75 (roughly equivalent to £10,000 today); see Kenneth D. Brown, *A Social History of the Nonconformist Ministry in England and Wales, 1800–1930* (Oxford: Clarendon, 1988), 147–61.

37. Spurgeon, "The Pastors' Advocate," *Sword and the Trowel*, January 1867, 17, 19.

38. Spurgeon, "Notes," July 1875, 344; Spurgeon, "Holy Service on Behalf of Poor Ministers," *Sword and the Trowel*, August 1880, 413.

should be poor, but glad that men can be found who are willing to preach the gospel in poverty. Such men ought to be helped." Spurgeon went on to say, "A poor preacher with seven children and £70 per annum, prizes a box of clothing as those can hardly imagine who roll in riches."[39] In a typical year, the Poor Ministers' Clothing Society distributed over twenty-five hundred articles of clothing, along with hundreds of shoes, blankets, sheets, and quilts.[40]

Spurgeon's interest in the plight of poor pastors also led him to suggest to his wife the idea of starting what became known as Mrs. Spurgeon's Book Fund. Susannah Spurgeon desired to make her husband's books available to ministers across the country, and she began to do so beginning in 1875 with copies of Spurgeon's *Lectures to My Students*.[41] Eventually, the catalog came to include a wide range of books, not just ones authored by Spurgeon himself. This modest effort eventually turned into one of the most celebrated of the Tabernacle's benevolent ministries. Spurgeon regularly contributed to the book fund and frequently promoted it in the pages of the *Sword and the Trowel*. Susannah Spurgeon oversaw the operation from its inception in 1875 until her death in 1903. During that time, the ministry distributed over two hundred thousand books to pastors across the country.[42]

Along with many other Victorian activists, such as Lord Shaftesbury, Spurgeon was greatly concerned about the working conditions of Britain's mills, workhouses, and factories. Thousands of men, women, and children worked long hours in grueling conditions for astoundingly low wages. Spurgeon believed that such people ought to be the objects of Christian compassion, and he was eager to take up their cause. In an 1877 sermon, he said, "Our mines, our railways, and our seas show a terrible toll of suffering and death. Long hours in poorly ventilated workrooms are accountable for thousands of lives,

---

39. Spurgeon, "Notes," July 1875, 344.
40. Spurgeon, "Evangelists: J. Manton Smith and W. Y. Fullerton," *Sword and the Trowel*, July 1884, 383.
41. Rhodes, *Susie*, 139.
42. Rhodes, *Susie*, 140.

and so are stinted wages, which prevent a sufficiency of good from being procured. Many a needlewoman's way of life is truly a path of blood.... Do you not agree with me that such persons ought to be among the first to receive of our Christian kindness?"[43] Spurgeon was an advocate for England's common man.[44] He felt solidarity with his concerns and identified with his plight. "[Spurgeon] was one of the most articulate—perhaps the most articulate of all—in arguing the claims of the people against the elite," writes David Bebbington. "His immense popularity therefore flowed not only from his pugnacious loyalty to the basics of the gospel. It was also a result of his doughty championship of the common man."[45]

Spurgeon did not only advocate for the needy but endeavored to bring help and relief to them when it was within his power to do so. A number of examples have been cited already in this book, but another important episode is worthy of special note. Only a year after Spurgeon first came to London, he found himself amid a massive cholera outbreak. Many in his own congregation perished during the epidemic, and Spurgeon went out almost daily to minister to those who fell prey to the disease. Spurgeon recalled, "During that epidemic of cholera, though I had many engagements in the country, I gave them up that I might remain in London to visit the sick and the dying. I felt that it was my duty to be on the spot in such a time of disease and death and sorrow."[46] For his part, Spurgeon felt quite certain that he, too, would contract the disease and die, as it was believed that cholera was contagious.[47] Nevertheless, he gave

---

43. C. H. Spurgeon, "The Good Samaritan," in *The Metropolitan Tabernacle Pulpit: Sermons Preached and Revised by C. H. Spurgeon* (Pasadena, Tex.: Pilgrim Publications, 1972), 23:352.

44. David W. Bebbington, "Spurgeon and the Common Man," *Baptist Review of Theology* 5, no. 1 (Spring 1995): 63–75. Mike Nicholls also identified concern for common people as "a keynote of [Spurgeon's] ministry." Nicholls, *C. H. Spurgeon*, 64.

45. Bebbington, "Common Man," 75.

46. *C. H. Spurgeon's Autobiography*, 1:372.

47. Amanda J. Thomas, *Cholera: The Victorian Plague* (Barnsley, U.K.: Pen and Sword Books, 2015).

himself eagerly to visiting the victims and their families until he was "weary in body, and sick at heart."[48]

Slavery: "The Foulest Blot"

One of the most notable examples of Spurgeon's advocacy for the poor and disenfranchised was his stand against slavery in America. He referred to slavery as the "crime of crimes, a soul destroying sin, and an iniquity which cries aloud for vengeance."[49] In 1856, early in his London ministry, Spurgeon said in a sermon, "Ah! Poor negro slave, every scar on your back shall have a stripe of honor in heaven."[50]

Few vices drew stronger censure from Spurgeon. On a Thursday evening in December 1859, Spurgeon opened his pulpit to a fugitive slave named John Andrew Jackson, who shared his experiences as a slave in America. After Jackson concluded his address, Spurgeon then spoke extemporaneously to the gathered audience, saying,

> Slavery is the foulest blot which ever stained a national escutcheon, and may have to be washed out with blood. America is in many respects a glorious country, but it may be necessary to teach her some wholesome lessons at the point of a bayonet—to carve freedom into her with a bowie knife or send it home to her heart with a revolver. Better far should it come to this issue, that North and South should be rent asunder, and the States of the Union shivered into a thousand fragments, than that slavery should be suffered to continue. Some American divines seem to regard it, indeed, with wonderful complacency. They have so accustomed themselves to wrap it up in soft phrases that they lose sight of its real character. They call it a 'peculiar institution,' until they forget in what its peculiarity consists. It is indeed a peculiar institution, just as the Devil is a peculiar angel, and hell is a peculiarly hot place. For my part, I hold such

---

48. *C. H. Spurgeon's Autobiography*, 1:371.
49. Carlile, *C. H. Spurgeon*, 160.
50. C. H. Spurgeon, "Consolation Proportionate to Spiritual Sufferings," in *The New Park Street Pulpit: Containing Sermons Preached and Revised by the Rev. C. H. Spurgeon, Minister of the Chapel* (Grand Rapids: Baker Book House, 2007), 1:103.

> miserable tamperings with sin in abhorrence, and can hold no communion of any sort with those who are guilty of it.[51]

On another occasion, Spurgeon remarked with equal opprobrium,

> I do from my inmost soul detest slavery anywhere and everywhere, and though I commune at the Lord's Table with men of all creeds, yet with a slave-holder I have no fellowship of any sort or kind. Whenever one has called upon me, I have considered it my duty to express my detestation of his wickedness, and I would as soon think of receiving a murderer into my Church or into any sort of fellowship, as a man-stealer.[52]

When it came to slavery, Spurgeon was unequivocally clear in stating that such a practice was sub-Christian and should be excoriated in the strongest of terms.

Spurgeon's stand against slavery cost him tremendously from the standpoint of his sermon sales in America.[53] Eventually, his sermons and books were consigned to mass book burnings across the American South. Pastors warned their people against reading books by Spurgeon. In North Carolina, some argued that the circulation of Spurgeon's sermons should be outlawed.[54] Severe criticism of Spurgeon in Southern Newspapers was not uncommon. One newspaper read, "Last Saturday, we devoted to the flames a large number of copies of Spurgeon's Sermons.... We trust that the works of the greasy cockney vociferator may receive the same treatment

---

51. Carlile, *C. H. Spurgeon*, 159–60.

52. Carlile, *C. H. Spurgeon*, 160–61.

53. Many scholarly sources have highlighted the controversy surrounding Spurgeon's sermons in the American South. The best and most recent treatment is found in Nathan Rose, "Spurgeon and the Slavery Controversy of 1860: A Critical Analysis of the Anthropology of Charles Haddon Spurgeon as It Relates Specifically to His Stance on Slavery," *Midwestern Journal of Theology* 16, no. 1 (2017): 20–37; see also Spurgeon Center, "The Reason Why America Burned Spurgeon's Sermons and Sought to Kill Him," *Spurgeon Center* (blog), September 22, 2016, https://www.spurgeon.org/resource-library/blog-entries/the-reason-why-america-burned-spurgeons-sermons-and-sought-to-kill-him.

54. "Rev. Mr. Spurgeon," *The Weekly Raleigh Register*, February 15, 1860, cited in Christian T. George, preface to *Lost Sermons of C. H. Spurgeon*, 1:xix.

throughout the South." The article went on to say, "If the Pharisaical author should ever show himself in these parts, we trust that a stout cord may speedily find its way around his eloquent throat."[55] Spurgeon's criticism clearly hit a nerve and also turned up the heat on defenders of slavery in the South. A correspondent in Boston wrote to a well-known London newspaper, saying, "Our Baptist papers are overflowing with indignation and call on all publishers and booksellers to banish [Spurgeon's books] from their counters.... The poor slave holders are at their wits' end and know not what to do to save their doomed system."[56]

Doing Good to All

Spurgeon's life was filled with acts of individual kindness and charity. He loved to do good to others and was ready to give his money, time, and energy to serve people in need. His home was both a refuge for visitors and a center for ministry. As Spurgeon encountered cases of injustice, cruelty, and hardship in the world, he naturally gravitated toward the needy and the disenfranchised. His instinct was to plead their cause and, when he was able, provide help and relief. When a case gripped his heart, he was not afraid to use his platform for influence. He was, at times, selective in his advocacy for various groups. Cases involving some form of injustice or acute need moved him the most, and he also spoke up for those who lacked the opportunities and advantages that others enjoyed. Like the Good Samaritan in Luke 10, Spurgeon eagerly applied himself to cases of need with Christian compassion and generosity. He established himself as a friend of London's poor and afflicted almost immediately after he arrived there in 1854. Whether it was London's widows and orphans, poor pastors, neglected seamen, the victims of the various cholera epidemics, or the city's forgotten blind, Spurgeon opened his arms wide to the needy and afflicted.

---

55. "Mr. Spurgeon's Sermons Burned by American Slaveowners," *The Southern Reporter and Daily Commercial Courier*, April 10, 1860, cited in George, preface to *Lost Sermons of C. H. Spurgeon*, 1:xviii.

56. As quoted in Carlile, *C. H. Spurgeon*, 161.

12

Social and Political Activism

One of Spurgeon's favorite anecdotes had to do with an occasion when he was to preach for a friend named John Offord. Having arrived uncharacteristically late to this preaching engagement, he explained that part of the reason for his tardiness was that he stopped to vote in a local election on his way to preach. Mr. Offord exclaimed, "To vote! But my dear brother, I thought you were a citizen of the New Jerusalem!" Spurgeon responded, "So I am! But my 'old man' is a citizen of this world." "Ah!" replied Mr. Offord, "but you should mortify your 'old man.'" Without missing a beat, Spurgeon shot back, "That is exactly what I did; for my 'old man' is a Tory, and I made him vote for the Liberals!"[1]

Spurgeon was not at all shy about his allegiance to the Liberal Party. One newspaper referred to him as "the greatest single influence in South London in favour of Liberalism, upon whose every word, thousands and thousands hang, as if it were the very bread of life."[2] Though this statement is somewhat exaggerated, it nonetheless highlights the significance of Spurgeon's voice in the public arena. He was London's leading preacher and a household name in the English-speaking world. He had the ability to influence thousands through his sermons and writings. Spurgeon was primarily a preacher and not a political activist. However, when an issue gripped his mind and

---

1. C. H. Spurgeon's Autobiography, Compiled from His Diary, Letters, and Records by His Wife and His Private Secretary (London: Passmore and Alabaster, 1899), 3:342.
2. "Eminent Radicals out of Parliament," Weekly Dispatch, November 9, 1879.

conscience, he did not hesitate to advocate for his convictions, even if doing so provoked some to label him "a political dissenter."[3]

Any treatment of Spurgeon's social concern would be incomplete without at least a survey of some prominent examples of his social and political activism. Though by no means exhaustive, this chapter highlights some of the foremost social and political issues that invited Spurgeon's public remarks. Though he was first a citizen of the New Jerusalem, he took seriously his citizenship on earth, and was willing to lend his voice in the public square when he felt that doing so could have a good effect. However, it must be remembered that on the whole, Spurgeon's involvement in politics was greatly limited. He only occasionally addressed political subjects, and generally only did so when he felt religious concerns were involved. This perspective should temper how the reader interprets the content of the present chapter. The issues highlighted below represent his main political contributions over four decades and were not the main features of his ministry.

Disestablishment

The subject that most animated Spurgeon in the political arena was that of the disestablishment of the state church. After breaking with the Roman Catholic Church in 1534 through Henry VIII's Act of Supremacy, England established a national church, referred to variously as the Anglican Church, the Established Church, or the Church of England. After the split from Rome, England endured 150 years of intense religious turmoil, which included a civil war and the criminalizing of non-Anglican worship. With the Toleration Act of 1689, Dissenters, or Nonconformists, as they became known, were finally granted freedom of worship outside the auspices of the Anglican Church. However, significant tensions remained between the state church and those who refused to conform to the church's confession

---

3. C. H. Spurgeon, "A Political Dissenter," *Sword and the Trowel*, March 1873, 106–9.

and liturgy. These tensions persisted throughout the eighteenth and nineteenth centuries.

Spurgeon was utterly opposed to the idea of a national church because he believed it represented an unhealthy mixture of politics and religion, and it inevitably led to the curtailment of religious freedom. The main Nonconformist bodies in England in Spurgeon's day were the Methodists, Congregationalists, Baptists, Presbyterians, and Quakers. Most Nonconformists aligned with the Liberal party partly because the Liberals usually advocated for greater religious liberty and equality in England. As a Nonconformist, a Baptist, and a Liberal, Spurgeon was an eager supporter of the disestablishment of the state church. Albert Meredith notes, "He never ceased to chafe under the conviction that, as a Nonconformist, he was relegated to the role of a second-class citizen in the ecclesiastical world."[4] This was indeed the case, and not just in the ecclesiastical world. For over three hundred years, Nonconformists were legally barred from holding political office, from enrolling in elite universities such as Oxford and Cambridge, and even from burying their dead in state graveyards if they refused to use the Anglican burial rites. Moreover, Nonconformists were required to pay taxes to support the Established Church. These and other Nonconformist grievances were often referred to as *disabilities*.

Spurgeon's upbringing conditioned him to be somewhat hostile toward the Established Church. He descended from a long line of Nonconformists, one of whom was imprisoned for his Nonconformist convictions.[5] Furthermore, Spurgeon imbibed a large amount of Puritan literature from an early age. Many of the Puritans suffered on account of their dissent, most infamously during the Great Ejection of 1662, when over two thousand Puritan ministers were expelled from their churches for their refusal to conform to the Anglican

---

4. Albert R. Meredith, "The Social and Political Views of Charles Haddon Spurgeon, 1834–1892" (PhD diss., Michigan State University, 1973), 72.

5. *C. H. Spurgeon's Autobiography*, 1:8.

confessional and liturgical standards. John Bunyan, who had been imprisoned for fourteen years as a Nonconformist, was one of Spurgeon's earliest heroes. Spurgeon also devoured *Foxe's Book of Martyrs* early in his childhood, which certainly fueled his antipathy toward the idea of a national church. He also received his early education in Anglican schools and spent a few years living in Cambridge, where he no doubt was made to feel his inferiority as a Nonconformist. Thus, it is not surprising that one should find Spurgeon speaking out against Anglicanism even in his earliest sermons as a teenager in Cambridgeshire.[6]

Most of the dissenting disabilities were gone by the 1870s, but Nonconformist resentment toward the Anglican establishment remained. In an 1873 sermon, Spurgeon said, "We shall never be satisfied until all religious communities stand upon an equal footing before the law.... An Established Church is a spiritual tyranny. We wear no chains upon our wrists, but on our spirits our oppressors have thrust fetters which gall us worse than bands of steel."[7]

Kruppa suggests that one of the reasons Spurgeon was able to be so outspoken for the cause of disestablishment was that he came to prominence at a time when Nonconformity was at the height of its powers.[8] Dissenting bodies such as the Congregationalists and Baptists were not nearly as large or as organized in previous generations as they were in Spurgeon's day. It was only in 1844 that the British Anti–State Church Organization was founded, a project that never could have materialized one hundred years prior. The organization later changed its name to the Liberation Society. That such an organization could not only exist but grow and expand in the 1850s and

---

6. See *The Lost Sermons of C. H. Spurgeon: His Earliest Outlines and Sermons Between 1851 and 1854*, ed. Christian T. George (Nashville: B&H Academic, 2016), 1:191–93.

7. C. H. Spurgeon, "Questions of the Day and the Question of the Day," in *The Metropolitan Tabernacle Pulpit: Sermons Preached and Revised by C. H. Spurgeon* (Pasadena, Tex.: Pilgrim Publications, 1971), 19:51.

8. Patricia Stallings Kruppa, *Charles Haddon Spurgeon: A Preacher's Progress* (New York: Garland, 1982), 294–95.

onward is evidence that a new day had dawned for Nonconformists.[9] Kruppa notes, "[Spurgeon's] career spanned the period of the most active drive to disestablish the Church of England, and for most of that period he was a prominent participant in the movement."[10] As Spurgeon was the most well-known Nonconformist of his generation, and one who commanded the power of the pulpit as well as the press, he was well positioned to be a spokesman for the disestablishment cause.

For many years, Spurgeon gladly hosted meetings of the Liberation Society at the Metropolitan Tabernacle, and he was an active member of the society himself. He often spoke at their rallies and events, and some viewed him as one of the society's foremost agitators for reform. While Spurgeon maintained many friendships with evangelical Anglicans, and though he at times could take an irenic posture toward the Church of England, he generally deprecated establishment and did not hesitate to unleash the full fury of his pulpit and pen on the Anglican Church. In 1864, he preached one of his most well-known and long-remembered sermons, which was on the subject of baptismal regeneration. He claimed that he felt moved to preach the message out of "an awful and overwhelming sense of duty."[11] In it, he lambasted the Anglican Church for holding to what he believed to be a duplicitous stance on the issue of baptismal regeneration. Throughout the message, he claimed that many in the Established Church publicly subscribed to the Church's articles of faith, which affirm baptismal regeneration, while in fact, they rejected the Church's plain confessional stance on the doctrine.

---

9. Chadwick suggests, "The nonconformist campaign for disestablishment was a sign of the strength of Victorian Christianity. For nonconformists were not afraid that if they weakened establishment they would weaken Christianity." Owen Chadwick, *The Victorian Church*, vol. 1, *1829–1859* (London: SCM, 1971), 438.

10. Kruppa, *Charles Haddon Spurgeon: A Preacher's Progress*, 296.

11. Spurgeon, "Baptismal Regeneration," in *Metropolitan Tabernacle Pulpit*, 10:314.

He said,

> For clergymen to swear or say that they give their solemn assent and consent to what they do not believe is one of the grossest pieces of immorality perpetrated in England, and is most pestilential in its influence, since it directly teaches men to lie whenever it seems necessary to do so in order to get a living or increase their supposed usefulness: it is in fact an open testimony from priestly lips that at least in ecclesiastical matters falsehood may express truth, and truth itself is a mere unimportant nonentity.... It is time that there should be an end put to the flirtations of honest men with those who believe one way and swear another. If men believe baptism works regeneration, let them say so; but if they do not so believe it in their hearts, and yet subscribe, and yet more, get their livings by subscribing to words asserting it, let them find congenial associates among men who can equivocate and shuffle, for honest men will neither ask nor accept their friendship.[12]

This infamous sermon would go on to be Spurgeon's most widely distributed sermon, selling 350,000 copies within a year of its publication, and would draw no small amount of criticism from various clergymen and members of the religious press.[13]

In the *Sword and the Trowel*, especially in the magazine's early issues, Spurgeon spoke derisively of the Church of England and could be unsparing in his attacks on the institution.[14] The magazine featured several tracts that contained cartoon portrayals of Anglican priests designed to satirize and ridicule the Established Church.[15] As

---

12. Spurgeon, "Baptismal Regeneration," 10:316–17.
13. Kruppa, *Charles Haddon Spurgeon*, 254–81.
14. For examples, see Spurgeon, "Mr. Spurgeon and the Church of England in 1861," *Sword and the Trowel*, March 1865, 110–13; Spurgeon, "The Holy War of the Present Hour," *Sword and the Trowel*, August 1866, 339–45; Spurgeon, "Best Oxford Soap," *Sword and the Trowel*, November 1867, 514–16; Spurgeon, "Sword and the Trowel Tracts, No. 30," *Sword and the Trowel*, May 1868, 203; Spurgeon, "A Political Dissenter," 106–9.
15. For examples, see Spurgeon, "Sword and the Trowel Tracts, No. 9," *Sword and the Trowel*, May 1865, 210; Spurgeon, "Sword and the Trowel Tracts, No. 16,"

time went on, Spurgeon became even more vocal in his support for disestablishment. In an 1873 article, Spurgeon went so far as to say, "It is to be hoped that no Nonconformist will vote for a man who will not aid in the disestablishment of the Anglican Church. Liberal and Tory alike are useless to us if they will not do this much for us."[16] In 1876, he wrote, "We can never rest till Episcopacy is disestablished and perfect religious equality is found everywhere.... There must be no patronage or oppression of any faith by the State, and all men must stand equal before the law whatever their creed may be; and until this is the case our demands will not cease.... The cause of disestablishment is no mere piece of politics, but a sacred inheritance for which we contend with our whole hearts."[17] Spurgeon vigorously and unequivocally denounced establishment and was clearly willing to use his significant public platform to decry the marriage of church and state as it came to expression in the Church of England.

Spurgeon never abandoned his support for disestablishment. However, in his later years, his zeal for the cause moderated, and he gradually adopted a more tolerant posture toward the Anglican Church. After the Burials Bill passed in 1880, allowing Nonconformists to bury their dead in national graveyards according to their own funeral rites, Spurgeon declared his hope for growing respect and mutual esteem between Anglicans and Dissenters, saying, "The struggle is over, and we are grateful for it: one less cause of stumbling now remains among Christian men.... Our hope is that the civilities of the grave-yard may lead on to courtesies, and these to intercourse and knowledge, and these again to esteem and Christian union; and these to happy times in which strifes between Christians shall be

---

Sword and the Trowel, August 1865, 357; Spurgeon, "Sword and the Trowel Tracts, No. 22," *Sword and the Trowel*, November 1865, 499; Spurgeon, "The Church of England the Bulwark of our Liberties (?)," *Sword and the Trowel*, May 1868, 227–28; Spurgeon, "Sword and the Trowel Tracts, No. 32," *Sword and the Trowel*, September 1868, 412–13.

16. Spurgeon, "Notes," *Sword and the Trowel*, October 1873, 476.
17. Spurgeon, "Notes," June 1876, 285–86.

impossible."[18] Though he never withdrew his endorsement of the disestablishment cause, Spurgeon did, in 1891, withdraw from the Liberation Society and ceased hosting their meetings at the Tabernacle. This was primarily because he believed the society contained within its fold some who were theologically progressive.[19] He nonetheless went to his grave with hopes that one day there would be a decisive break between church and state in England.

Foreign Policy and British Imperialism

The latter half of the Victorian era was the heyday of British imperialism. Britain involved itself in many foreign lands exercising jurisdiction, influencing trade, and conducting military campaigns. Benjamin Disraeli embodied the aggressive foreign policy of the age with his interventionist philosophy and ambitions for imperialist expansion. Spurgeon, for his part, stridently opposed Disraeli's foreign policy.[20] Against the currents of his age, Spurgeon was an outspoken opponent of imperialism. He was especially eager to speak out against the government's treatment of the peoples of other countries whom he believed were harmed by Britain's interventions. He would not stand idly by and watch Britain "bully Russia, invade Afghanistan, pour out our wrath upon the Zulus, and stand sword in hand over against Burmah."[21] Though he always remained proud of his country, he nonetheless believed that Britain was guilty of perpetrating great evils in the world. An example of one such evil was the opium trade. In Spurgeon's estimation, guilt for introducing the trade lay with the British nation. He wrote, "The opium trade, by almost universal consent, is one of the most iniquitous, most deadly, and most accursed evils of the nineteenth century. If war is slaying its thousands, the opium trade is slaying its tens of thousands. The

---

18. Spurgeon, "The Burials' Bill," *Sword and the Trowel*, October 1880, 506.
19. David W. Bebbington, "The Political Force," *Christian History* 10, no. 1 (1991): 39.
20. Meredith, "Social and Political Views," 88.
21. Spurgeon, "The Work of God in Paris," *Sword and the Trowel*, July 1879, 338.

mournful tale of its immoral and destructive effects is faithfully and fearlessly told.... The responsibility for its origin, its extension, and its enforcement, in spite of remonstrances and prohibitions, is clearly shown to sit with the British Government of India and consequently with England and the British Crown."[22] Though he was in many ways a proud nationalist, Spurgeon was not shy about acknowledging his country's wrongdoings, at home and abroad.

Spurgeon was not a pure pacifist, but he hated war and only made allowance for armed conflict in the rarest of circumstances.[23] David Nelson Duke's succinct summary of Spurgeon's view is correct, "Though Spurgeon was not a pacifist, he had nothing good to say about war."[24] He said, "War is to our minds the most difficult thing to sanctify to God."[25] Spurgeon believed that Christian principles were antithetical to war, and he advanced this position many times in his sermons and in the *Sword and the Trowel*. Shortly after Disraeli's second government came to an end in 1880, Spurgeon wrote,

---

22. Spurgeon, "Notice of Books," *Sword and the Trowel*, January 1880, 38.

23. Some, such as David Swartz, have argued erroneously that Spurgeon was a complete pacifist; see David Swartz, "Unexpected Sites of Christian Pacifism: Charles Spurgeon Edition," *Anxious Bench* (blog), *Patheos*, September 3, 2014, https://www.patheos.com/blogs/anxiousbench/2014/09/unexpected-sites-of-christian-pacifism-charles-spurgeon-edition/. Swartz cites a handful of quotations indicating that Spurgeon had a negative view of war, which is certainly true. However, Swartz fails to address the many places in Spurgeon's sermons and writings in which he indicates that war is, in rare circumstances, just, necessary, and even noble. Spurgeon held Oliver Cromwell in the highest esteem and generally supported the cause of the Parliamentarians in the English Civil War. He glamorized Britain's victories at Waterloo and Trafalgar, and he believed the American Civil War was justified due to the moral atrocity of slavery. It is most accurate to say that Spurgeon hated war, often spoke out against the wars of his own country and those of others, and believed that Christian principles led to the promotion of peace. And yet, at the same time, he recognized that war was, on rare occasions, necessary to advance or defend just causes in the world.

24. David Nelson Duke, "Charles Haddon Spurgeon: Social Concern Exceeding an Individualistic, Self-Help Ideology," *Baptist History and Heritage* 22, no. 4 (October 1987): 51.

25. Spurgeon, "A Peal of Bells," in *Metropolitan Tabernacle Pulpit*, 7:410.

Politically, we have come back to a condition in which there will be a respect to righteousness, justice, and truth, rather than for self-assertion and national gain and conquest. We shall no longer be steered by a false idea of British interests, and the policy which comes of it.... We are up to the hilt advocates of peace, and we earnestly war against war. I wish that Christian men would insist more and more on the unrighteousness of war, believing that Christianity means no sword, no cannon, no bloodshed, and that, if a nation is driven to fight in its own defence, Christianity stands by to weep and to intervene as soon as possible, and not to join in the cruel shouts which celebrate an enemy's slaughter.[26]

It was the subject of unjust war, among other issues, that induced Spurgeon to publish and circulate a tract in the boroughs of Lambeth and Southwark during the 1880 election in South London, representing perhaps his most direct foray into politics. In the tract, he explicitly denounced the Tory party and urged his readers to vote Liberal in the upcoming election. He wrote, "Are we to have another six years of Tory rule? This is just now the question. Are we to go on invading and slaughtering, in order to obtain a scientific frontier and feeble neighbours? How many wars may we reckon upon between now and 1886. What quantity of killing will be done in that time, and how many of our weaker neighbours will have their houses burned and their fields ravaged by this Christian (?) nation? Let those who rejoice in War vote for the Tories; but we hope they will not find a majority in Southwark."[27] As noted in an earlier chapter, Spurgeon was usually reluctant to enter the political fray and try to influence politics. In this case, however, his extreme aversion to war moved him to violate his normal policy and take direct action in the political arena.

---

26. Spurgeon, "Inaugural Address," *Sword and the Trowel*, July 1880, 321.
27. C. H. Spurgeon, *To the Liberal Electors of Southwark* (London: printed by the author, 1880), reproduced in Mike Nicholls, *C. H. Spurgeon: The Pastor Evangelist* (Didcot, U.K.: Baptist Historical Society, 1992), 65.

Irish Home Rule

Spurgeon was an ardent supporter of the Liberal Party.[28] David Bebbington has gone so far as to say, "Spurgeon could hardly have been closer to the heart of Liberalism."[29] Spurgeon was a vocal backer of the foremost Liberal leader of the day, William Ewart Gladstone, who held the premiership four times between 1868 and 1894. Spurgeon enjoyed a warm personal friendship with Gladstone and often spoke highly of him in the *Sword and the Trowel*.[30] Only on rare occasions did Spurgeon break from Gladstone publicly on political and social issues. By far, the most notable example was on the question of Irish Home Rule.[31]

The Irish Home Rule movement campaigned for the right to self-government for Ireland through the establishment of a parliament in Dublin. For centuries Ireland sent members of Parliament to London, which, by the mid-nineteenth century, was seen by many as simply impractical. Some believed the most efficient and amicable solution was to grant Ireland a kind of semi-independence that allowed them a measure of self-governance while still maintaining a connection with the British government in certain affairs. Various politicians proffered their schemes for Home Rule, but as different arrangements were contemplated, complexities multiplied. Furthermore, opposition to Irish Home Rule was vigorous as some believed

---

28. Nonconformists in Spurgeon's day generally sided with the Liberal Party, while most Anglicans sided with the Tories; see John Wolffe, *God and Greater Britain: Religion and National Life in Britain and Ireland, 1843–1945* (London: Routledge, 1994), 130–32; Hugh McLeod, *Religion and Society in England, 1850–1914* (New York: St. Martin's, 1996), 93–99.

29. Bebbington, "Political Force," 39.

30. For examples, see Spurgeon, "Be Just, and Fear Not," *Sword and the Trowel*, November 1868, 509–10; Spurgeon, "Notes," March 1875, 141; Spurgeon, "Notes," January 1880, 40.

31. Lawrence J. McCaffrey, *The Irish Question: Two Centuries of Conflict*, 2nd ed. (Lexington: University Press of Kentucky, 1995); David George Boyce, *The Irish Question and British Politics, 1868–1986*, 2nd ed. (London: Palgrave Macmillan, 1996).

it would harm Ireland economically, destabilize the British Empire, and betray Protestants within Ireland.

Gladstone presented two Home Rule bills in Parliament, one in 1886 and the other in 1893. Spurgeon was deceased when Gladstone introduced his Second Home Rule Bill, which passed through the House of Commons but was ultimately defeated in the House of Lords. However, in 1886, Spurgeon came out publicly in direct opposition to Gladstone on the Irish question. In an article in *The Times*, Spurgeon was quoted as saying,

> We feel bound to express our great regret that the great Liberal leader should have introduced his Irish Bills. We cannot see what our Ulster brethren have done that they should be cast off. They are in great dismay at the prospect of legislative separation from England, and we do not wonder. They have been ever our loyal friends, and ought not to be sacrificed. Surely something can be done for Ireland less ruinous than that which is proposed? The method of pacification now put forward seems to us to be full of difficulties, uncertainties, and unworkable proposals. It is well meant: but even the best and greatest may err. Is it not possible for those who desire the welfare of Ireland and the unity of the Empire to devise a more acceptable scheme? We cannot look forward with any complacency to Ulster Loyalists abandoned and an Established Irish Catholic Church; and yet these are by no means the greatest evils which we foresee in the near future should the suggested policy ever become a fact.[32]

Spurgeon also criticized Gladstone privately. In a letter to his pupil T. W. Medhurst (who supported Gladstone's bill), Spurgeon wrote, "I believe [the bill] to be a fatal stab at our common country, and I am bound to oppose it. I am as good a Liberal as any man living, and my loving admiration of Mr. Gladstone is the same as ever, hearty and deep, but this bill I conceive to be a very serious error."[33] Spur-

---

32. "Mr. Spurgeon on Home Rule," *The Times* (London), June 3, 1886.
33. C. H. *Spurgeon's Autobiography*, 4:126–27.

geon's opposition was partially due to his conviction that Gladstone's bill would generate some measure of volatility for Ireland in being separated from England. His opposition was also shaped, in part, by the fact that about 80 percent of the Irish population was Roman Catholic, and Spurgeon feared that Protestants would become the objects of discrimination if Ireland received political autonomy.[34] In the end, this fear was never realized since Gladstone's attempts at achieving Home Rule for Ireland ultimately failed.[35]

Public Education
Though often suspicious of educated elites and at times cynical about the purported worth of academic degrees, Spurgeon nonetheless highly valued education. Even though he never attended college himself, Spurgeon received a strong middle-class education and was exceedingly bright and eager to learn as a boy. He was a voracious reader and excelled in mathematics, science, and Greek and Latin. Spurgeon's hunger for knowledge, reading, and study continued into adulthood. He always believed education was essential to the stability and progress of any great nation. He once wrote, "Rest assured, dear reader, that next to godliness, education is the mainstay of order."[36] Spurgeon's career bears witness to the high valuation he placed on education—he founded the Pastors' College, offered evening classes to working-class people, and promoted education among poor children through his various Sunday schools, ragged schools, and the schools connected to the Stockwell Orphanage and the Tabernacle almshouses. He clearly believed education was crucial to the development and well-being of the individual as well as society as a whole.

Despite remarkable advances socially, culturally, and politically in the eighteenth and nineteenth centuries, Britain lacked a system

---

34. Bebbington, "Political Force," 39.
35. The Republic of Ireland was eventually established in 1937, while Northern Ireland, consisting of six counties, remained a part of the United Kingdom.
36. C. H. Spurgeon, *Feathers of Arrows; or Illustrations for Preachers and Teachers* (London: Passmore and Alabaster, 1884), 209.

of public education until the passing of the Education Act of 1870. The bill essentially made the education of all children under the age of thirteen mandatory. It continued aid to voluntary schools (what many in America think of today as private schools) and introduced thousands of elected school boards across the nation to fill in the gaps where no schools existed.

Prior to 1870, the education of children was provided primarily through the voluntary efforts of various denominational schools. Anglicans and Nonconformists alike did their part to educate the masses of poor children through the founding of thousands of schools across the country. Nonetheless, for most children of working-class people, a solid education was out of their reach. In his famous sociological study of London, Henry Mayhew estimated less than 10 percent of the working classes could read.[37]

By the late 1860s, almost all agreed that a system of public education was not only desirable but utterly essential for any developing nation with the sort of global influence that Great Britain possessed and hoped to maintain into the future. However, the discussion leading up to the Education Act of 1870 was nonetheless controversial. The controversy revolved largely around the question of whether the education offered at state-sponsored schools should be religious in nature or if it should be purely secular. For several years leading up to the passage of the Education Act, most Nonconformists opposed a system of public education, believing any such system was destined to privilege the Church of England by promoting the teaching of the Anglican articles of faith. For many Nonconformists, if there were to be state-sponsored schools at all, they must proceed without denominational preference. The easiest solution, then, was to keep religious teaching out of the schools and leave such instruction to churches and families.

---

37. Henry Mayhew, *London Labour and the London Poor: A Cyclopedia of the Condition and Earnings of Those That Will Work, Those That Cannot Work, and Those That Will Not Work* (London: Griffin, Bohn, 1861), 1:22.

Spurgeon entered the debate surrounding public education and made his voice heard in the years leading up to the Education Act of 1870. Spurgeon supported the idea of implementing a system of public education in Britain.[38] As Meredith notes, "He was convinced that public schools were necessary if Britain were to retain her position as a power in the modern world. He was also convinced that religious instruction of some sort was imperative if the country were to maintain its moral principles."[39] Though Spurgeon believed religious instruction was pivotal to the well-being of the masses, his early position on the issue of public schools seems to be consistent with most Nonconformists—namely, that religious teaching should be kept out of any system of public education. As many were debating the issue, Spurgeon commented in the spring of 1868, "The great question of the hour seems to be a national system of education. We should like to see a system of universal application which would give a sound education to children, and leave the religious training to the home and the agencies of the church of Christ."[40] A month later, in an article titled "Can Nothing More Be Done for the Young?," Spurgeon said,

> Are we to regard Sabbath-schools as the climax of all Christian effort for the young?... The laudable efforts of our tens of thousands of Sunday-school teachers are a mere installment of the debt which is due from the church of Christ to the little ones around us.... Taking it at its best, and rating it at its highest supposable value, we are Radical enough to assert that it is not all that the children of this age require, nay, nor one half of what might be, and must be done for them if England is to become a Christian country. Education of a secular sort has been too long withheld by the bickering of rival sects; the nation is now in such a humor that it will have no more of such unenlightened bigotry, but will insist upon it, that every child shall be taught to read and write. Since the Sectarian system

---

38. Spurgeon, "Memoranda," *Sword and the Trowel*, March 1868, 139–40.
39. Meredith, "Social and Political Views," 110–11.
40. Spurgeon, "Memoranda," March 1868, 139.

> has in England most evidently failed to reach the needs of millions, a purely secular system will be established, and will be thrust upon us whether we will or no. There will be a great outcry about the divorcing of religion from education, but we shall not join in it, partly because it is useless to cry over spilt milk—the thing must be, and there is no preventing it; and yet more, because we see our way to a great real gain out of a small apparent loss.[41]

Though Spurgeon's position seemed clear enough in 1868, it appears he moderated his view by 1870, when the actual Education Act was put forward for debate. Though Spurgeon wanted nonsectarian schools and the absence of religious instruction favoring one or another of the denominations of England, he did not ultimately favor a fully secular method of education. Spurgeon believed strongly that the reading of Scripture in state-sponsored schools should be allowed and that any effort to rid the public schools of the Bible should be rejected. Thus, though Spurgeon believed the schools should be unsectarian in terms of denominational or confessional commitment, he nonetheless believed the Bible should be prized and read in all of Britain's public schools.

By the time the bill that became the Education Act was being debated in 1870, Spurgeon was openly advocating the inclusion of the Bible in the proposed public schools. He said, "Our cry is undenominational education, but the Bible read in the school by all children whose parents wish them to read it; and these we trust will be the great majority of the nation." He went to the extent of saying he would "counsel Christians to refuse to send their children to the schools if the Bible be excluded."[42] In June 1870, two months prior to the passage of the Education Act, Spurgeon participated in a public rally in Exeter Hall centered around a discussion of the bill. After due deliberation, the assembled congregation voted overwhelmingly

---

41. Spurgeon, "Can Nothing More Be Done for the Young?" *Sword and the Trowel*, April 1868, 147.

42. Spurgeon, "Memoranda," June 1870, 285.

to approve the use of the Bible in England's public schools. Spurgeon celebrated this victory, noting,

> The Education Meeting at Exeter Hall over which we presided, was an extraordinary triumph for those who would preserve our national liberties in connection the proposed new schools.... When the resolution, that the Bible be permitted to be read in the National Schools by those children whose parents wished it, was put to the meeting, it was carried amid a tumult of cheers, about twenty hands only being held up for the secularist amendment. The working men of London are not prepared to withhold from their children the book of God.[43]

The version of the Education Act that was finally approved required the public schools to be free of denominational commitment but still permitted Bible reading in the schools. This was precisely the arrangement Spurgeon desired. One of the bill's provisions, however, was especially controversial among Nonconformists, particularly the amendment that allowed for state aid to go to children too poor to pay for admission to either the public or voluntary schools. This aid made it possible for poor students to attend Anglican schools, which gave credence to the long-standing Nonconformist complaint that their taxes were used to subsidize the state church. In the end, though he did not get everything he wanted, Spurgeon largely supported the new measure. He referred to the bill as a "compromise" and encouraged people to give the bill a fair trial.[44] He celebrated the provision of public education for children and appeared to be optimistic that the bill would ultimately produce great good, not only for children but for the British nation as a whole.

Summary

As the most popular preacher of the day, Spurgeon carried influence

---

43. Spurgeon, "Memoranda," July 1870, 332.
44. Spurgeon, "Members of School Boards," *Sword and the Trowel*, November 1870, 528.

with tens of thousands of people, not only in London but all over the nation. Moreover, he was the leading English Nonconformist at the height of Nonconformity's power in England. In his day, Spurgeon possessed a singular command of the pulpit and the printed page. He also collected a host of influential friends and contacts over the years, some of whom occupied the highest positions of power and authority in the land. In light of these facts, it is striking that Spurgeon was not more active than he was in the political arena. Surely, he could have influenced national events across a vast array of important issues. When it came to politics, however, he generally exercised restraint. His political commentary was occasional and limited. He never abused his position and rarely spent his spiritual capital on political influence. The subjects outlined above were among the rare political issues that invited his public appraisal.

Spurgeon believed the work of the church and the building of Christ's kingdom were at the center of his calling. He was primarily a Christian preacher, not a politician. Therefore, politics could never occupy a position of primacy for Spurgeon. Meredith's assessment of Spurgeon's political engagement is close to the mark: "Nowhere in all of Spurgeon's sermons or publications does he ever indicate that political ends take precedence over spiritual ends. While it is true that he was vitally concerned about political affairs and considered it his Christian duty to make his mark in that area of his life, the end was always the enlargement of the Kingdom of God. Never did political considerations become an end in themselves."[45] Soul winning and the expansion of God's kingdom were always central to Spurgeon. Political matters were secondary and never ultimate. They were relevant insofar as they related to the greater Christian principles that were dear to Spurgeon. Though a faithful and active citizen of the British nation, his most precious citizenship was in heaven. His energies were ultimately bound up with that latter kingdom, and its concerns were always his greatest priority.

---

45. Meredith, "Social and Political Views," 98–99.

Conclusion

Spurgeon died peacefully in the Hotel Beau Rivage in Mentone, France, on January 31, 1892. In the days that followed, memorial services were held across Britain as thousands mourned the loss of the greatest preacher of the age—perhaps, of any age. In America, services were held in cities such as Philadelphia, New York, Boston, and Chicago. Famous men and women of the day shared their condolences and recorded their tributes in letters and articles. Newspapers all over the world carried the story of the passing of the storied Prince of Preachers. One of London's leading papers opened with the following statement: "The Nonconformist Churches, and indeed all churches, have lost in Mr. Spurgeon a man of considerable powers and of immense influence, which was persistently and strenuously exerted to do good."[1]

To do good was, in a sense, the theme of Spurgeon's life. Of course, he believed the greatest good he could do was to introduce sinners to the Savior in whom they could find everlasting life. But he also sought to do good through thousands of acts of charity, both small and great, that truly benefited scores of needy people. Tens of thousands of poor Londoners had a benevolent champion in Charles Spurgeon. He rescued orphans from the streets, widows from grinding poverty, and the poor from utter ruin. Spurgeon rose

---

1. From *The Spectator*, cited in H. L. Wayland, *Charles H. Spurgeon: His Faith and Works* (Philadelphia: American Baptist Publication Society, 1892), 284.

each morning, put on his overcoat, and stepped out his door in the direction of London with the singular aim of doing good to others.

I come now to conclude this book, and in so doing, I wish to provide a brief summary of the book's overall argument and analysis, as well as some parting lessons Christians can learn from Spurgeon's example.

Summary

In part 1, I presented Spurgeon's views related to how benevolence and social ministry fit into the overall conception of the Christian life and the ministry of the local church. Spurgeon believed good works of mercy and charity are not merely optional or preferable but, indeed, essential to the individual Christian life and the work of the church. He believed that acts of benevolence are the inevitable product of the new birth—that each Christian is "a philanthropist by profession, and generous by force of grace."[2] Spurgeon also stressed that true obedience to Christ's commands and imitation of His example will lead disciples to give themselves to mercy ministry and care for the needy.

Spurgeon carefully articulated the proper relationship between gospel proclamation and social ministry. He believed that the proclamation of truth unto the winning of souls and the building up of believers is at the heart of the church's mission. Social concern is never to be seen as primary but rather serves the larger mission of promoting the gospel by showing forth the power of grace and commending the character of Christ to a needy world. The church is ultimately meant to be like a city on a hill and a light to the world; the good works of believers are meant to shine forth in a dark world, drawing needy souls to the light of truth.

---

2. C. H. Spurgeon, "Christian Sympathy," in *The Metropolitan Tabernacle Pulpit: Sermons Preached and Revised by C. H. Spurgeon* (Pasadena, Tex.: Pilgrim Publications, 1969), 8:628.

Conclusion

In part 2, I provided a historical survey of Spurgeon's actual work in the realms of benevolence, philanthropy, and social concern. Central to Spurgeon's life and ministry was the burden of winning souls through preaching the gospel. Everything else for Spurgeon flowed out of his calling to preach the Word. His preaching ultimately gave shape to all his philanthropic enterprises. The Pastors' College was the foremost of his benevolent institutions and invited more of his energy and attention than any of his other organizations, save his local church. The Pastors' College was designed by Spurgeon to provide training especially for men who operated under educational or economic disadvantages. Spurgeon would help such men develop into preachers for the masses who were peculiarly suited to reach needy people from among the working classes.

Spurgeon was responsible for no less than sixty-six benevolent ministries that operated out of the Metropolitan Tabernacle. Prominent among these institutions were the Stockwell Orphanage, the Tabernacle Almshouses, the Sunday schools and ragged schools for needy children, and a host of other ministries. Each of these institutions displayed something of Spurgeon's commitment to minister to the practical concerns of a vast array of needy people. Beyond his formal ministries, he also gave himself privately to various forms of philanthropy, from giving money away to the poor to ministering to the sick and the dying in London's various cholera epidemics. He advocated for poor English pastors, forgotten Spanish sailors, and afflicted American slaves. His heart was always open to the disenfranchised and oppressed.

Though Spurgeon was not a political preacher, he nonetheless made his mark in the political arena, occasionally speaking about political issues, especially when they touched upon religious matters. Spurgeon spoke about issues such as the disestablishment of the state church, Irish Home Rule, British foreign policy, slavery, and public education. These subjects invited Spurgeon's commentary because he believed that they in some way touched upon the concerns of

Christ's kingdom. When such was the case, he felt that politics was encroaching on his turf, not the other way around.

In all of this, we have a portrait of a man who was devoted to good works. Spurgeon dedicated untold hours and massive sums of money to helping London's poor and indigent. His life was marked by a ceaseless effort to bring good to needy people. Spurgeon the preacher is well-known and greatly beloved. But he appears as an altogether *greater and grander man* when one appreciates this lesser-known man, one marked by enormous care and concern for the poor and afflicted.

Concluding Lessons

I conclude this book by highlighting a few prominent features of Spurgeon's ministry as they relate to mercy ministry and social concern. These features can be instructive to pastors and churches today as they think through the pivotal place of mercy ministry in the overall ministry of the church.

First, *Spurgeon reminds Christians of the indispensability of good works in the Christian life and in the ministry of the local church.* Spurgeon expected that works of mercy and compassion, done in true love and regard for others, would populate the Christian life and, indeed, give it its unique savor. The good works of Christians flow from a transformed heart and a renewed nature. They are meant to have a certain apologetic power and evangelistic appeal in the eyes of the world. Spurgeon reminds believers that mercy ministry and benevolent care for the needy should be as characteristic of Christians as any other trait. Christians are those who love and care for the poor, the oppressed, and the afflicted. Dogs bark. Birds fly. Christians love. Such compassion has marked believers since the earliest days of the Christian movement, and it must continue to mark the Lord's people as a distinctive and dynamic attribute of the Christian character. Christians are truly to be a people zealous for good works (Titus 2:14).

Furthermore, Spurgeon would urge local churches to regard mercy ministry as an imperative feature of basic church work.

Conclusion

Churches must be places where needy people can go to find aid and relief. Of course, the ultimate help the church must give is spiritual in nature. It is of no lasting good to feed a belly for a lifetime, only for it to starve in hell for eternity. Nonetheless, concern for the physical needs of people is by no means at odds with concern for their spiritual needs. The relieving of physical burdens is often important in creating a context for the more manifestly spiritual work of the church. After all, who would be open to hearing about good news from people who are evidently selfish, parsimonious, and illiberal? The most effective evangelists are typically those who are marked by compassion, generosity, and genuine regard for the needs of others. The benevolent lives of Christians on display in the church can create an atmosphere and context for the spiritual work of the church to go forward without impediment. But Spurgeon calls churches to recognize that mercy ministry is not only required as a matter of witness but as a simple matter of basic Christian faithfulness to the commands of Scripture. Christ wants His churches to have regard for the needs of the poor among them and in their communities. Mercy ministry is not an optional or preferable feature of church ministry but rather an essential part of the work of the church.

Second, *Spurgeon shows churches a way forward in how to think about the relationship between mercy ministry and gospel proclamation.* At the time of writing, this issue seems especially relevant to many Christians. However, it is likely that the same could be said in almost any era of church history. How to understand the relationship between social ministry and the church's call to proclaim the gospel is a perennially relevant and crucial issue. Sadly, careless and imbalanced thinking seems to abound in discussions on this topic. Too many have given into a social gospel, with its overemphasis on social ministry and fixation on creating a kind of kingdom of heaven on earth, along with its concomitant negligence of teaching doctrine and proclaiming spiritual salvation. However, many of those who have emphasized the preaching of truth are regrettably not known for their zeal for good works or their commitment to benevolence and mercy. In fact, some may even eschew social ministry as unimportant, unnecessary, or even a distraction from what is to be the church's main work of preaching the gospel.

Spurgeon shatters the false dichotomies and faulty assumptions that undergird these distortions. He understood the church's main work to be the proclamation of the revealed will of God unto the saving of souls and the building up of the church, but nonetheless, he preserved a vital place for the priority of social ministry in the work of the church. The church's mercy ministry is meant to support and sweeten the church's preaching of the gospel. It gives tangible expression to the love of Christ and the power of grace. Thus, though the preaching of truth can never be removed from its place of preeminence in the mission of the church, social ministry can still occupy a pivotal and indispensable, albeit secondary, place of importance in the church's ministry.

In this approach, Spurgeon provides churches with a way forward while avoiding errors on either side. His example makes plain that one can be passionately committed to the preaching of truth *and* earnestly devoted to caring for the poor without losing the gospel or neglecting the needy. The quote from Lewis Drummond mentioned in chapter 4 bears repeating: "Almost unparalleled in church history, the ministry of Charles Haddon Spurgeon epitomized the perfect blending of evangelistic fervency and deep social concern."[3] Spurgeon's faithful example can serve and instruct churches today as they seek to prioritize the preaching of the gospel while also maintaining the importance of good works in the church's ministry.

Third, *Spurgeon stimulates local churches to more significant engagement with needy people*. It is unlikely that many churches will be able to achieve what Spurgeon achieved in London in terms of the scope and breadth of his benevolence ministries. The administration and coordination of so many ministries and organizations

---

3. Lewis A. Drummond, *Spurgeon: Prince of Preachers*, 3rd ed. (Grand Rapids: Kregel Publications, 1992), 398.

require a certain scale and concentration of resources unavailable to the vast majority of churches. However, the scriptural motivations that induced Spurgeon to engage in benevolent ministry to the needy can and should be shared by all true churches. Spurgeon was proactive in his pursuit of practical avenues of ministry to the poor and afflicted in his community. He was the friend of orphans, widows, poor and uneducated children, prostitutes, the blind, police officers, and working mothers and fathers who fought just to scratch out a living. It was as though no one fell outside the sphere of his compassion and concern. Why may it not be so with more ministers and more churches? Though it is not possible to help every needy case, all churches can organize themselves to provide what aid they can with the resources God has given them. It is as though Spurgeon, standing upon a mountain of good works which God enabled him to carry out, says to us, "What have you done for the needy in your own community? What will you do for foster children, the hungry, the sexually abused, the addicted, the homeless, the battered, the broken? Are there needy people within your reach? Then go to them and help them, and as you do, tell them about Jesus who has taught you to care for others in this way."

Perhaps you are a pastor reading this book, and you have thought to yourself while reading that you would like to lead your church to do more in the realm of benevolence ministry. Do not start by trying to do all that Spurgeon did. Consider what particular needs are prominent in your own community and what might be reasonably accomplished to meet those needs through your own church's resources. Step out in faith, believing that God will sovereignly assist and attend your church's efforts to do good. Perhaps you are a church member wishing to see more done through your local church for needy people in your community. Consider setting up a meeting with your pastor. Give some thought before you do, and go to him humbly with a concrete plan for what you think your church can begin to do to minister to those in need in your area. If you can, tell him you would be willing to head up this new ministry yourself, with the help of some fellow church members. Remember, Spurgeon's efforts in benevolence never appeared grand at their beginning, but they were sincere, practical, and achievable, and they were wrought in love for God and neighbor. His example is stimulating and empowering to Christians who, like Spurgeon, love mercy and are zealous for doing good.

Fourth, *Spurgeon invites those outside of Christ to behold a bright vision for a transformed community devoted to doing good.* There are many things that Spurgeon is known for today—his preaching, his Calvinism, his love of the Puritans, his stand for orthodoxy in the Downgrade Controversy, etc. He is lesser known for his benevolent care for needy people and his eagerness to provide aid and relief for the suffering and the sinning. Spurgeon's work in this arena should be better known because it gives a certain brightness and sanctified charm to his witness. Spurgeon wanted outsiders to know that Christianity produces benevolence and good works for those in need. The gospel creates a people zealous for good works. Playing off the words of the prophet Elijah, Spurgeon once said, "The God that answereth by orphanages, let him be God!"[4] Dallimore captured a similar idea with a great line in his biography regarding Spurgeon's benevolences. He said, "The Almshouses and the orphanage were, of course, the fruit of Christianity."[5] In other words, Spurgeon viewed care and concern for the needy as the inevitable fruit of Christian belief. It was as though Spurgeon, through all his philanthropy and benevolent work, said to the world, "This is what Christianity produces. This is what the gospel creates."

The history of the Christian movement attests to this. Wherever Christians have gone, good works have gone with them. Whether it is the founding of hospitals and orphanages all over Europe in the early centuries of the church or the explosion of benevolent institutions

---

4. As quoted in H. L. Wayland, *Charles H. Spurgeon: His Faith and Works* (Philadelphia: American Baptist Publication Society, 1892), 171–72.

5. Arnold Dallimore, *Spurgeon: A New Biography* (Edinburgh: Banner of Truth, 1985), 129.

and agencies that accompanied the evangelical revivals, Christians have always been a people zealous for good works. Christians are the people who help. They are those who show compassion and care for the needy. As Spurgeon said, "To me a follower of Jesus means a friend of man.... Wide as the reign of sorrow is the stretch of his love."[6] Christians embrace the needs of the poor, the afflicted, and the oppressed. They seek to bind up the wounds of the suffering as they tell them about salvation in Jesus. They work to release captives as they preach to them about the one who brings freedom from sin's bondage. They advocate for the oppressed as they point men and women to the Savior who delivers from oppression. Christians work to undo and beat back sin's effects as they preach the good news of the one who is coming to make all things new. Spurgeon preached a gospel of forgiveness and redemption in Christ that brought in its train a host of good works. This is a ministry worth emulating.

---

6. Spurgeon, "Christian Sympathy," in *Metropolitan Tabernacle Pulpit*, 8:628.

Appendix
Spurgeon and Social Ministry in Historical Perspective

Social ministry can often sound like a "four-letter word" in the ears of many conservative evangelicals today. Thus, a book that rings the note of Spurgeon's expansive benevolence work may sound dissonant to some, particularly when played in the context of the more familiar chords of his evangelical theology. Some view Christian activism and ministries of mercy among the poor as an impulse of theological liberalism. This is not altogether surprising, as theological liberals often promote social activism as part of the church's primary purpose in the world. Of course, when one abandons belief in hell, penal substitutionary atonement, and the exclusivity of Christ, there is not much left of Christianity besides a kind of sentimental love for neighbor. Thus, when one finds a group of Christians who are passionate about social justice, helping the poor, and feeding the hungry, the assumption is often made that the group must be theologically liberal or, at least, must be acting out the instincts of liberalism.

This assumption is understandable given the history of evangelicalism in the twentieth century. The early 1900s saw the clash of the modernists and fundamentalists over some of the most basic tenets of the Christian faith. As modernists denied many orthodox Christian doctrines, such as the infallibility of the Bible, the virgin birth, and the necessity of the atonement, the social gospel began to sound more plausible. Perhaps the church's main mission should be located in social reform, cultural renewal, and the alleviation of human suffering and poverty. Talk of the kingdom coming, justice rolling, and the lame walking began to replace the old gospel of repentance, faith, and the quiet hope of everlasting life beyond the grave. Couple this trend in the theological arena with the optimistic anthropology and eschatology of the secular progressive movement ascendant in the wider culture, and all at once, classical evangelicalism began to sound hopelessly quaint and passé in the ears of those who adopted a more sophisticated and modernized faith with its commitment to social engagement and its denial of an ever-growing body of foundational Christian doctrines. It is possible that conservative evangelicals, for their part, began to see concerns over social renewal, clothing the naked, and feeding the hungry as the reflex of a liberal program that increasingly abandoned the core doctrines of the faith.

What's more, political and economic developments, especially in the twentieth century, caused a net deflation in the value of Christian social ministry, as many advanced Western countries launched government-subsidized welfare programs to care for their neediest citizens. What some had once understood to be the responsibility of churches and charitable organizations (usually founded by conservative evangelicals) in the nineteenth century was, by the early to mid-twentieth century, increasingly believed to be the responsibility of the wider body politic, mediated through local and national taxation. It is at least plausible, then, that the twin developments of the rise of theological liberalism on the one hand, and the massive expansion of state paternalism on the other, had the effect of sapping conservative evangelicalism of what had been its characteristic zeal for mercy ministry.

The foregoing is all supplied to provide context for why Spurgeon's approach to faith-based social concern may seem unusual to some evangelicals today. Perhaps in reading these pages on Spurgeon's extensive and far-reaching social ministries, readers have been bothered by an uneasy feeling that Spurgeon's benevolent program is outside the typical conservative evangelical program. This book—and this appendix—were written, in part, to address such a concern.

While Spurgeon was busy administrating dozens of benevolent ministries in the heart of metropolitan London, he had no sense he was acting out the impulses of liberalism. When he organized ragged schools, advocated for American slaves, and cared for needy orphans and widows, he was by no means championing a social gospel. It goes without saying that Spurgeon was no theological liberal. But how then does one account for his charitable work among the poor and needy? Was Spurgeon some sort of evangelical anomaly? Did he deviate from the Calvinistic and Reformational traditions in which he was reared? Did his zeal for social ministry represent a departure from the evangelical beliefs and practices of men such as Whitefield and Wesley?

These questions betray a contemporary consciousness shaped more by modern cultural and theological debates than a serious and sustained reflection on the heritage of the reformed and evangelical traditions. In order to properly understand Spurgeon's commitment to social ministry, one must appreciate that Spurgeon saw care and concern for the needy as springing forth from his understanding of the Bible, as well as the body of doctrine he had received from his theological forebears. Without question, Spurgeon would have seen himself as living out the consistent social implications of Reformed and evangelical theology. He also would have understood himself as being in continuity with the example set by many of his great heroes of the faith. When one studies how many Protestants, beginning in the sixteenth century, prioritized care for the poor and needy, Spurgeon begins to look more like the norm. Meanwhile, many twentieth- and twenty-first-century evangelicals suspicious of social concern begin to appear like more of a departure from their historical and theological heritage.

This point can be illustrated first by a brief consideration of the confessional record left for us in various Reformed statements of faith. The Belgic Confession requires, in article 30 on the government of the church, that the church be properly organized and ordered, in part, "so that also the poor and all the afflicted may be helped and comforted according to their need." In the Thirty-Nine Articles of the Anglican Church, article 38 states, "Every man ought, of such things as he possesseth, liberally to give alms to the poor, according to his ability."[1] The Second Helvetic Confession, in chapter 18, teaches that ministers are "to commend the necessity of the poor to the church," and in chapter 28, that the church should use its resources "especially for the succor and relief of the poor."[2] In answer to the question, "What is God's will for you in the fourth commandment?," the Heidelberg Catechism gives as part of its answer, "to bring Christian offerings for the poor" (HC 103). A passage in John Knox's First book of Discipline is worth quoting at length,

> Every several kirk[3] must provide for the poor within itself; for fearful and horrible it is, that the poor, whom not only God the Father in his law, but Christ Jesus in his evangel, and the Holy Spirit speaking by St Paul, hath so earnestly commended to our care, are universally so contemned and despised. We are not patrons for stubborn and idle beggars who, running from place to place, make a craft of their begging, whom the civil magistrate ought to [compel to work, or then] punish: but for the widow and fatherless, the aged, impotent, or lamed, who neither can nor may travail for their sustentation, we say, that God commands his people to be careful: and therefore, for such, as also for persons of honesty fallen into decay and poverty, ought such provision to be made, that of our abundance their indigence may be relieved.[4]

In addition to what the Reformers *said* in their confessions, one may also consider what they themselves *did* in their actual practice. Two of Spurgeon's Reformation heroes, Martin Luther and John Cal-

---

1. John H. Leith, ed. *Creeds of the Churches: A Reader in Christian Doctrine from the Bible to the Present*, 3rd ed. (Louisville: Westminster John Knox, 1982), 280.

2. Leith, *Creeds of the Churches*, 159, 187.

3. I.e., *church*.

4. *The History of the Reformation of Religion in Scotland, by John Knox; to Which are Appended Several Other Pieces of His Writing; Including the First Book of Discipline, etc.* (Glasgow: Blackie, Fullarton, & Co, 1831), 494.

vin, gave significant attention to social ministry. Samuel Torvend ably expounds Luther's understanding of the priority of benevolence and mercy ministry in his book *Luther and the Hungry Poor*.[5] Calvin scholar Scott Manetsch has noted that in Calvin's Geneva, pastors "defended the cause of helpless orphans, poor laborers, mistreated prisoners, despised refugees, and social misfits." They also "worked to root out social and economic injustice" and were specially tasked to provide help and aid in times of plague.[6]

Beyond the Reformation era, one may also look to the evangelical movement in Britain and America, the origins of which are typically located in the awakenings of the early eighteenth century. It has been argued that Spurgeon embodied the ideals of classical evangelicalism perhaps better than any other figure in nineteenth-century England.[7] He is, in some ways, an heir of the evangelical movement. When the movement first emerged in the eighteenth century, it exploded with benevolent activity. The historian David Bebbington, a great expositor of historic evangelicalism, has identified activism as one of the leading traits of the evangelical tradition.[8] In the century before Spurgeon's birth, evangelicals committed themselves to social ministry on an unprecedented scale, spawning all kinds of social ministries, benevolent institutions, and charitable agencies. The establishment of orphanages, such as the one founded by George Müller in Bristol, was representative of the evangelical impulse to serve the neediest members of society. The Clapham

---

5. Samuel Torvend, *Luther and the Hungry Poor: Gathered Fragments* (Minneapolis: Fortress, 2008).

6. Scott M. Manetsch, *Calvin's Company of Pastors: Pastoral Care and the Emerging Reformed Church, 1536–1609* (Oxford: Oxford University Press, 2013), 215–16.

7. See David W. Bebbington, *The Dominance of Evangelicalism: The Age of Spurgeon and Moody* (Downers Grove, Ill.: InterVarsity, 2005), 40–45; See also Alex J. DiPrima, "'An Eagerness to Be Up and Doing': The Evangelical Activism of Charles Haddon Spurgeon" (PhD diss., Southeastern Baptist Theological Seminary, 2020), 43, 54–70.

8. David W. Bebbington, *Evangelicalism in Modern Britain: A History from the 1730s to the 1980s* (New York: Routledge, 1989), 10–12.

Society, a group of evangelicals within the Church of England led by William Wilberforce, were famous for their philanthropic efforts and their advocacy for the poor and the disenfranchised. Wilberforce once said, "If to be feelingly alive to the sufferings of my fellow-creatures and to be warmed with the desire of relieving their distresses, is to be a fanatic, I am one of the most incurable fanatics ever permitted to be at large."[9] The Moravians, who were tremendously active in the arena of social ministry, articulated their own commitment to universal benevolence in article 5 of the Moravian Covenant, which says, "Together with the universal Christian Church, we have a concern for this world, opening our heart and hand to our neighbors with the message of the love of God, and being ever ready to minister of our substance to their necessities (Matthew 25:40)."[10]

The evangelical impulse to do good on behalf of the needy reached its zenith in Victorian England during Spurgeon's tenure in London. This was the heyday of street missions, ragged schools, and almshouses. This was the age of Lord Shaftesbury, that greatest of England's philanthropists and Spurgeon's close personal friend, who gave his life to social reform on behalf of factory workers, poor children, and England's disenfranchised. This was the era of men such as William Booth of the Salvation Army, who launched missions to prostitutes, alcoholics, and orphans in London's overcrowded East End. This was also a time for women who had unprecedented opportunities to participate in social ministry. Examples included the Anglican Josephine Butler, who fought against prostitution and human trafficking, and the Quaker Elizabeth Fry, who labored for the reform of England's prisons.[11] "It was a representative impulse to do good to the

---

9. Robert Isaac Wilberforce and Samuel Wilberforce, *The Life of William Wilberforce* (London: John Murray, 1839), 4:290.

10. "Moravian Covenant for Christian Living," Moravian Church, last modified November 19, 2018, https://www.moravian.org/2018/06/moravian-covenant-for-christian-living/.

11. For a study of female activism in Victorian England, see Frank K. Prochaska, *Women and Philanthropy in Nineteenth-Century England* (Oxford: Clarendon, 1980).

less fortunate members of society," Bebbington states, "a symptom of the large-hearted sense of mission that motivated evangelicals of the Victorian era."[12] The historian Kathleen Heasman writes,

> The most striking feature of Evangelical charity in the Victorian era is its vast dimensions. There were societies of all sorts and descriptions to meet a widespread variety of needs. Some were large; others small. Some were run by a committee; others were entirely under the control of a particular individual. Some were nation-wide in scope; others were completely local. It would be difficult to point to a need which was not catered for in one way or another. Societies dealing with children and young people vied with those helping the sick and the aged. There were organisations to cope with the aberrant groups in society—the criminals, the prostitutes and the drunkards. There were others to make life more bearable for the handicapped. The sailor and soldier and some other working men and women came in for their share; and finally there were the general missions which regarded few things as outside their scope of action.[13]

Simply put, Victorian evangelicals understood social ministry to be their God-given responsibility. Charity, benevolence, and philanthropy were seen as basic Christian duties and flowed naturally out of a belief in the unmerited grace of God and the call to love one's neighbor.

Spurgeon understood his commitment to social ministry not to be an aberration from his historical and theological heritage but rather the consistent outworking of it. Evangelicals before Spurgeon viewed social concern, particularly in the form of care and provision for the neediest members of society, as an integral part of the ministry of the Christian community. It was only in later generations after Spurgeon's death that some evangelicals began to view social

---

12. Bebbington, *Dominance of Evangelicalism*, 39–40.
13. Kathleen Heasman, *Evangelicals in Action: An Appraisal of Their Social Work in the Victorian Era* (London: Geoffrey Bles, 1962), 285.

ministry as part of a program grounded in theological liberalism or, still yet, as the primary responsibility of the state.

It is possible my diagnosis of the reasons why conservative evangelical zeal for social ministry began to wane beginning in the early twentieth century is incomplete or in need of further nuance. However, what cannot be denied is that an evident change in attitude toward social concern took place over the course of the twentieth century among those who were the natural heirs of the evangelical tradition.[14] Rare were the appeals of figures such as Carl F. H. Henry, who advocated for a muscular social agenda within the framework of conservative evangelical theology. Though many evangelicals today remain engaged in works of benevolence and mercy ministry, such efforts, on the whole, have descended the scale of priorities in most conservative churches and among many conservative denominations.

Could it be that the recession of evangelical efforts in the realm of social ministry is influenced more by a reaction to liberal theology or progressive government policies than by sound biblical exegesis or serious reflection on the history of social concern among evangelicals of the past? Could it be that widespread Western affluence has insulated evangelicals today from the concerns of the poor and, thus, enfeebled Christian benevolence? Could it be that some modern-day evangelicals are turning their backs on what used to be a hallmark of the evangelical movement and one of its most attractive traits? And might evangelicals, who perhaps have faltered in this arena in recent decades, one day see within their own ranks a revival of practical concern for the poor and the afflicted?

A genuine recommitment to evangelical social engagement requires neither the adoption of a social gospel nor the endorsement of a progressive political agenda. A successful renewal of social min-

---

14. This fact is widely recognized among scholars. For just one example, consider David O. Moberg, *The Great Reversal: Evangelism Versus Social Concern* (Philadelphia: Lippincott, 1972).

istry among conservative evangelicals must be grounded firmly in a more thorough commitment to evangelical and Reformed theology, which originally was all that was needed to move Christians to compassion and care for the neediest members of fallen humanity. All the resources for a vibrant social ministry are found in the evangelical tradition. But more importantly, they are found in the Scriptures themselves, which call Christians to love their neighbors, to do good to all, and to be a people zealous for good works.